After the Velvet Revolution

After the Velvet Revolution

Václav Havel and the New Leaders of Czechoslovakia Speak Out

Edited by Tim D. Whipple

Focus on Issues, No. 14

Freedom House

First published in 1991.

Cover design by Emerson Wajdowicz Studios, Inc., N.Y.

Library of Congress Cataloging-in-Publication Data

After the velvet revolution : Václav Havel & the new leaders of Czechoslovakia speak out / edited by Tim D. Whipple.
p. 328 cm. -- (Focus on issues : no. 14)
Includes index.
ISBN 0-932088-62-7 (cloth). -- ISBN 0-932088-61-9 (paper)
1. Czechoslovakia--Politics and government--1989- I. Whipple, Tim D. II. Series: Focus on issues (Freedom House (U.S.)) : 14.
DB2238.7.A35 1991
943.7--dc20 90-49104
CIP

Distributed by arrangement with
National Book Network
4720 Boston Way
Lanham, MD 20706

3 Henrietta Street
London, WC2E 8LU England

Dedication

For those who did not live to see the day

Contents

Political Figures and Independents

Contributors are listed under the titles held in June 1990.

Preface

THE AIM OF this book is to let Czechoslovakia's new political leaders describe, in their own words, their analyses of the present and hopes for the future.

Of the major events in recent history, the collapse of communism in central and eastern Europe has been given perhaps the fullest—and glossiest—coverage the world has seen. But in the rush of events there was much that was missed. Correspondents report what they see and tailor their remarks for the audience at home. They rarely have the time or space to reproduce what the people involved are actually saying to one another.

This book is a collection of interviews, speeches and articles by Czechoslovakia's new political leaders. It is intended as an introduction: to the post-Communist political climate, and to the tone and substance of the discussions that will shape the country's future. Almost all of this material is drawn from the Czechoslovak press, and reflects what these figures are saying to the public, as well as how they are saying it. Some of the selections are my own interviews; in them I have tried to focus on current issues and the nature of the domestic situation, and to avoid the superficial generalities to which foreigners are prone.

The contributors all played major roles in the "velvet revolution" of November 1989, and have since been catapulted into positions of national or party leadership. Many were former dissidents, and all were initially involved in the opposition movements Civic Forum and Public Against Violence—except, of course, the Communist party First Secretary Vasil Mohorita, whose answers to my questions are offered as an example of what the opposition of today sounds like. The contributors also represent Czechoslovakia's emerging political spectrum: from the Christian Democrats Benda and Carnogursky, and the rightist Bratinka, through the center—the majority—to the social democrat Battek and the reformed Communists Kusy and Dubcek. All are prominent figures and will help define the contours of their emerging democracy.

I have tried to place myself between their words and the reader as little as possible, providing footnotes and definitions only where it seemed unavoidable. To be coherent, however, a mosaic like this requires a frame, a context into which the pieces may be fitted. The introduction opens with a chronological commentary of the events that led from the crushing of the "Prague Spring" in 1968 to the collapse of communism in 1989, and gives a day-by-day analysis of the revolution itself. "Images of the Revolution" offers photographs of the major events in November and December 1989. "After the Velvet Revolution" describes the achievements and problems of the first six months, including the legislative, political and economic reforms enacted before the free elections in June 1990. The Czechoslovak revolution was every bit as merry as it was velvet, and political cartoons are scattered throughout the book as alternative social commentary.

The material for this book was drawn from a variety of newspapers, journals and magazines. Of the Czech periodicals, the richest source has been *Lidové noviny* ("People's News"), the independent paper that was started as an underground weekly in January 1988 and became a leading (and openly published) daily in January 1990. Another "new" newspaper is *Respekt*: edited by a younger generation of former dissidents, it is the current (and enormously popular) incarnation of *Informacní servis* ("Information Service"), an opposition paper prominent during the revolution. *Fórum* is the Civic Forum weekly. *Mlady svet* ("Young World") was an official youth movement magazine under the Communist regime, but has since acquired a new editorial board and something of a fresh image. *Evokace* is one of the myriad new publications that have sprouted since the revolution, and is published by the Fund for Democratic Initiatives. The other Czech sources—*Bulletin Krest'ansko-demokraticke strany* ("The Christian Democratic Party Bulletin") and *Tydeník vlády Ceské republiky* ("Weekly News of the Czech Republican Government")—are self-explanatory. *Radost* is a new and privately owned studio, and provided the photographs of the revolution.

Two Slovak periodicals are former official publications that are trying to carve out a new identity. *Literárny tyzdenník* ("Literary Weekly") was one of the more liberal (i.e., less conformist) pre-revolutionary periodicals in Slovakia. It has continued to be controversial since the revolution, criticizing Public Against Violence and printing some Slovak nationalist pieces. *Mladé rozlety* ("Young Inspirations") is the Slovak equivalent of *Mlady svet*. *Verejnost'* ("The Public") is a weekly put out by Public Against Violence. Other published sources used were *l'Unitá* ("Unity"), the Italian Communist Party newspaper, *Reason,* an American magazine focusing on libertarian and classical liberal issues, and Manchester University Press, whose forthcoming *Spring in Winter* (edited by Gwynn Prince) will include Jan Urban's piece. All other material was obtained directly from the authors.

I thank these agencies and publications for the use of their material, which is reprinted or translated with their permission.

Of the many who offered their time and advice, there are several to whom I would like to express my gratitude. In Prague, Jarmila and Petr Mares were hospitable, critical and informative in ideal measure. In Bratislava, Gabriela and Ján Langos shared their home, experience and friends, while Ingrid Antalová (the administrative heart and soul of Public Against Violence) was a cheerful source of suggestions and information. Clare Brooks translated, edited and encouraged, but her sense of humor was the biggest boon of all. Finally, great thanks go to the members of my family: for encouraging my Bohemian tendencies, and for offering support and advice as a new baby—this time a book—was brought into the world.

Most of all I would like to thank the contributors to this collection. Many of them found time in the aftermath of a revolution for conversations with an interested foreigner. All of them have struggled and suffered for their beliefs, and have seen—in the words of the Czechoslovak student slogan—justice and truth prevail over hatred and lies. There is much that we can learn from them.

Tim D. Whipple
McLean, Virginia
Prague and Bratislava
June 1990

From 1968 to 1989: A Chronological Commentary

1968

On 21 August, Czechoslovakia is invaded by the armies of five Warsaw Pact countries. This puts an end to the "Prague Spring" reform movement headed by Alexander Dubcek. Czechoslovak leaders are arrested and flown to Moscow, where they are forced to sign the "Moscow Protocols." This "agreement" forces acceptance of the invasion and a "temporary" Soviet troop presence in Czechoslovakia. It also rescinds reform legislation and forces the resignation of its architects. Their replacements are hard-line Communists responsive to Moscow.

On 26 September, Soviet *Pravda* publishes the "Brezhnev Doctrine": whenever the Soviet Union sees the interests of socialism being threatened in another Communist country, it has a right and obligation to come to that country's aid, that is, to interfere in that country's internal affairs.

1969

16 January: to protest the continuing replacement of reformers by

Soviet-approved hard-liners, Jan Palach (a student at Charles University) commits suicide by self-immolation on Prague's Wenceslas Square. Large demonstrations follow.

On 28 March, the Czechoslovak national ice hockey team defeats the Soviet Union in Stockholm. Crowds celebrate throughout Czechoslovakia. Hard-liners portray this as proof of Dubcek's again losing control of the country.

After almost eight months of increasing powerlessness, Dubcek finally resigns on 17 April. The new general secretary of the Czechoslovak Communist Party is Gustáv Husák. Dubcek is banished to an ambassadorial post in Turkey. Six months later he will be expelled from the Communist party and relegated to the rank of mechanic in a Slovak forestry enterprise.

This opens the way to unrestrained "normalization," the process of pulling Czechoslovakia back under Soviet control by restoring totalitarian order and extirpating the reforms—and reformers—of the 1960s. Censorship is reestablished. 170,000 flee the country by 1971; 244,000 will have left by November 1989. 500,000 members are purged from the Communist party, a full third of its membership. Hundreds of thousands suffer professional discrimination and other harassment. All expression of dissent is severely repressed through surveillance, arrest and political trials. The "normalizers" strike a cynical deal with society: social peace and political conformity—or nonparticipation—in return for state-subsidized consumer comforts.

1971

The XIV Congress of the Communist Party takes place in May. Postponed for three years since 1968, the Congress proves the total control of Party personnel that the Husák regime has established since the Soviet-led invasion. In the November national elections, Communist-selected candidates—the only contenders—receive over 99 percent of the vote.

1975

In one of the first publicly dissident actions of the 1970s, Václav

Havel sends his "Open Letter to Gustáv Husák" to protest the effects of "normalization" (8 April). On 29 May, Husák becomes president of the Czechoslovak Socialist Republic.

In late July and early August, Czechoslovakia signs the Helsinki Final Act of the Conference on Security and Cooperation in Europe (CSCE). The Act's human rights covenants automatically become part of Czechoslovak law and theoretically commit the government to upholding these United Nations-approved norms.

1976

After performing semi-legally for five years, members of the popular "underground" rock group *Plastic People of the Universe* are arrested and imprisoned for "disturbing the peace." This harsh extension of the "normalization" process to the younger generation and cultural sphere provokes widespread resentment and gives rise to some of the first petition drives and dissident groups.

The first East European dissident group to focus on establishing cooperation between workers and intellectuals is founded in Poland: The Committee for Workers' Defense (KOR).

1977

Charter 77 is established on 1 January. Drawing much of its inspiration from the Helsinki agreements, it aims not to serve as a political opposition, but to put pressure on the government to adhere to its own laws and human rights obligations. It also offers to open a "dialogue" with the government on resolving the country's problems. Over 200 people sign. The first trio of spokesmen includes the philosopher Jan Patocka, the Prague Spring foreign minister Jiri Hájek, and the playwright Václav Havel, who describes the group as "an icebreaker with a kamikaze crew." The group starts to circulate reports and documents despite police persecution. In March, Patocka dies after police interrogation.

1978

The Committee for the Defense of the Unjustly Prosecuted (VONS) is founded on 27 April. As opposed to the more general human rights concerns of Charter 77, VONS focuses on individual cases of unjust persecution, providing documentation and legal advice.

The first openly proclaimed independent political group since 1968 is founded: the Independent Socialists, who register with the Socialist International.

During August and September representatives of the Polish KOR (Committee for Workers' Defense) and Charter 77 meet illegally on the Polish-Czechoslovak frontier.

On 22 October, Karol Cardinal Wojtyla, Polish archbishop of Kraków, is elected Pope John Paul II. His visits to Poland (beginning in June 1979) and his attention to Eastern Europe bolster religious sentiment and opposition to the Communist regimes in the region.

1979

Large-scale police action against VONS signatories climaxes in May. In October six founding members are sentenced to long prison terms.

1980

The Czechoslovak government acknowledges negative GNP growth for the first time and announces that only 2 percent of the country's products match the technological level of the developed world.

After widespread factory strikes protesting government policy, an independent trade union, Solidarity, is founded in Poland on 31 August. The Gierek government falls; Wojtech Jaruszelski, an army general, takes over leadership of the Communist party and country. Having won the right to exist and to strike, the trade union will be joined over the next eighteen months by more than 10 million students, workers and intellectuals. Clandestine working ties are also established with dissident groups in Czechoslovakia, including Charter 77. By the time of its first and last national congress in October 1981, Solidarity is facing increasing inflexibility and pressure from the government and Moscow. As Soviet and other Warsaw Pact troops amass on Poland's borders, Jaruszelski declares martial law on 13 December 1981, outlawing Solidarity and arresting its leaders.

1985

Mikhail Sergeevich Gorbachev becomes general secretary of the Communist Party of the Soviet Union.

1986

24-28 March: The XVII Congress of the Czechoslovak Communist Party gives formal support to Mikhail Gorbachev's *perestroika* program, and promises accelerated economic and social reform. It soon becomes clear, however, that no more than lip service is being paid to Moscow's initiatives.

The Czechoslovak leadership is faced with a dilemma. If it does not follow Moscow's lead and embrace reform, its rule will come under increasing attack both at home and abroad. But if it does take up Gorbachev's repudiation of the past, it will implicitly be attacking itself. Czechoslovakia's "normalizers" have no Brezhnev to blame the "years of stagnation" on: they were the perpetrators themselves.

1987

Prime Minister Lubomír Strougal emerges in January as an advocate of limited change when he speaks of rehabilitating some 1968 reforms (though not the reformers) and criticizes the "excessive caution" of "normalization."

Leaders of the Union of Musicians' semi-official Jazz Section are jailed for publishing uncensored materials.

Gorbachev visits Prague in March, raising hopes of liberalization and accelerated reform in Czechoslovakia—hopes that are not fulfilled. Gorbachev does announce that the Soviet Communist Party has no "monopoly on the truth" (something the "Brezhnev Doctrine" claimed it did have in 1968), but no further criticism of the Husák regime is shown.

Moravian workers write to President Husák asking him to step down.

Friends of Czechoslovak-Polish Solidarity is formed in July after six years' clandestine existence.

Democratic Initiative is founded in September to urge democratization and public discussion of political and economic reform. The unofficial movement describes itself as "liberal democratic."

As the year proceeds, a number of senior Soviet officials hint that a revision of 1968 is overdue. Prague ignores the suggestions. Criticizing "fashionable" interest in Soviet developments, the Husák regime pressures the Society for Czechoslovak-Soviet Friendship to be more "moderate" in its activities.

In October, the Slovak environmental movement publishes the first in a series of reports, *"Bratislava nahlas"* ("Bratislava Aloud"). Based on officially published data, they document the severity of Slovakia's ecological problems. The government is unsure how to respond, first permitting publication, then confiscating and destroying most copies. The movement remains in the grey area of tolerated criticism: it is granted official status in 1988, but will also see many of its participants persecuted as dissidents.

Dubcek's telegram to Gorbachev in November, wishing him luck with his reform program, is reported in the official Soviet and Hungarian media, prompting rumors of Dubcek's rehabilitation.

On 15 November, Romanian workers in the industrial city of Brasov demonstrate against food shortages and government privileges in one of the first public stirrings in Ceausescu's glacial Romania. Protesters are shot at, beaten, arrested and tortured.

Milos Jakes, one of the leaders of the post-1968 purges, replaces Husák as general secretary of the Czechoslovak Communist Party. Husák retires with full honors and retains the ceremonial post of president. Limited economic reforms are announced. Jakes soon proves to be in the "normalizer" mold, and will remain out of tune with the tenor of Gorbachev's reform rhetoric for the rest of his tenure.

1988

More than 600,000 people—both religious and lay supporters—sign a petition demanding more religious freedom. Catholic demonstrations in Prague and Bratislava take place in March, and in September 60,000 make the religious pilgrimage to Sastin in western Slovakia.

The Academy of Science's Institute for Economic Forecasting produces a controversial report on the seriousness of Czechoslovakia's economic and social problems and recommends radical reform and democratization. Prime Minister Strougal uses the report to call for reform, but is ousted by the conservative Jakes leadership later in the year.

More than 280,000 Catholics make the pilgrimage to Levoca in Slovakia during July.

On 21 August, the twentieth anniversary of the Warsaw Pact invasion, 10,000 people participate in a spontaneous demonstration in Prague, the largest since 1969. Police use dogs and tear gas to disperse the crowd.

The Movement for Civil Liberties (HOS) is founded on 15 October. Rejecting the Communist party's leading role in all areas of society, HOS is a loose asociation of movements and clubs that run across the political spectrum. It produces a journal, *Alternativa*, and issues its manifesto "Democracy for All."

28 October: For the first time in thirty-five years, the anniversary of the 1918 founding of the Czechoslovak Republic—the "bourgeois" First Republic—is declared a national holiday. Independent demonstrations are held in Prague despite the arrest of some 190 organizers the night before.

Charter 77 and other groups organize demonstrations in Prague to celebrate 10 December, International Human Rights Day. The crowd calls for the release of political prisoners and freedom of religion, travel, association and the press.

1989

Spontaneous and massive demonstrations commemorate the twentieth anniversary of Jan Palach's self-immolation on Wenceslas Square. Six days of public protest ensue, with crowds chanting for democratization and the release of dissident activists arrested while attempting to lay flowers at the site of Palach's suicide. Police use tear gas, dogs and baton charges to disperse the demonstrators.

The government passes legislation dramatically increasing penalties for "disturbing the peace." Both dissident and official cultural figures start signing a petition condemning the police brutality and calling for the activists' release.

The government declares over one hundred major Czechoslovak enterprises bankrupt, but will continue to bail them out.

Obroda ("Revival"), "A Club for Socialist Restructuring," is founded on 16 February. Comprising former officials from the Prague Spring who still adhere to some form of communism, it supports Gorbachev's line in the USSR and calls for more rapid reform in Czechoslovakia. It starts a journal, *Dialog 89*.

Hungarian television airs an interview with Dubcek on 4 April, provoking angry denunciations from the Czechoslovak government.

Round-table talks between Solidarity and the government in Poland lead in April to the legalization of Solidarity and an agreement to hold "semi-democratic" elections in June.

In May the Socialist party, a Communist party satellite, calls for more political freedom for non-Communist parties.

Hungary opens its border with Austria, prompting a wave of East German refugees seeking a way to the West.

On 14 June, the Czechoslovak government praises the Chinese crackdown on Tiananmen Square.

On 16 June, Imre Nagy, leader of Hungary's 1956 rebellion against Moscow's domination, is reburied in a massive ceremony from which the Communist party is excluded. The rehabilitation of the 1956 uprising is decried by the Czechoslovak government.

Solidarity trounces the Communists in the Polish elections.

29 June: the petition named "A Few Sentences" is signed by both official and unofficial artists. Calling for democratization, it will be signed by more than 40,000 people in five months.

6 July: Gorbachev announces in Strasbourg that all countries have the right to choose and change their social systems free of outside interference, effectively declaring the "Brezhnev Doctrine" to be dead.

21 July: Polish Solidarity leaders—fresh from their election triumph—visit Czechoslovakia.

8 August: The first East German refugees reach the West Ger-

man embassy in Prague. More than 11,000 will cram into the embassy grounds until allowed to emigrate to West Germany in October.

11 August: the Polish senate unanimously condemns the 1968 invasion and apologizes to the people of Czechoslovakia for Poland's participation. On the same day, the Czechoslovak Communist Party newspaper *Rudé právo* rules out any dialogue with independent initiatives, which it calls "illegal structures."

After widespread arrests and detainments the night before, a demonstration on 21 August (the anniversary of the Soviet-led invasion) is broken up by police.

In September, the Communist party's stance continues to harden with ideologist Jan Fojtík calling for only limited and cautious reform, "avoiding the excesses of *glasnost*."

Hungary allows tens of thousands of East German refugees to leave for the West.

30 August: the State Planning Agency declares that 30 percent of Czechoslovak industrial enterprises are "uneconomical" and recommends closure.

25 September: the biggest demonstration in East German history takes place in Leipzig, calling for reforms and democracy.

28 September: the Hungarian parliament condemns the 1968 invasion of Czechoslovakia.

14 October: the "Stream of Rebirth" group is formed in the People's Party, a Communist party satellite, and accuses the old leadership of betraying the party's Christian values.

After growing demonstrations throughout the country, East German leader Erich Honecher resigns on 18 October.

25 October: After continued persecution of "A Few Sentences" signatories, official journalists and the Czech Philharmonic, led by Václav Neumann, announce a boycott of Czechoslovak television.

28 October: On the anniversary of the founding of the Czechoslovak Republic—October 28—tens of thousands of demonstrators fill Prague, chanting for civil rights and democratic reform.

4 November: over 1 million people demonstrate in Berlin for free

elections and democracy. The East German politburo and hundreds of other officials resign; elections are announced.

6 November: Hungarian television airs an interview with Havel, which the Czechoslovak government denounces.

9 November: the Berlin Wall and the East German government fall.

11 November: Todor Zhivkov is ousted as leader of Bulgaria. His replacement Petar Mladenov promises to build a "modern democratic state."

13 November: Democratic Initiative declares itself the first independent political party since 1948, and applies for registration. Demonstrations protesting environmental devastation take place in Western Bohemia.

15 November: a demonstration protesting the government's ecological policy is prevented by police from entering Prague's Hradcany Castle.

The "Velvet Revolution" of 1989

11.17 Students hold an officially sanctioned demonstration to commemorate the closing of Czech universities under German occupation and remember the death of Jan Opletal, a student executed by the Nazis for participating in an anti-German protest on 28 October 1939. The gathering attracts large numbers of people and, about 100,000 strong, turns into a demonstration for freedom and democracy. As the crowd moves up Národní avenue towards Wenceslas Square, thousands of people are caught in a trap manned by police and "Red Beret" special forces. Forced to run a gauntlet of truncheon-wielding police to escape, hundreds of men, women and children are injured and one student is reported killed (this rumor later proves to be false).

11.18 Protesting the police violence of the previous evening, students occupy university buildings and call for a public show of support in a general strike on 27 November. Police surround some buildings, but do not force entry: a major boost for the demonstrators' morale and confidence. Students meet with actors in the Realistic Theatre. Prague's acting community decides to boycott all performances, and theatres become political discussion centers.

11.19 Civic Forum is formed in Prague's Cinoherní Klub. It is an association of opposition groups, students and others, including members of the hitherto satellite Socialist and People's parties. It becomes the leader of the revolution in the Czech Republic, and its headquarters are moved to the Magic Lantern Theatre.

More than 20,000 demonstrate in Prague and demand the resignation of Communist Party General Secretary Milos Jakes. The police close some streets and stand by—but do not attack.

11.20 Public Against Violence, the Slovak equivalent of Civic Forum, is founded in Bratislava.

200,000 people gather on Wenceslas Square to voice demands for political pluralism, freedom of the press and the resignation of compromised Communist leaders. Demonstrations begin to spread to other cities: Bratislava, Ostrava, Brno, Olomouc etc. Strike committees and Civic Forum/Public Against Violence representatives begin to appear in factories, schools, hospitals and offices. The Czech and Slovak republican governments announce their intention to "restore order." The previously obedient satellite Party press publishes articles denouncing the police violence of 17 November.

11.21 200,000 again gather on Wenceslas Square. Václav Havel addresses the crowd for the first time, and threatens a general strike on 27 November unless their demands are met for an investigation of 17 November, the release of all prisoners of conscience, and freedom of press and information. Student strikes spread throughout the country.

11.22 More demonstrations on Wenceslas Square, with students now camped around the statue of the country's patron saint. Busfulls of the Communist Party's People's Militia begin to arrive in Prague.

At a 100,000-person demonstration in Bratislava, Alexander Dubcek makes his first public speech in Czechoslovakia since 1969.

11.23 300,000 gather on Wenceslas Square. 10,000 workers from the enormous CKD engineering works join the demonstrators, declaring the support of "the workers." Tens of thousands protest again in Bratislava.

Czechoslovak Television employees protest slanted coverage of recent events, with the result that the first shots of the Prague demonstrations are aired. This proves to be crucial in spreading word of the revolution throughout the country, much of which has been starved of information until now.

11.24 The Communist Party Central Committee dismisses Jakes and his presidium, but conservatives block radical changes in personnel. The hard-liner Karel Urbánek is made general secretary, and the Prague first secretary responsible for the 17 November police attack, Miroslav Stepán, is retained.

Dubcek makes his first speech in Prague since 1969 to a crowd of 200,000.

Professional sportsmen and women proclaim their support for the demonstrators by boycotting all competition.

11.25 Czech Primate Frantisek Cardinal Tomásek conducts a mass celebrating the canonization of Agnes Premyslid, patron saint of Bohemia. Tens of thousands of pilgrims from all over Czechoslovakia participate, and the service is broadcast on television. Almost three-quarters of a million people then gather on Prague's Letná Plain, where Havel appeals for public pressure on the government to accept opposition demands, which at this point are still limited to the resignations of compromised government members, and increased civil liberties.

General Secretary Urbánek announces that the authorities are ready for talks with the opposition. Miroslav Stepan and other hard-liners resign.

11.26 Prime Minister Ladislav Adamec heads the government delegation* that meets in Prague's City Hall with Civic Forum representatives led by Havel, and agrees to further talks with the opposition.

More than half a million people gather on Letná Plain. Adamec speaks to the crowd, and promises that the government will accede to all demands "within our competence." At the end of the demonstration a human chain is formed from Letná Plain to Prague Castle.

Public Against Violence repeats calls for support of the 27 November general strike at large demonstrations in Bratislava.

Approximately 6,000 strike committees have formed, challenging the official trade union organization and preparing for the general strike the following day.

Civic Forum adopts its program "What We Want," calling for civil rights, an independent judiciary, political pluralism, economic reform and changes in environmental and foreign policy.

11.27 A general strike is mounted throughout the country between 12:00 and 2:00 P.M. Four-fifths of the total labor force stop work. Town squares all over the country are filled with people as bells, horns and sirens accompany people rattling their keys in celebration. This enormous show of popular support allows Civic Forum and Public Against Violence to increase their demands to full political pluralism and representation in a new government. At a celebratory demonstration that afternoon, students demand Adamec's resignation.

The Communist-controlled Ministry of Culture releases books and films that have previously been censored for political reasons. This

---

* While the government was of course controlled by the Communist party, there was a formal distinction drawn between the federal government and party apparatus in Soviet-style systems. Civic Forum was careful to begin by negotiating with the government of Czechoslovakia; it only later (30 November 1989) started direct talks with the monopoly party that happened to control that government.

is one in a series of "concessions" that the Party will grant in an attempt to deflect protest.

11.28 Adamec meets with Civic Forum and pledges to abolish the Communist party's leading role by 29 November and to have a compromise government drawn up by 3 December.

11.29 After forty-one years of Communist party monopoly rule, the constitution's article on the Party's leading role in all areas of society is rescinded. In talks between Civic Forum and the Communists, negotiations on control of various state agencies and positions begin, and a commission to investigate 17 November is set up. Adamec suggests talks with the Soviets on the withdrawal of their forces from Czechoslovak soil.

11.30 Civic Forum holds its first direct talks with a Communist party delegation headed by the new secretary of the Communist party Central Committee, Vasil Mohorita.

Public Against Violence meets with the Slovak republican government to discuss leadership changes.

12.1 Communist Party Central Committee Secretary Mohorita admits that 1968 was "a mistake."

12.3 Adamec proposes a new government that is "only three-quarters" Communist. Civic Forum and Public Against Violence reject his proposal and answer this test of their strength by calling for country-wide demonstrations. Threats are made of another general strike, on 11 December.

12.4 Hundreds of thousands of people gather on Prague's Wenceslas Square to protest the Adamec proposals. Civic Forum demands the recall of compromised Federal Assembly deputies, an agreement to free elections by June 1990, and that a representative government, i.e., one including more opposition figures, be agreed upon by 10

December. Otherwise a general strike will be called for 12 December. Students decide to continue their occupation of university buildings until these demands are met.

Prime Minister Adamec and General Secretary Urbánek go to a Warsaw Pact meeting in Moscow at which the 1968 invasion is condemned by the five countries that took part in it: the USSR, East Germany, Bulgaria, Hungary and Poland.

The Communist government cancels all visa requirements for its citizens' travel abroad.

12.5 Adamec holds new talks with Civic Forum, Public Against Violence, the former satellite parties and *Obroda* ("Revival").

12.7 Adamec and his government, unwilling to bow to opposition demands, resign. Jakes and Stepán are expelled from the Communist Party for "political mistakes." Marián Calfa, a Communist party member, is designated next prime minister.

12.8 President Husák announces a general amnesty for political prisoners. Calfa opens talks with the major political forces over the constitution of the new federal government.

12.10 International Human Rights Day

A new "government of national understanding" is announced that for the first time since 1948 leaves the Communists in the minority. Of the twenty-one members, seven are nominated by the opposition, two by the Socialist party, two by the People's party, and ten by the Communist party. The Czech and Slovak republican governments will also have a Communist minority. A vast demonstration on Wenceslas Square celebrates the announcement that afternoon.

12.11 Artists, actors, theatre and museum workers call off their strikes, but students decide to continue, fearing continuing Communist party strength throughout the country.

Pacem in Terris, an organization of Catholics subservient to the

Communist party, and never recognized by the Vatican, is disbanded.

12.15 Defense Minister Miroslav Vacek announces that all Communist party activities in the armed forces have been suspended.

12.19 In a speech to the Federal Assembly, Prime Minister Calfa announces that there will be no further "experiments" in economic reform: his government will work to establish the conditions for transition to a full market economy.

12.20 The Communist party holds an extraordinary congress at which it changes its structure, abolishing the position of general secretary and replacing it with two positions, Party chairman and first secretary (filled by Adamec and Mohorita respectively). It declares its support for a multi-party system and promises democratization of its internal affairs. It also disbands the People's Militia, its paramilitary arm, and apologizes to the Czechoslovak people for events following 1968.

12.21 State Security (StB) is placed under collective government control as the Communists and opposition fail to agree on a minister of Internal Affairs.

12.28 As agreed in talks on 22 December, a number of deputies resign from the Federal Assembly, allowing the coopting of opposition representatives into the national parliament. This newly constituted Federal Assembly elects as its chairman Alexander Dubcek, the Prague Spring leader.

12.29 The Federal Assembly unanimously elects Václav Havel—the dissident playwright who had been in prison just two months before —president of the Czechoslovak Republic.

Images of the Revolution

17 November 1989, 6:00 P.M.: The commemoration of Jan Opletal's death becomes a demonstration for freedom and democracy.
(Photo by Tomki Nemec)

17 November 1989, 8:00 P.M.: Riot police surround demonstrators on Národni Avenue, one of the main streets leading off of Wenceslas Square. Demonstrators offer flowers and call on the police not to use violence.

(Photo by Tomki Nemec)

17 November 1989: Demonstrators offer flowers to riot police.
(Photo by Pavel Stecha)

17 November 8:15 P.M.: Peaceful stand-off between riot police and demonstrators on Národni Avenue. The banners read "Democracy For All" and "We Don't Want Violence."
(Photo by Jan Sibik)

17 November 1989, 8:15 P.M.: The lull before the storm.
(Photo by Tomki Nemec)

17 November 1989, 8:30 P.M.: Armored cars and riot police begin to drive demonstrators into a side street. There they will have to pass through a cordon of truncheon-wielding policemen. Hundreds are wounded, some seriously.

(Photo by Jan Jindra)

21 November 1989: Candles mark the sight of the police brutality.
(Photo by Petr Rosicky)

25 November 1989: Three-quarters of a million people gather on Pragues' Letná Plain to support Civic Forum demands. St. Vitus' Cathedral in Prague Castle is in the background.
(Photo by Jiri Vsetecka)

26 November 1989: A gathering on Prague's Letná Plain.
(Photo by Zdenek Lhoták)

24 November 1989, Wenceslas Square: Rita Klimova (now ambassador to the United States) congratulates Alexander Dubcek on his first public speech in Prague since 1969.
(Photo by Pavel Stecha)

26 November, Prague City Hall: Negotiations with the government begin. Prime Minister Ladislav Adamec is talking; Václav Havel faces him in the foreground. Marián Calfa, to Adamec's left, will replace him as prime minister two weeks later.
(Photo by Pavel Stecha)

29 December 1989, Prague Castle: The new president in inaugurated.
Finance Minister Václav Klaus congratulates Václav Havel.
(Photo by Tomki Nemec)

"After you, comrade..."

Introduction

After the Velvet Revolution: The First Six Months

IN THE MONTHS following the revolution, one of Prague's most stirring sights was an outdoor exhibition on Na príkope, a pedestrian shopping street off of Wenceslas Square. Copies of old newspaper articles, treaties and political posters covered pillars lining the street; shop windows showed videotapes from the last forty years, including the Prague Spring; and previously censored facts and figures about Czechoslovakia's past were revealed. An artists' collective turned a wall into a mock podium, with effigies of past Communist leaders grinning down on the crowds. A statue of Tomás Masaryk—founder of Czechoslovakia and first president of what the Communists dubbed the "bourgeois" First Republic (1918-38)—was put up to head the proceedings. This multimedia display gave one of the country's first honest portrayals of recent history since 1968.

At the far end of the street, facing Masaryk's statue, was a museum devoted to relics of the Communist past: secret police eavesdropping systems, film of Party members' speeches (now a source of great amusement), riot control equipment. In the same museum, there were booths offering information on Czechoslovakia's new political parties and the free elections to be held in June 1990. The juxtaposition said it all. The past was being objectified, analyzed, defined. With the reestablishment of democracy and civil rights, Communist rule was becoming a museum exhibit, a gruesome monument to a theory run amok.

What Czechoslovakia achieved in November and December 1989 was a revolution in the sense of political overthrow. What has begun to happen since then has made it a revolution in another sense: that of returning to a starting point, completing a circuit, closing a circle. The mood in late 1989 was one of restoration and renaissance. Czechoslovakia could now pick up where it left off in 1938-39, when first Nazi occupation, then Communist totalitarianism isolated the country from its pre-World War II stable democracy, economic prosperity and international stature. In the words of the new president, Václav Havel, the years of paralysis under the unchanging mask of "socialism" were over. History had returned to Czechoslovakia.

After decades of dissatisfaction and more less open disagreement with their government, it took Czechs and Slovaks just twenty-three days to shrug themselves free of Communist rule. But after the excitement of November and the euphoria of December, January dawned as the morning after. Opposition activists were now amateurs in power, taking stock of the situation they had inherited. The selections in this book describe what they found: A comatose economy, the worst pollution in Europe, the legal, political, social and psychological distortions of forty years of totalitarianism. History was certainly returning to the country, bringing with it an understanding of the severity and urgency of the country's predicament. How has the new political leadership addressed these problems during the six months leading up to the June 1990 elections, and what course has it charted out of the perversions of its past?

Philosopher president

Václav Havel's election as president of Czechoslovakia came on 29 December 1989, and was the velvet revolution's crowning moment. A dissident playwright whose work had been officially banned for two decades, Havel had spent the last thirteen years under constant police surveillance for his uncompromising criticism of the government's abuse of citizens' rights. Five of those years passed in prison. In September 1989, the Communist prime minister Ladislav Adamec had dismissed Havel as an "absolute zero." By December the prime minister was negotiating with an opposition movement led by this "zero," who just two months before had been behind bars.

Enjoying enormous moral authority at home, and building on an already considerable reputation abroad, Havel has come to personify for the West the best in the East European revolutions of 1989. His insistence on morality and reconciliation, the philosophical tone of his speeches, and his interest in Central European cooperation, reflect a conscious effort to recall the founder and first president of Czechoslovakia, Tomás Garrigue Masaryk. Writer, philosopher and historian, Masaryk personified the liberal humanism of Czechoslovakia's stable, tolerant democracy and prosperous economy between the wars.

Havel has cast himself in Masaryk's mold of the intellectual and liberal statesman who guarantees stability by remaining above the domestic political fray. Czechoslovakia is traditionally a parliamentary democracy, not a presidential republic; the new constitution that will be drafted after the June 1990 elections will likely confirm this. But as one of the contributors to this book, Pavel Bratinka, has put it, Havel has become "a cross between St. Theresa and George Washington." A new father-figure to his country, hailed as a moral messiah abroad, Havel has brought vast authority to the office of president.

Foreign relations

Nowhere has this been clearer than in foreign policy. Havel has used his own prestige and that of the "velvet revolution" to put Czechoslovakia back on the world's political map. The major thrust of this foreign policy has been consistent with the president's tone at home: morality should be the cornerstone of all human relations, whether on the local, national or international level. Czechoslovakia's experience of two totalitarianisms—first Nazi occupation, then Communist rule—are seen as qualifying it for a leading role in this moral regeneration.

Havel's policy has focused on the European unity that, with the end of the Cold War, he considers to be more achievable than ever. The era of military blocs is over: the future that Havel and his foreign minister, Jirí Dienstbier, see lies in collective European security. To this end they have proposed accelerating the Helsinki process and establishing a "European Security Commission" to guarantee peace and adjudicate disputes (Dienstbier's *Central and Eastern Europe and a New European Order* goes into this idea in more detail). The initial rush of starry-eyed rhetoric has been tempered by on-the-job experience: there has been some reconsideration of the usefulness of NATO as the Warsaw Pact disintegrates, and calls for its disbandment have been muted. But the notion of a "democratic" security framework for all of Europe remains at the center of the new foreign policy.

One of the features that this policy shares with the Masaryk years is the idea of Czechoslovakia as a crossroads between eastern and western Europe. The new president's first few visits abroad were to West and East Germany, Poland and Hungary: a conspicuous break with the tradition of a president's first trip taking him to Moscow. Emphasizing the need for the countries of the former East bloc to make a "coordinated return to Europe," Havel suggested the creation of regional political structures to replace the architecture of blocs. The "Pentagonal Group," including Czechoslovakia, Austria, Hungary, Italy and Yugoslavia is one such structure fostering closer cultural and trade ties. The president's February 1990 visit to the United States was a dazzling success, proof of the president's enormous popularity abroad. His speech to a joint session of Congress brought an unaccustomed but healthy tone to that assembly, discussing being, consciousness and the ethics of politics. Talks with President George Bush resulted in important U.S. trade concessions (including a promise of most favored nation status), and a pledge of U.S. support of Czechoslovakia's application for membership in the International Monetary Fund, the World Bank and other international institutions. There was more good news on this front when the Coordinating Committee on Multilateral Export Controls (COCOM) reduced its tight limits on high-tech exports to Eastern Europe and China.

In late February 1990 Havel finally did make his trip to Moscow, where he signed an agreement on the withdrawal of all Soviet troops from Czechoslovakia by June 1991. Treaties of mutual respect were also signed; but the symbolism of Havel's previous itinerary was unmistakable. The new Czechoslovakia was going to look West, not East, for support, advice and models. This distancing from Moscow was emphasized in another moral moment in Czechoslovak foreign policy: it was one of very few countries officially to condemn Soviet treatment of Lithuania after its declaration of independence.

The establishment of diplomatic relations with Israel, South Korea, Chile and the Vatican are part of this redefinition of Czechoslovakia's foreign policy. Repudiation of the country's diplomatic past has occasionally brought problems, however. When Havel visited Germany in January 1990, there was talk of Czechoslovakia apologizing for the expulsion of 2 to 3 million Germans after World War II; a flood of public dismay and memories of the Nazi occupation removed the item from the president's agenda. In one of the symbolic acts that have characterized Havel's presidency, he also invited the Pope and the Dalai Lama to visit Czechoslovakia. When the Dalai Lama arrived on a purportedly "private" trip, the Chinese government protested and cancelled billions of dollars in trade agreements—a high price for a country embarking on fundamental economic reform.

There has been grumbling in Czechoslovakia that the president has been spending too much time abroad, making grand, symbolic gestures, and not enough at home where the most difficult days of reform still lie ahead. Ultimately, these gripes seem to have been outweighed by the surge in international prestige that Havel has brought the country.

Prague has also made numerous offers to mediate in various negotiations: between the Soviet Union and the United States, Israel and Palestine, Lithuania and Moscow. None of these offers has yet been accepted, but they do illustrate the role Havel has tried to carve out for Czechoslovakia. The new policy has tried to act on the credit it inherited from the revolution and to shed Czechoslovakia's old image as Moscow's colorless, albeit efficient, sidekick. That stigma is gone; relations with the rest of the world have been normalized; and Czechoslovakia once again has a personality of its own. That personality is presently inseparable from the person of Václav Havel, who more than anyone else has provided the inspiration and expression for the innovations of the first six months.

Domestic policy

When elected, the new president enjoyed enormous popularity in his country, but was effectively a caretaker until free elections were held in June 1990. The situation he faced was a tricky one. As many of the contributors to this collection point out, the problems of socialist society were clear enough to its members; but the new leaders were not prepared for the sheer scope and number of the crises they would face in government. There was also the question of popular support for the painful adjustments that would be necessary to reform the political and particularly economic system. After the euphoria of late 1989 and the rapid relinquishing of power by the Communist party, a period of post-revolutionary disillusionment was bound to set in. The task Havel set himself was to guarantee the holding of free elections in June 1990, and to use his office to encourage the social, institutional and legislative climate for the reforms that the new government would undertake.

The revolution had left the opposition with a majority in the government and control of all but two of the major ministries: Defense, held by a Communist, Miroslav Vacek, and Internal Affairs. Negotiations having failed to reach agreement on these particularly sensitive portfolios, they were under collective government supervision. One of Havel's first acts as president was to appoint a practicing Catholic, Richard Sacher, minister of internal affairs. Havel also pressed for, and won, an agreement for 120 deputies of the Federal Assembly (the parliament) to resign, allowing the co-option of opposition deputies in their place. In this way the Communists lost their parliamentary majority and, with it, control of the last major state body they had dominated.

There was a host of other personnel changes that Havel initiated: new prosecutors-general; a new chairman of the Supreme Court; new ambassadors to the United States, the Soviet Union, West Germany and other countries; a major restructuring of the State Defense Council (Czechoslovakia's version of the United States' National Security Council); new rectors of the country's major universities. One of his more controversial moves was the establishment of a "college" of presidential advisors. Drawn mostly from Havel's pre-revolutionary personal friends, the group was conspicuous for its lack of specialists with experience in politics or economics. The president claims that he needed a reliable corps of devoted followers to help him gain a foothold in the hostile government bureaucracy, and that their inexperience has thus far worked to his advantage. Others have resented the influence of this "retinue," however, and suspect that as the powers of the presidency expand under Havel, so the (unconstitutional) authority of these advisors has grown.

Havel's domestic tone is consistent with his moral stance in foreign policy. One of his first acts in office was the traditional gesture of a new leader: an amnesty of about 25,000 prisoners, symbolizing the start of a new era. He has repeatedly called for reconciliation and acceptance of shared responsibility for the totalitarian past so that the country can move on to a free and democratic future. The emphasis is always on personal morality and the responsibility of every citizen to engage in public affairs on some level. This has not meant that the president has decided to close the book on the Communist past: his speeches have eloquently denounced the previous regime's practices, and give graphic descriptions of the legacy that they have bequeathed. But Havel has called for tolerance towards the Communist party, and he rejects the notion of its past and present members' collective guilt for the wrongs it perpetrated. The Party, he maintains, should not be abolished by government decree, but ought to have the good conscience to dissolve itself and start afresh—something it has yet to do. The revolution is to proceed by absolutely legal means. Slow and complicated this may be, but accusations of a new totalitarianism will be avoided.

There have been several criticisms of Havel's presidency. The most pervasive is that he has been too "velvet," too smooth in his treatment of the Communist party, which has been allowed to continue its existence relatively unchanged, with much of both its legal and illegal assets intact. At least in the early days of his presidency, he also tended to paint a too-rosy picture of rapid economic transformation to Western European levels. Since then, he has appeared to act as something of a restraint on the economic reform process, particularly with the appointment of a cautious economic advisor, Richard Wagner. In this and other areas, his approach has sometimes seemed to take a populist bent: a desire to be all things to all people, and not to take the difficult and unpopular decisions that must be a part of radical change. It is often suggested that this has led to squandering of the revolutionary enthusiasm of the first few months, when the momentum for deep and painful change still existed. Havel the president has also distanced himself from Havel the Civic Forum leader, much to the exasperation of the movement's other members as the June elections approached.

Like Masaryk, Havel has adopted the role of the "great conciliator," remaining above the din of party politics. Like other participants in this intellectual-led uprising, he has been acutely aware of how revolutions tend to devour their own children. Recognizing the danger of replacing Communist totalitarianism with the absolutism of anti-Communist vindictiveness, he has also tried to avoid even the appearance of Civic Forum usurping the "leading role" of the Communist party. Playwright that he is, he has probably been most successful on the international stage, or in evoking the symbols and prestige to re-moralize his country. Despite his insistence that he accepted the presidency only temporarily, and was looking forward to returning to writing, it now seems that Václav Havel will remain President Havel for some time to come. Could it be that the author, who was always as much a moral philosopher and social commentator as a playwright, has found his true vocation? As the writer Ivan Klíma has said, "I sometimes feel that Havel became a playwright by mistake, that he really should have been a politician. His essays are better than his plays."*

The government and federal assembly

The "government of national understanding" that took office on 10 December 1989 was the result of round-table negotiations between the Communist party, satellite parties and opposition forces. The Federal Assembly (the Czechoslovak parliament) had been reconstituted through a two-tier process of opposition deputies being coopted to replace a number of Communist members. In both cases, it was the opposition that named the new representatives, with the result that Czechoslovakia's government and parliament—which then elected Havel president—were not democratically elected. As was the case with the president, they were a temporary bridge-measure for governing the country until free elections could be held in June.**

One of the deputies coopted in December 1989, and subsequently elected chairman of the Federal Assembly, was Alexander Dubcek. Leader of the Communist party during the Prague Spring reforms, he had been ousted from office and banished to a series of menial positions. He was given an enormous popular welcome in November when, after twenty years of virtual silence, he gave his first speeches to the demonstrators in Bratislava and Prague. He was a symbol of the freedom and hope—and disappointment—of an earlier reform period. There was even talk of his becoming president, but his moral

---

* Quoted in Elie Abel's *The Shattered Bloc* (Houghton Mifflin, Boston: 1990), p. 68.

** The same situation prevailed in the Czech and Slovak republican governments, the so-called National Councils: they too were "reconstructed" with coopted deputies in December 1989 and January 1990. The Czech Republic includes the "Czech lands" of Bohemia and Moravia; the Slovak Republic is Slovakia. Together they form the Czech and Slovak Federative Republic.

authority never approached that of Havel. There is still much questioning of how Dubcek managed the events of 1967-68 and of how he reacted to the Soviet invasion: the interview "1968 Revisited" gives the flavor of these reproaches. Dubcek had never been active in the dissident movement and was reputedly still devoted to some form of communism. All in all, he seemed to be yesterday's man. His impact as a political leader has remained minimal, but he has continued to be important as a symbolic link with 1968.

The undemocratic government and parliament did, however, enjoy a solid popular mandate. Polls in late January 1990 showed 86 percent satisfaction with developments, and 84 percent of the respondents agreed with the economic and social reforms being discussed. The Federal Assembly and government announced that they would use this popular support to set up the legislative framework for economic, political and legal reforms which could then be expanded by the freely elected government that would take over in June 1990.

Legislative achievement

In a flurry of legislative activity, the parliament adopted a number of new laws in record time. Perhaps the most important, or visible, was the election law, which stipulated 10,000 members or signatures for participation in the elections, thus cutting down the vast number of parties that sprang up in the revolution's wake. Representation in parliament was made contingent on receiving 5 percent of the vote in one of the two republics, prompting some criticism for limiting the opportunities of individual candidates or representatives of the country's several ethnic minorities.

Other laws set the president's and parliamentary deputies' terms at two years. Freedom of association, assembly, petition and the press were codified, making *de facto* abolishment of censorship *de jure.* In the area of religious rights, the state renounced the right to license priests and reached agreement with the Vatican on filling bishoprics long empty because of the Communist leadership's unwillingness to let the Pope fill them. A law on rehabilitation allows reversal of unjust verdicts in the past and makes the state accountable for compensation to victims or their family members. The death penalty was abolished, and the language of prosecution procedures tightened to rule out political abuse. Legal restrictions on travel were all but abolished. Education reform increased universities' autonomy, strengthened the role of student organizations, and restructured postgraduate study, bringing Czechoslovakia's advanced degree system into line with that of Western Europe and the U.S., and away from that of the Soviet Union.

New laws on military reform were also passed. In December 1989, the Communist Defense Minister Miroslav Vacek had announced a moratorium on all Party activities in the armed forces; but the fact still remained that 82 percent of all officers, and 55 percent of noncommissioned officers were Party members. As mentioned above, Havel attacked part of this problem by restructuring the State Defense Council and by replacing several senior officers.

In March 1990, the Federal Assembly made a number of further changes. The Czechoslovak Army was no longer the "People's Army"; military service was cut from twenty-four to eighteen months, with the option of civilian service offered to conscientious objectors; freedom of religious practice was codified; political activity and membership were banned from the services; the army's role in internal security was limited; women were excluded from peacetime drafts (although they may volunteer); and the armed forces were banned from being used in industry and agriculture. Cuts in army personnel and funding were tied to progress in the Vienna talks, though the government's March budget included a 12.5 percent reduction in defense expenditures.

There was some confusion over reform of the armaments industry, one of Czechoslovakia's most profitable enterprises. Havel and Dienstbier had initially proposed to abolish it, but the Foreign Ministry subsequently backed away from that proposal. The government did provide sobering information on the Communist regime's sale of Semtex, a virtually undetectable plastic explosive favored by international terrorists. Large amounts had been sold to various states suspected of sponsoring terrorists, including as much as 1,000 tons to Libya over the past two decades.

The economy

Of all the problems facing the government and country, the one that looms largest is the economy. Before World War II Czechoslovakia was the seventh most industrialized state in the world. By the 1980s it had been relegated to seventieth place, and was plagued with the problems of all Soviet-style economies: over-centralization, blocked initiative, state subsidies and distorted price structures, "socialist construction's" emphasis on heavy industry, and vast monopolies at the expense of small- and medium-size firms. Irresponsible state management had also led to one of the worst environmental pollution problems in Europe and decreasing life-expectancy.

Despite this devastating record, Czechoslovakia still has perhaps the best prospects for economic recovery in Eastern Europe. The prewar traditions of political stability and economic prosperity are distant but still remembered. More important today are the country's small foreign debt, an extensive industrial base, relatively well-trained labor force and adequate agricultural production. The task facing the new government and parliament is straightforward: to build the framework for turning this potential into the reality of a flourishing economy.

The government's economic team was headed by former members of the Academy of Sciences' Institute for Economic Forecasting: Deputy Prime Minister and Chairman of the State Planning Commission Vladimír Dlouhy, Finance Minister Václav Klaus and First Deputy Prime Minister Valtr Komárek. The institute, headed by Komárek, had produced influential reports in the late 1980s advocating radical market reforms, as well as democratization of the political process to re-engage the public in social affairs.

Transition to a market economy has had the virtually unquestioned support of the population and political parties. There was also consensus on what stood in reform's way: state monopolies, price distortions, "soft" currency and so on. But disagreement flared over the speed of reform, pitting political considerations against economic projections. Komárek spoke for the cautious and the populists when he forecast "economic agony" resulting from too rapid a move to market economics. Klaus advocated swifter austerity measures, claiming that putting them off would only make the job harder. By the time of the June 1990 elections, Klaus' camp had emerged the winner, and his are the policies that will most likely guide the process of reform.

In the general terms that have been used so far, this program begins by setting the legislative framework for privatization and market relations. State monopolies are then to be broken down and most state-owned enterprises privatized. Reformed price structures will follow, along with liberalized foreign trade and capital flow. The last stages include making the Czechoslovak crown convertible and cutting prices free of state control. Privatization is to take place in two stages. "Minor privatization" will begin in late 1990, and will lead to private ownership of trade and service outlets (restaurants, shops etc.) by one of two means: restitution of property nationalized by the Communist government to the original owners or their heirs, or sale by auction to the public. The so-called "major privatization" of larger state holdings has required an improvised solution in a capital-poor country. Vouchers are to be distributed to the population as selected state-owned enterprises become joint-stock companies. People can then use the vouchers to buy shares, with demand creating a measure of value. The priority sale of shares in a given enterprise will be to its employees, but Czechoslovak citizens will also be able to purchase extra investment coupons at a price higher than the basic voucher cost. Profits from sales of enterprises to private persons—Czechoslovak or foreign—will contribute to the establishment of a State Property Fund, which in turn will help defray denationalization and restructuring costs. Even the classical liberal Klaus admits that up to 40 percent of the economy will remain state-owned for the foreseeable future. The March 1990 budget started the reform process by turning a 10 billion crown deficit (approximately $800 million) into a 5.4 billion crown surplus. It also cut subsidies to state enterprises by 10 percent, defense by 12.5 percent, and wage and price subsidies by 14 percent. State support of the Communist party (over 1 billion crowns a year) and its satellites was officially curtailed.

In the six months after the revolution, the Federal Assembly managed to pass much of the legislation necessary for these moves. The process began with establishing unemployment benefits, and devaluing the crown's artificially high exchange rate. The different forms of ownership (state, private and cooperative) now enjoy equal status. This is also true in agriculture, where members of cooperative farms may now leave to repossess family land taken from them, or receive an equivalent patch elsewhere. Foreign trade is no longer a state monopoly: individual businesses can now operate abroad without state approval. Czechoslovak and foreign citizens have equal rights for setting up businesses in Czechoslovakia with foreign capital (although foreigners are not yet allowed to purchase real estate). Joint-stock companies can be formed at any level: there is no limit on the number of employees allowed, state approval is not required, and foreigners can hold up to 100 percent interest. Shares may be distributed to employees, who have the right to be advised of strategy and management decisions, but operation of the enterprise remains securely in the hands of management. The government has also been given the power to break up monopolies and privatize at its discretion.

These measures form the skeleton for economic reform, and will put on flesh as more subsidies are cut in mid-1990, privatization begins in late 1990, and price reform takes off in earnest in 1991. The program laid out so far has won the approval of the International Monetary Fund, which has announced its intention to grant Czechoslovakia membership in 1990. The government has also won respect for its withdrawal from the Council for Mutual Economic Assistance (CMEA)* monetary system, and for its refusal of large doses of foreign aid. Aware that the economy is currently incapable of benefitting from a simple injection of capital, it is waiting to com-

* The former Soviet bloc's economic alliance.

plete basic structural reforms before asking for help. In theory, this all paints a rosy picture; but after the first six months, theory and the legislative framework are more or less all the country has had time to produce, and the real test is only just beginning.

Problems with state security

During these six months of feverish legislative activity, several problems arose that took some of the sheen off the velvet revolution. They are likely to remain major issues in the future.

There was never any doubt over what would be one of the most painful wounds to heal in all the Eastern European countries: the state security apparatus. When Havel appointed the Catholic Richard Sacher minister of internal affairs, he was the first non-Communist to hold that position for more than forty years. He initially seemed to be moving quickly to neutralize this most dangerous of ministries, one that controlled domestic and foreign intelligence, special military units and as many as 140,000 informers in a total population of only 15 million. Sacher immediately closed secret police departments, and in late January 1990 abolished State Security (StB) altogether, replacing certain arms of the service with new departments (foreign intelligence, protection of government members, a rapid deployment force and so on). He also established commissions to investigate the records of officers he was removing from active service.

As what seem to have been unfounded rumors of a secret police coup filled Prague in early 1990, these moves were welcomed by the public. But problems soon began to accumulate. It was Civic Forum that had pressed hard for the abolition of State Security; when Sacher finally did react, he fired officers but kept them on payroll for a further six months. The public, not surprisingly, found the argument that the law guaranteed severance pay hard to swallow. Wasn't this another example of the revolution being too "velvet" for its own good?

As the year progressed, accusations spread that Sacher was stalling on purges of his ministry and the secret police. The first major scandal broke when Sacher went to extraordinary lengths to find a deputy internal affairs minister from the previous regime a good position: first as his own deputy, then, as protest mounted, in an embassy and the Ministry of Defense. The officer, a General Alojz Lorenz, was finally retired with a large pension and bonus. When official investigation of his past began, Lorenz was arrested for breaches of the law under the Communist regime. Sacher insisted that he never knew of Lorenz's unsavory past.

A crisis, which the press was quick to dub "Sachergate," developed in April. The background to the affair was the screening of officials' and candidates' pasts to ensure they were "clean" of any dealings with the secret police.* It started with Sacher subordinates leaking information on a senior Civic Forum official, Oldrich Hromádko, who happened to be one of Sacher's most vocal critics. These documents alleged that Hromádko had worked in the 1950s as a concentration camp guard in the uranium mines, and contained what seemed to be his own report on killing inmates who were trying to escape. Civic Forum defended Hromádko by pointing out that the same accusations had been made against him in the 1960s, but had never been proven.

What had been simmering suspicion now burst out into the open. Sacher was a member of the People's Party, a traditionally Catholic party that had been an officially sanctioned satellite of the Communist party for the past forty years. The party had managed to regain much prestige during and after the revolution, and by May 1990 seemed to be attracting much of the Christian Democrat vote. The Hromádko leak appeared to be a campaign tactic to discredit the powerful Civic Forum, and demands were made for the minister's resignation. Accusations of abuse of ministerial privilege abounded, and the Federal Assembly decided to discuss the matter. A compromise that was never made public was reached between Sacher and his critics, and the minister stayed in office until the June 1990 elections.

---

* Václav Benda's "Open letter" goes into this in more detail.

At the same time several deputy ministers of Internal Affairs accused Sacher of ordering investigations of leading government and Federal Assembly members. They also suggested that he had been blocking the screening of certain election candidates' pre-revolutionary activity. Being a member of a former collaborationist party, Sacher seemed to have every reason to want the past left undisturbed. Once again, however, the minister weathered the storm, and even won the dismissal of the mutinous deputies. An important new appointment was made to replace them: Jan Ruml, editor of a leading independent newspaper, *Respekt* (one of Sacher's harshest critics), and a former Charter 77 spokesman. With these impeccable credentials, Ruml has taken over purging State Security and running the process for screening officials' pasts.

The nationality question

It was always clear that State Security would be a Pandora's box. But there was another issue that had been muted for many years and that surprised people with the vehemence of its reappearance: nationalist resentment. Many of the contributors to this book discuss this issue at some length, but a few words of background will help put their comments in context.

Since the founding of Czechoslovakia in 1918, there is nothing that annoys a Slovak, or a Czech, more than to suggest that their cultures and languages are the same. The two nations have had distinct histories, with the Czech lands (Bohemia and Moravia) falling under Austrian and German influence, while Slovakia was more closely associated with Hungary. During the First Republic (1918-38), the notion of "czechoslovakism" was encouraged as a way of creating a unified nation-state. This was resented by the minority Slovaks (they form about a third of Czechoslovakia's total population), and contributed to the rise of fascist and secessionist movements in the 1930s. When the the Nazis occupied the Czech lands in 1938-39, the Slovaks finally did establish an "independent" fascist puppet state.

The country reunited after World War II, but what limited autonomy the Slovaks won was lost in the Stalinist centralization that followed the 1948 Communist takeover. Little regional or cultural independence from Prague center was possible, even after the 1968 establishment of a federal structure. Slovaks resented Czech domination of their political and economic affairs; Czechs resented the financial and social burden of developing "backward" Slovakia. In the 1940s Slovakia was indeed less developed than the Czech lands, and, strongly Catholic, had shown less initial support for communism. The Communist regime reacted by investing heavily in Slovak development, and created an affirmative action program to increase Slovak participation in government and the Party. Czechs naturally resented this preferential treatment, particularly the fact that many of the most hard-line "normalizers" of the post-1968 period were Slovak.

A tight lid was kept on nationalist resentment, which ranged beyond Czech-Slovak rivalry to friction with other ethnic minorities: the Hungarians, Poles, Germans, Ruthenians, Romanians and particularly Gypsies, reviled by virtually everyone. That these sentiments would emerge after the revolution was predictable; but the speed with which this happened, and the forum in which it took place, was a surprise. Havel proposed to the Federal Assembly that the word "socialist" be removed from the official name of the Czechoslovak Republic. The Slovak desire for equal federal status prompted some to seize the opportunity to demand a symbolic change in the country's name. Tired of foreigners who refer to the people of either the Czech lands or Slovakia as "Czechs," they insisted on a hyphen in the name—Czecho-Slovakia—to emphasize their separateness. For a host of reasons,* and with demonstrations brewing in Slovakia, the Federal Assembly had difficulty finding a compromise acceptable to both nations. In an example of this young democracy's parliamentary inexperience, the harangues were allowed to continue longer than they need have, and several versions of the country's new name were adopted before a final version was accepted: the Czech and Slovak Federative Republic. This drawn-out affair was given amused

* Best described by Carnogursky in "Physics, Psychology and the Gentle Revolution," and by Urban in "The Politics of Power and Humiliation."

coverage in the international press and was a source of acute embarrassment to many Slovaks and Czechs.*

There is another area in which ethnic tensions have turned violent. In a situation all too familiar from other parts of the world, economic malaise and political uncertainty have combined to produce ultra-right chauvinists. There have been several cases of Gypsies and Vietnamese being attacked in some of Czechoslovakia's industrial cities, and in May 1990 there was even a racist rampage of two hundred skinheads and punks in Prague. Like any "nation within a nation," Gypsies have long been a target for national frustrations in Europe. In Czechoslovakia they are notoriously alienated and under-educated, the butt of jokes and much discrimination. The Vietnamese are students and guest workers who make up 35,000 of the 46,000 foreigners employed in Czechoslovakia. Under the previous regime, these workers and students from other Communist countries were invited to Czechoslovakia for training, and have always been resented by a population indifferent to policies of supporting "fraternal socialist states." The government has tried to calm the situation by announcing that this category of foreign workers will have to leave the country by 1995.

It is currently fashionable to write about the reemergence of nationalism in post-totalitarian Eastern Europe. Like any generalization that contains some truth, this one should not be overextended. Decades of "proletarian internationalism," rejection of "bourgeois nationalism," and centralization led to the suppression of ethnic and national identities. As Czechoslovakia starts on the path of painful reform, a reasonable dose of patriotism and national identity, and even rivalry, may be healthy. Much of President Havel's symbolic politics has in fact aimed at encouraging a sense of national pride and cohesion. Few Slovaks support outright independence, with even the Nationalist Party program of June 1990 claiming that it stands only for in-

---

* The translations in this book have mimicked the form of the country's name that contributors have chosen to use. Thus both "Czechoslovakia" and "Czecho-Slovakia" appear, with the former more common in Czech, and the latter preferred in Slovak.

creased autonomy. Certainly there are serious concerns among both Czechs and Slovaks, and much sensitivity and accommodation will be needed as new federal and republican governmental roles are established; but violent conflict or secession were not yet in the air by June 1990.

The political landscape

As the Federal Assembly overcame its teething problems (muddled procedure and chaotic debate) and passed a remarkable array of reform legislation, a new political landscape was taking shape. A burst of independent political activity followed the revolution, with more than seventy parties being formed in the first few months. The election law reduced this chaos by requiring 10,000 members or signatures for participation in the June 1990 national elections, but there were still twenty-three parties that met this requirement. Lack of definition and clear conceptualization was not surprising after four decades of single-party rule. Different candidates' programs tended to be virtually identical, seldom offering more than a call for pluralist democracy and a market economy. The traditional political extremes of right and left failed to emerge, and the basic distinction was between the Communist party and the rest.

The June 1990 elections identified the major political groups in the new Czechoslovakia. The vote was essentially a referendum on Civic Forum and Public Against Violence, the Czech and Slovak opposition movements formed during the revolution. Their first six months in power was up for popular approval, which they unambiguously won. Over 96 percent of eligible voters turned out, and gave Civic Forum 53.15 percent in the Czech Republic, while Public Against Violence won 32.54 percent in Slovakia.* The Communist

* Percentages given are for seats in the Federal Assembly's House of the People, which divides its seats in proportion to the size of the two republics: 101 for the Czech Republic, and 49 for the Slovak. The second chamber is called the House of Nations, and divides its seats equally between the republics.

party came a surprise second, with 13.48 percent in the Czech Republic and 13.81 percent in Slovakia. The Christian Democratic Union had been expected to rival Public Against Violence in the heavily Catholic Slovakia and was running strongly in polls in the Czech lands just a few weeks before the elections. After a series of problems (discussed below), it finished a disappointed third, with just 16.66 percent of the Slovak vote, and 8.69 percent of the Czech. Strong ethnic identities in unhomogeneous Czechoslovakia were reflected in support of minority parties. The Slovak National Party won 10.96 percent in Slovakia: a strong showing, but far from being a landslide of Slovak nationalism. A coalition of smaller groups (Poles, Germans and Hungarians) won 8.58 percent in Slovakia. 7.89 percent of the Czech Republic's voters supported The Society for Moravia and Silesia-Democratic Self-Administration's call for greater regional autonomy.*

What follows is a brief review of the major political forces that have developed over the six months following the revolution.

Civic Forum and Public Against Violence

Civic Forum and Public Against Violence are the products of the revolution. They were established as umbrella organizations to coordinate opposition pressure on the government, and negotiated the Communist party's transfer of power. As such they are enormously broad and amorphous, which has been the source of both their strength and weakness.

Civic Forum was the first to form, and drew on the relatively well-developed dissident circles in Prague, as well as cultural figures and student leaders. The voice of the revolution in the capital of the country, it is based in the Czech Republic and has remained more visible and influential than its sister organization, Public Against

---

* These were the only parties to gain the 5 percent minimum required for representation in the Federal Assembly; there were others that satisfied the 3 percent requirement for the republican parliaments, notably the Greens, the Slovak Democratic Party and the Social Democrat Party.

Violence. The latter is a Slovak movement and has made its presence most felt in that republic's parliament.

Both Civic Forum and Public Against Violence were determined to remain "civic movements" until at least the June elections. The very idea of politics has been discredited by decades of rigged elections and government deception of the population. For many, the word "party" reeks of the Communist past, political bureaucracies and abuse of power. The new movements established a loose structure without membership and tried to practice what Havel has dubbed "nonpolitical politics": civic activism without the power struggles and deception of traditional party politics. Local representatives in factories, offices and villages worked through the "Coordination Centers" in Prague and Bratislava. In this sense these movements have been highly successful. They have to a great extent overcome the "capital-provinces" and "intellectual-worker" barrier, and have established a truly broad base of support.

The first problem that faced these movements hit Civic Forum particularly hard. As new ministers and government officials were appointed in early 1990, there was a constant exodus of their top leadership. The president and government members represented in this book were all previously Civic Forum or Public Against Violence Coordination Center members. Once in office, they were effectively excluded from participation in day-to-day leadership of these movements by the demands of their new positions. The sheer scale of their work kept them away: people who weeks before had been dissidents, actors, even in prison, had to learn and govern at the same time. As members of the "government of national understanding," they were also expected to show political equanimity in the execution of their duties. They were of course highly visible, and their affiliation to the opposition movements was clear; but the movements missed their leadership, and often wished that they would use their prestige more to benefit their election efforts.

The looseness of these movement's structures caused other problems. There were cases of opportunists trying to use local Civic Forum and Public Against Violence offices for personal advancement, no surprise in a loosely-organized and recently victorious revolutionary movement. Its size and success created another fear: that Communist one-party rule would be replaced with that of a new totalitarianism. The Socialist party was particularly critical of the movements' "unfair advantage," pointing to their control of most of the government and the fact that they alone had representatives in factories, offices and farms. The Socialist party had in fact enjoyed a few advantages of its own during the forty years it was an obedient satellite of the Communist party, and its sniping did little either to hurt Civic Forum or to help itself (it received just under 2 percent of the national vote). The consistently "velvet" management of the revolution and the government was a convincing counter-argument.

Civic Forum and Public Violence's all-embracing nature have caused their most serious problems. Their tolerance of a whole range of political and religious opinion was drawn from dissident days, when groups like Charter 77 and the Movement for Civil Liberties welcomed a wide array of activist groups.* As the post-revolutionary situation developed, some parties under these movements' umbrella—the Christian Democrats, for instance, or the Social Democratic Party—split away to run in the elections as independents. But others stayed: usually for financial reasons, but also because running with the popular Civic Forum or Public Against Violence would bring representation in parliament, while the independents would struggle to break the 5 percent barrier.

There was thus a certain tension built into the situation. The "civic movements" spanned the whole political spectrum, from classical liberals (such as Pavel Bratinka or Václav Klaus, contributors to this book) to the neo-Trotskyist, "revolutionary Marxist" Petr Uhl (a former dissident and human rights activist who has become Director of the Czechoslovak Press Agency (CTK)). If incompatibilities were easily overcome in the theoretical discussions of dissent, they were a source

* See "From 1968 to 1989: A Chronological Commentary" (1977 and 1988) for a description of these groups.

of tension and conflict when it came to practice and the formulation of policy.

Another, related source of friction in Civic Forum and Public Against Violence tended to follow generational lines. Many of the initial members of Charter 77 were former Communist party members who had been expelled for their roles in the Prague Spring reforms of the late 1960s. They were critical of the "normalization" regime, which they saw as a perversion of socialist principles, but often remained devoted to the ideals of Marxism. The younger generation tended to be more thorough-going in its rejection of both the totalitarian communism of Husák and Jakes, and the "reform communism" of a Dubcek or Gorbachev. As far as they were concerned, it was not the application that was flawed, but the entire approach.

The conflict in Civic Forum's Brno headquarters epitomized this friction. In this, the capital of Moravia, two former dissidents clashed over Forum policy, and particularly over how to deal with local Communists still in power. The older Jaroslav Sabata was a regional Communist party secretary in 1968. Expelled in the purges that followed the Soviet-led invasion, he was twice a spokesman for Charter 77 and was imprisoned for his opposition to the "normalization" regime. Like many of the dissidents of his generation, Sabata favored the "velvet" approach of negotiations and compromise. He was opposed on this by Petr Cibulka, a younger exdissident who advocated demonstrations and more militant anti-Communist measures. A serious and embarrassing power struggle ensued, with demonstrations by supporters and occupations of public buildings. In the end both Sabata and Cibulka had to be demoted from the Civic Forum Council in Brno. The importance of all this is not so much in the direct political sense, although Brno did not benefit from the tussles. Rather what happened there may be a harbinger of things to come for Civic Forum and Public Against Violence in general. As the economic situation becomes more serious and what post-revolutionary unity there still is dissipates, political and generational tensions like this will only increase.

Civic Forum and Public Against Violence's rallying call for the

June 1990 elections had a single major theme: the "return to Europe," with the pluralist democracy, market economy and cultural traditions which this was held to imply. This vague platform was typical of the political climate six months after the revolution—although these were also the only groups to warn how much reform would demand of the population, adopting as their own John F. Kennedy's slogan: "Ask not what your country can do for you; ask what you can do for your country." As movements that were formed in opposition to communism tried to become political actors in their own right, the incompatibilities of some of the umbrella's constituent groups seemed bound to cause friction and fracture.

The government, dominated by the two movements, has established the framework for reform. But the pace and extent of that reform (the role of the state, the division of power between the federal and republican governments, or the timing of price reform, for example) are not yet clear. As policies are planned and executed, the most important support *and* criticism will likely come from the ranks of Civic Forum and Public Against Violence themselves. The umbrella's fabric will have to rip, for it is an unnatural agglomeration of groups whose only reason for unity—opposition to the Communist regime—is fast disappearing. Public Against Violence was already hinting at a split before the elections, with some members forming a political party and others starting a social aid group to help the poor and needy as reform gets under way. Civic Forum will probably follow suit, with some members striking out on their own, while others establish one or, perhaps, several centrist political parties.

The Communist party

The velvet revolution was less the overthrow of a regime by a political opposition than the collapse of a discredited and corrupt system that had long since ceased to be at all effective. The Communist party that ran this system had felt the effects of its isolation from the population well before November 1989: Party membership was down, and the average age of Party members by late 1989 was over forty-five. Inertia and apparent totalitarian power kept the regime alive until the public outcry on 18 November 1989. As the ruling Party was forced to relinquish power, the hemorrhage began.

By February 1990 the Party had lost a full third of its members, including three members of the new government: Prime Minister Marián Calfa, First Deputy Prime Minister Valtr Komárek, and Deputy Prime Minister Vladimír Dlouhy. Gestures at reforming its structure, leadership and program at the extraordinary Party conference on 20 December 1989* made some cosmetic changes, but were not enough to stop a number of mutinous groups splintering from the Party. The Czechoslovak Communist Party did not follow the example of some of its East European counterparts, dissolving itself or adopting a new name. Instead, with much of its old membership intact, its tactics were to lay low.

The "gentle" revolution was not pressing for disbandment or prosecution of the Party as a whole—although several members of the leadership were arrested for their roles in ordering the police brutality of 17 November and others were arraigned on charges of "crimes against peace" in 1968. The Party opted not to counter what questions and accusations were leveled at it, hoping thus not to provoke public condemnation. It let the opposition government take over its Augean stables, and contented itself with occasional sniping at its "amateur" efforts. President Havel's amnesty, it suggested, had encouraged a rising crime rate; the new government was fueling nationalist tensions; economic reform was threatening the social security that the Party had guaranteed during its tenure.

For the most part, the Party remained quiet. As the Czech proverb says, *kdo mlci, priznává se*: he who is silent admits his guilt. Public censure grew as Havel spoke repeatedly of the devastation wrought by the old regime. Books and articles on crimes committed under communism started to appear, and even linked the new first secretary, Vasil Mohorita, to a secret police operation against dissidents in the early 1980s.

The single greatest issue that emerged was the Communist party's

---

* See "From 1968 to 1989: A Chronological Commentary" for details.

enormous assets. The only true party in a single-party state, it had been inseparable from the government in terms of both its power and finances. When the Communist government fell in December 1989, the Party retained most of its real estate holdings, cars and financial assets, granted to it by its own government. No reliable estimates of the size of these assets existed, although guesses ranged into billions of dollars. The consistently legal and velvet revolution respected rights of property, but pressured the Party to relinquish some buildings, which it did.

Popular dissatisfaction with this state of affairs began to flare in April 1990, when a symbolic ten-minute strike was called to demand that the Party release other assets. Then the Prague prosecutor-general, Tomás Sokol, threatened to commence legal proceedings against the Party for its past breaches of the law, including illegal gain and "propagation of fascism." Sokol's superiors promised disciplinary action for this unauthorized action, but he was supported by Civic Forum and much of the public. Repeated demonstrations and even a hunger strike were held in his support. When the Federal Assembly produced a report detailing vast Communist party assets (including state funding and large, mysterious hard currency withdrawals from the State Bank, which were then sent to Moscow), further protests were held.

Havel and parliament stood by their commitment not to ban the Communist party, but pressure in Prague continued to grow for some sort of punitive action. Former satellites of the Communist party—the People's, Socialist and Democratic parties—joined the Social Democrats in calling for abolition of the Party before the June elections. Clearly an attempt to clear the left for the Social Democrats, and to rid the satellites of their collaborationist past, the move was denounced by Civic Forum and others as "politically immature"—but contributed to the general tone of condemnation. Just before the elections, the Czech Republic's prosecutor-general pressed charges against the Party for stealing from the state, and the government announced that all Party property would be confiscated as of 1 June 1990.

The Communist party weathered this storm surprisingly well for a number of reasons. It still has the largest membership of all the political parties in Czechoslovakia and benefits from the nationwide apparatus set up during its rule. *Rudé právo,* its newspaper, is the best distributed source of news in the country, and presents the Party's view of the world to a large audience. And there still is a large audience for what the Party has been saying. Certain sections of the population are nervous at what the economic reforms will do to their standard of living or job security: workers in heavy industry, for example, or pensioners. The Party has continuously hinted at the effects of cutting state social security subsidies, although the new government had been careful to keep a comprehensive safety net in place.

Czechoslovak agriculture was relatively effective (by Soviet standards), and enjoyed large state subsidies and low quality control under the old regime. Somewhat distanced from the "intellectuals' revolution" in Prague (although this has been much less of a problem than in, say, Bulgaria), some farmers are not overjoyed at future competition with Western Europe in terms of either quality or productivity. And then there is the vast, grey army of bureaucrats, whose jobs were guaranteed by toeing the Party line. Marketization will streamline this apparatus and will trim considerable fat from the bloated administration of Soviet-style centralism. These people will have to prove their effectiveness to keep their jobs, and not just rely on Party membership. The combination of these various interests, together with a small core of Marxist-Leninists who still believe despite it all, gave the Communist party second place in the June 1990 elections: far behind Civic Forum and Public Against Violence, but with a solid 13 percent of the national vote.

This collection's interview with Vasil Mohorita, first secretary of the Communist party, shows the type of image the "new" Communists are trying to create for themselves. Assuring the population that it is now a "modern, democratic, leftist party," the Party that was so long out of step with Moscow's reform beat has now adopted very Gorbachevian rhetoric. Too little too late, perhaps. The Party hopes to regain some support during the social upheavals of reform. But if a credible leftist alternative emerges—the Social Democrats are the traditional candidate—the disintegration of the Communist party that started even before November 1989 is likely to continue.

The Christian Democrats and other parties

As elsewhere in Eastern Europe, one of the strongest political currents to emerge from the revolutions of 1989 was the Christian Democrats. The Catholic church had been one of the most important structures for opposition to the Communist regime, though not as vocal or organized as in Poland. After the November revolution, two religious activists who had been active in the dissident movement broke from the civic movements' ranks to found Christian Democratic parties. Jan Carnogursky, first deputy prime minister in the federal government, former leader of Public Against Violence and one of Slovakia's leading dissidents under communism, headed the Christian Democratic Movement in predominantly Catholic Slovakia. Václav Benda—a leading figure in Charter 77, the Movement for Civil Liberties and other dissident groups—founded the Christian Democratic Party in the less religiously active Czech lands of Bohemia and Moravia.

Pope John Paul II's visit to Czechoslovakia in April 1990 gave these parties added prestige in the eyes of a number of people. Calling for a rejection of the collectivist anonymity of the Communist past, and a return to individual responsibility, the Pope also suggested the first synod to include all European bishops. This meeting would discuss the implications of a post-Communist Europe and the role the church would play in it. This dovetailed with the Czech and Slovak Christian Democrats' increasing cooperation with West European parties of a similar inclination (particularly in West Germany), which they hoped would boost their standing as the party to lead the country back to morality and Europe.

An election coalition was formed between the Czech and Slovak parties, which were joined by the former satellite People's Party. After forty years of subservience to the Communist party, the People's Party had been at pains to break with the past during and after the revolution, electing a new leadership and working closely with Civic Forum during negotiations with the Communist party. Increasingly popular in the Czech Republic, the People's Party was still well-funded under the laws covering its former satellite status. Running an efficient and highly visible campaign, it hoped to bolster Benda's new, small and under-funded Christian Democratic Party.

A series of setbacks showed that the People's Party had not yet managed to escape its past. The scandals surrounding Richard Sacher, minister of Internal Affairs and senior People's Party official, were described above. Another of the party's representatives in government, Frantisek Reichel, was fired for incompetence. Just before the elections, Deputy Foreign Minister Vera Bartosková dropped out of the race: the implication had to be that her past was less than clean. But the most telling blow came when the new Deputy Minister of Internal Affairs Jan Ruml announced that the chairman of the People's Party, Josef Bartoncík, had been a paid secret police informer since 1971. In the wake of Sacher's apparent hesitancy to purge State Security, and his reported blocking of some screenings of candidates' pasts, this was a crippling blow to the credibility of the People's Party. The largest party in the Christian Democratic Union, its fall turned what was expected to be a strong showing into a disappointing third place. In Slovakia, where Carnogursky's movement was expected to defeat even Public Against Violence, the coalition came a distant second, only just beating the Communist party. In retrospect, alliance with the People's Party was a tactical disaster. With time and restructuring of the coalition, however, the other Christian Democratic parties are still sure to be a major force in future elections.

Three other parties won representation in the Federal Assembly: the Slovak Nationalist Party, the Society for Moravia and Silesia, and Coexistence (a Slovak coalition of Polish, Hungarian, German, Ruthenian and Jewish interests). Supporting increased regional autonomy and minority rights, these groups will encourage the current trend towards greater concentration of power in the republican governments.

There was a series of other parties that may not have enjoyed vast support in the June 1990 elections, but was expected to play an important political role in years to come. In a country that some consider the most polluted in Europe, the Greens attracted much interest in the early days of 1990. The enormity of this ecological disaster meant that all the other parties made environmental issues part of their platforms, however, and they coopted the Greens' most important policies. The Greens had also suffered from secret police penetration and had trouble establishing credibility as an independent organization. Perhaps most damaging in a national election was its concentration on local issues and its failure to produce a leader of visible stature. The Greens won about 4 percent in the national elections, but can be expected to do better in the local elections in November 1990.

The Socialist Party was a satellite of the Communist party under the old regime and enjoyed the funding and staff that went along with this as it prepared for the June elections. It tried to call on the traditions of its predecessor, the National Socialist Party, which had been a major political power between the wars. With the demise of the Communist party—not as complete as some anticipated—the Socialists hoped to inherit the role of leading spokesman for the left. The party had also played a visible role in the revolution: speeches to the vast demonstrations on Wenceslas Square were given from its building, and its newspaper became one of the revolution's mouthpieces. This, together with a professional election campaign and a new, young party leader were meant to regenerate the appeal of socialism. These assets, together with occasionally heavy-handed criticism of Civil Forum, failed to save the party from the shadow of its past collaboration, however, and it won less than 1 percent of the vote in June.

The Social Democrats should have been an important factor in these elections. One of the First Republic's strongest political forces, the party had been forcibly merged with the Communist party in 1948. Party traditions were kept alive both in emigration and at home, and it was reestablished in November 1989. A split in the leadership soon followed, however, pitting the former dissident and human rights activist Rudolf Battek against leaders of the emigré organization, who had returned to Czechoslovakia after the revolution. Offering considerable financial and logistical aid, the latter won control of the party leadership and broke with Civic Forum. Battek's Social Democratic Club opted to stay under the Civic Forum umbrella, though they have not ruled out reconciliation with the party in the future. If differences can be overcome and a possible merger with other leftist groups achieved, the Social Democrats stand to win much more in the future than the 4.11 percent they won in the Czech Republic, or the 1.81 percent they received in Slovakia.

There is not a strong tradition of rightist political parties in Czechoslovakia. The strongest conservative voice has been the Christian Democrats, whose strong defense of individual responsibility and rights sometimes verge on libertarianism. The Slovak Democratic Party uses similar Christian rhetoric, and although it did not win the 5 percent needed for representation in the national parliament, it will play a major role in Slovak politics. Other voices from the right come from within Civic Forum's ranks. Pavel Bratinka's Civic Democratic Alliance and Emanuel Mandler's Democratic Initiative both ran under Civic Forum's umbrella in the June elections, and consequently won representation in the Federal Assembly and the republican parliaments. Other rightist parties won virtually no support in the national elections and are not likely to rebound very quickly. The rightist cause may be difficult to advance as the government adopts a market economy, and forty years of socialism ends with what much of the population will probably see as enough of a move to the center.

• • •

A JOKE MADE the rounds of Prague in early 1989 that captured the mood of the moment. The leaders of the Soviet Union, the United States and Czechoslovakia are each granted one question of God. Mikhail Gorbachev goes first. The Soviet leader wants to know what his country will be like in twenty years' time. "Capitalist," says God, at which Gorbachev collapses in tears. George Bush gloats and asks the same question about the United States, but God's reply is "Communist," whereupon Bush starts to wail as well. Undaunted, Milos Jakes, general secretary of the Communist party, asks what the future holds for Czechoslovakia—and it's God who weeps, with pity.

With the unimaginably rapid collapse of the Communist system in November and December, God finally seemed to be cracking a wary smile over Czechoslovakia's future. The initial rush of optimism and energy has quickly been tempered, however, as people recognize the lasting effects of political and economic distortion, on both individuals' attitudes and society as a whole. The first six months since the revolution have seen the new president, government and political leaders set the framework for the transformation from Soviet-style socialism to a market economy, and from totalitarianism to democracy. The most basic groundwork for these institutional changes has been laid, but represents no more than a start in the right direction. More radical—and painful—reforms must now be expanded, requiring the resolve and sustained consensus of both government and people. This is the stage, just now underway, that will test the mettle of the velvet revolution.

Václav Havel

BORN IN 1936, Havel was denied university education until the mid-1960s because of his family's prominence during the "bourgeois" First Republic (1918-38). He was finally admitted to the Academy for Dramatic Arts and graduated in 1967. Continuing to write the "absurdist" plays that were already bringing him international recognition, Havel worked as a stage hand and program director in Prague. During and immediately following the Prague Spring, he chaired the Circle of Independent Writers and was an outspoken critic of censorship and repression.

Following the Soviet-led invasion in August 1968, Havel and his works were blacklisted. Fired from his theater job, he finally found work in a brewery in northern Bohemia. In 1975 he wrote an open letter to President Gustáv Husák protesting the moral decay of the post-invasion "normalization" process. In 1977 he was a founding member of Charter 77 and one of its first spokesmen. In April 1978 he co-founded the Committee for the Defense of the Unjustly Prosecuted (VONS). After repeated interrogations, constant surveillance and harassment, Havel was sentenced in 1979 to four-and-a-half years in prison along with other VONS members. He refused an opportunity to emigrate and served out his sentence until pneumonia and international pressure forced his early release in 1983. He continued his dissident activities under continued police persecution. He was arrested in January 1989, after the mass demonstrations in Prague, and was sentenced to eight months in jail for "incitement." He was released in May 1989 after serving about half his term. Sporadic detainment and harassment continued, with Havel's last imprisonment coming less than a month before the start of the "velvet revolution" on 17 November 1989.

The most prominent figure in Czech and Slovak dissent throughout the 1970s and 1980s, Havel is perhaps best known as a dramatist, although he has also written on political, philosophical and ethical subjects. These works were all published in the underground and foreign press. He is also the recipient of numerous international awards and honorary degrees. He quickly became the unofficial leader of the November 1989 revolution, and headed the opposition delegation that negotiated the Communist relinquishment of power. On 29 December 1989, the Federal Assembly unanimously elected him president.

Address to a Joint Session of the United States Congress

I

MY FRIENDS ADVISED me to speak to you in Czech. I don't know why. Perhaps they wanted you to hear the sweet sound of my mother tongue.

The last time I was arrested, on October 27th of last year, I didn't know if it would be for two days or for two years. When the rock musician Michael Kocab told me exactly one month later that I would probably be proposed as a candidate for president, I thought it was one of his usual jokes. When, on December 10th 1989, my actor friend Jiri Bartoska nominated me Civic Forum's presidential candidate, I thought it inconceivable that the parliament we had inherited from the previous regime would elect me.

Twelve days later, when I was unanimously elected president of my country, I had no idea that in less than two months I would be speaking to this famous and powerful assembly; that millions of people who had never heard of me would listen to my speech; and that hundreds of politicians and political scientists would study every word I say.

When I was arrested on October 27th, I was living in a country ruled by the most conservative Communist government in Europe.

Our society slumbered beneath the pall of a totalitarian system. Today, less than four months later, I speak to you as the representative of a country that has started on the road to democracy, that has complete freedom of speech, that is now preparing for free elections, and that wants to create a prosperous market economy and an independent foreign policy.

It is all very strange indeed.

But I am not here to speak of myself or my feelings, or merely to talk about my country. What I have just said is a small example, drawn from what I know well, that illustrates something general and important.

We live in extraordinary times. The face of our world is changing so rapidly that none of the political speedometers we have are adequate.

We playwrights, who have to be able to cram a whole human life or historical epoch into a two-hour play, can scarcely keep up with this speed. And if it gives us problems, then imagine the trouble political scientists must have, since they spend their lives studying the realm of the probable and must have even less experience of the improbable than we dramatists.

I shall try to explain why I think that the speed of change in my country, in Central and Eastern Europe and of course in the USSR itself has had such a significant impact on the shape of today's world, and why this concerns the fate of us all, including you Americans. I would like to examine this first from a political perspective, and then from a point of view we might call philosophical.

II

THE WORLD HAS been threatened with catastrophe twice in this century. Twice this catastrophe was born in Europe, and twice you Americans, with others, were called upon to save Europe, the world and yourselves.

The first rescue mission was a great boon to us Czechs and Slovaks. Thanks to the strong support of your President Wilson, our first president, Tomas Garrigue Masaryk, could found our modern state. He based it, as you know, on the same principles that underpin the United States of America, as his manuscripts held by the Library of Congress testify.

At the same time, America itself was making great advances. It became the most powerful nation on earth, and understood the responsibility that accompanied this strength. Proof of this are the hundreds of thousands of your young citizens who gave their lives for the liberation of Europe, and the graves of American pilots and soldiers on Czechoslovak soil.

But there was something else that was also happening. The Soviet Union appeared, started to grow, and transformed the enormous sacrifices of its people, suffering under totalitarian rule, into such strength that after World War II it was the second most powerful state in the world. It was a country that rightly terrified people, for no one knew what its rulers would think of next, what country they would decide to conquer and drag into their sphere of influence, as it's called in political language.

All this taught us to see the world in bipolar terms, as two vast forces, one a defender of freedom, the other a source of terror. Europe became the point of friction between these two powers, and so turned into one huge arsenal divided in two. Half of this arsenal belonged to the force of terror, while the other—the free half—bordering on the ocean and not wanting to be driven into it, had to work with you to devise a complex security system. It is probably thanks to this system that we still exist.

This may be the third time that you have rescued us Europeans, the world and yourselves. You have helped us survive until now by waging not a hot war, but a cold one.

And now what is happening is happening. The totalitarian system is breaking down in the Soviet Union and in most of its satellites, and our nations are looking for a way to democracy and independence.

The first act in this fascinating drama began when Mr. Gorbachev and his allies were faced with their country's sad reality and initiated their policy of "perestroika." They clearly had no idea of what they were setting in motion, or how rapidly events would unfold. We knew a lot, of course, about the vast number of growing problems that lay beneath the honeyed and unchanging mask of socialism. But I don't think any of us knew how little it would take for these problems to reveal themselves in all their enormity, or for the aspirations of these nations to emerge in all their strength. The mask fell away so quickly that in the flood of work that has ensued, we've literally had no time to be surprised.

What does all this mean for the world in the long run? Several things are clear. I'm convinced that what we are witnessing is a historically irreversible process and that Europe can begin again to seek its own identity now that it need not be an armory split in two. Perhaps this is reason to hope that sooner or later your boys won't have to guard Europe's freedom, or come to our rescue, since Europe will at last be capable of standing watch over herself.

But this is still not the main point. The most important thing, it seems to me, is that these revolutionary changes will allow us to abandon the antiquated straightjacket of seeing the world in bipolar terms so that we may finally enter an era of multipolarity. That is, an era in which all of us—large and small, former slaves and former masters—will be able to create what your great president Lincoln called "the family of man." Can you imagine what a relief this would be to that part of the globe we call the "Third World," even though it is the largest?

I don't think it's appropriate simply to generalize, so let me be specific:

1. As you certainly know, over the centuries most of Europe's major wars and other conflagrations have traditionally begun and ended on the territory of modern Czechoslovakia, or else they were somehow related to that region. The Second World War was the most recent example. This is understandable: whether we like it or not, we are located in the very heart of Europe, which is why we have no view of the sea and no real navy. I mention this because political stability in our country has traditionally been important for the whole of Europe. This is still true today. Our government of

national understanding, our current Federal Assembly, other state offices and I myself will personally guarantee this stability until we hold free elections, in June 1990.

We understand the terribly complex reasons, above all the domestic political reasons, why the Soviet Union cannot withdraw its troops from our territory as quickly as they arrived in 1968. We understand that the arsenals built there over the past twenty years cannot be dismantled and removed overnight. Nevertheless, in our bilateral negotiations with the Soviet Union we would like to have as many Soviet units as possible moved out of the country before the elections, in the interests of political stability. The more successful our negotiations, the better those who are elected in our place will be able to guarantee the political stability of our country after the elections.

2. I often hear the question: how can the United States of America help us today? My reply is as paradoxical as the whole of my life has been. You can help us most of all by helping the Soviet Union on its irreversible but immensely complicated road to democracy. Its path is far more complex than that of its former European satellites. You yourselves know best how to give prompt support to the non-violent evolution of this vast, multinational colossus towards democracy and autonomy for all its peoples. I would not presume to offer you advice. I can only say that the sooner and the more peacefully the Soviet Union begins to move towards genuine political pluralism, respect for the rights of nations to independence, and towards a working—that is, a market—economy, the better it will be, not only for Czechs and Slovaks, but for the whole world. The sooner this happens, the sooner you yourselves will be able to reduce the burden of the military budget born by the American people. To put it metaphorically: the millions you spend on the East today will soon return to you in the form of billions in savings.

3. It is not true that the Czech writer Václav Havel wants to dissolve the Warsaw Pact tomorrow and then NATO the next day, as some eager journalists have written. Václav Havel simply thinks what he has already said here, that American soldiers shouldn't have to be separated from their mothers for another hundred years just

"This is the department of blunders and mistakes.
Crimes are next door."

because Europe is incapable of guaranteeing peace, which it ought to do, in order to make some amends, at least, for having given the world two world wars.

Sooner or later Europe has to recover and come into its own, and decide for itself how many of whose soldiers it needs for its own security—and everything that depends on that security—so that it can shine as an example of peace to the whole world. Václav Havel cannot make decisions about things it is not proper for him to decide. He is merely putting in a good word for genuine peace, and for achieving it quickly.

4. Czechoslovakia thinks that the projected summit conference of countries participating in the Helsinki process should take place soon and that, in addition to what it already has planned, it should aim to hold the so-called Helsinki Two conference earlier than 1992, as originally scheduled. We feel it could be something far more significant than has so far seemed possible. We think that Helsinki Two should be something that has never been held, a European peace conference that would finally put a formal end to World War II and all its unhappy consequences. Such a conference would officially accept a unified, democratic Germany in a new pan-European structure that could decide about its own security system. This system would naturally involve some links with the part of the globe we might call the "Helsinki" part, stretching west from Vladivostok to Alaska. The borders of the European states (which incidentally ought to become increasingly unimportant) should finally be legally guaranteed by a common treaty. It should be absolutely clear that the basis for such a treaty would have to be general respect for human rights, genuine political pluralism and free elections.

5. Naturally we welcome the initiative of President Bush, which was essentially accepted by Mr. Gorbachev as well, concerning a radical reduction in the number of American and Soviet troops in Europe. This is a magnificent shot in the arm for the Vienna talks and creates favorable conditions not only for our own efforts to secure the quickest possible withdrawal of Soviet troops from Czechoslovakia, but also indirectly for our aim of making considerable cuts

in the Czechoslovak army, which is disproportionately large in relation to our population. If Czechoslovakia were forced to defend itself against anyone, which we hope will not happen, then it will be capable of doing so with a considerably smaller army, for this time its defense would be—for the first time in decades, even centuries—supported by the common and indivisible will of both its nations and its leadership. Our freedom, independence and newborn democracy have been purchased at great cost, and we will not surrender them. For the sake of clarity, I should add that whatever steps we take are not intended to complicate the Vienna disarmament talks, but rather to facilitate them.

6. Czechoslovakia is returning to Europe. In both its own and the general interest, it wants to coordinate this return—both politically and economically—with the other returnees, which means above all with our neighbors the Poles and the Hungarians. We are doing what we can to coordinate these returns. We are also doing what we can so that Europe finds itself able to welcome us, its wayward children. We hope that Europe will open itself to us, that it will set about transforming its structures—which are formally European but *de facto* Western European—to allow the participation of its eastern half. Not of course in such a way that this will be to its detriment, but rather to its advantage.

7. I have already said this in our parliament, but I would like to repeat it here, in this Congress, which is architecturally far more attractive. For many years Czechoslovakia has been someone's insignificant satellite, and has refused to face up to its responsibility in the world. It has a lot to make up for. If I dwell on this and so many other important things here, it is only because I feel—along with my fellow citizens—a sense of guilt for our former reprehensible passivity, along with a rather ordinary sense of indebtedness.

8. "Last but not least,"* we are of course delighted that your country is so readily lending its support to our reemerging democ-

* In English in the original.

racy. Both our peoples were deeply moved by the generous offers made a few days ago at Prague's Charles University, one of Europe's oldest, by your secretary of state, Mr. James Baker. We are ready to sit down and discuss them.

III

LADIES AND GENTLEMEN,

I've only been president for two months, and I've never attended any schools for presidents. My only school was life itself. Therefore I don't want to burden you any longer with my political thoughts, but instead will move on to an area that is more familiar to me. This is what I earlier called the philosophical aspect of those changes taking place in our corner of the world, changes that affect people everywhere.

As long as people are people, democracy in the full sense of the word will never be more than an ideal. One can approach it as one would a horizon, in ways that may be better or worse, but it can never be fully attained. In this sense you too are merely working towards democracy. You have thousands of problems of all kinds, as all countries do. But you have one great advantage: you have been moving towards democracy uninterruptedly for more than two hundred years, and your journey towards that horizon had never been cut short by totalitarianism. Czechs and Slovaks, despite their humanist traditions going back to the first millennium, have worked towards democracy for a mere twenty years, between the two world wars, and now for the three and a half months since November 17th of last year.

The advantage that you have over us is obvious.

The Communist version of totalitarianism has left both our nations, Czechs and Slovaks—as it has all the nations of the Soviet Union and the other countries that the Soviet Union has subjugated in its time—a legacy of countless dead, an infinite spectrum of human suffering, profound economic decline, and above all enormous human humiliation. It has brought us horrors that fortunately you have not known.

At the same time, however—unintentionally, of course—it has given us something positive: a special capacity that sometimes allows us to see a little further than someone who has not undergone this bitter experience. A person who cannot move and live an even partially normal life, because he is pinned under a boulder, has more time to think about his hopes than someone who is not trapped in this way.

What I am trying to say is this: we all have things to learn from you, from how to educate our offspring or elect our representatives to how to organize our economic life so that it will lead to prosperity, not poverty. But it needn't only be a question of the well-educated, the powerful and the wealthy offering assistance to someone who has nothing and who therefore has nothing to offer in return.

We too can offer you something: our experience and the knowledge that springs from it. This is a subject for books, many of which have been written, and many of which have yet to appear. I shall therefore limit myself to a single idea.

This specific experience I speak of has given me one great certainty: that consciousness precedes being, and not the other way around, as the Marxists claim.

For this reason, the salvation of our world can be found only in the human heart, in the power of humans to reflect, in human meekness and responsibility.

Without a global revolution in the sphere of human consciousness, nothing will change for the better in the sphere of our being as humans, and the catastrophe towards which this world is headed—be it ecological, social, demographic, or a general breakdown of civilization—will be unavoidable. If we are no longer threatened by world war, or by the danger of absurd mountains of nuclear weapons blowing up the world, this does not mean that we have finally won. This is actually far from being a final victory.

We are still a long way from the "family of man"; in fact, we seem to be receding from the ideal rather than drawing closer to it. Interests of all kinds—personal, selfish, state, national, group and, if you like, corporate—still considerably outweigh genuinely common and global concerns. We are still under the sway of the destructive and enormously arrogant belief that man is the pinnacle of creation, and not just a part of it, and that he is therefore permitted everything.

There are many who say that they are concerned not for themselves but for the cause, while it is obvious that they are out for themselves and not for the cause at all. We are still destroying the planet that was entrusted to us, along with its environment. We still close our eyes to the world's growing social, cultural and ethnic conflicts. Every once in a while we say that the anonymous megamachinery that we have created for ourselves no longer serves us but rather has enslaved us yet still we fail to do anything about it.

In other words, we still don't know how to put morality above politics, science and economics. We are still incapable of understanding that the only genuine grounding for all our actions—if they are to be moral—is responsibility. Responsibility to something higher than family, country, company, success. Responsibility to that level of being where all our actions are indelibly recorded and where they will be properly judged.

The interpreter or mediator between us and this higher authority is what is traditionally referred to as human conscience.

If I subordinate my political behavior to the imperative given me by my conscience, then I can't go far wrong. If, on the contrary, I were not guided by this voice, then not even ten presidential schools with 2,000 of the best political scientists in the world could help me.

That is why I ultimately decided, after much resistance, to accept the burden of political responsibility.

I'm not the first, nor will I be the last intellectual to do this. On the contrary, I feel that there will be more and more of them all the time. If the hope of the world lies in human consciousness, then it's clear that intellectuals cannot forever avoid their share of responsibility for the world, hiding their distaste for politics under a supposed need for independence.

It's easy to have independence on your program, leaving it to others to put that program into action. If everyone thought that way, pretty soon no one would be independent at all.

I feel that you Americans should have no difficulty understanding all this. Did not the best minds of your country, people we might call intellectuals, write your famous Declaration of Independence, your Bill of Rights, your Constitution; and didn't they—most important of all—take upon themselves the responsibility of putting these ideas into practice? The worker from Branik in Prague to whom your president referred in his State of the Union message this year is far from being the only person in Czechoslovakia, let alone the world, who is inspired by these great documents. They inspire us all. They inspire us despite the fact that they are over two hundred years old. They inspire us to be citizens.

When Thomas Jefferson wrote that "Governments are instituted among Men deriving their just Powers from the Consent of the Governed," it was a simple and important act of the human spirit.

What gave meaning to that act, however, was the fact that the author backed it up with his life. It was not just his words, but his deeds as well.

I shall close by repeating what I said at the beginning: history has accelerated. I believe that once again it will be the human mind that perceives this acceleration, comprehends its shape, and transforms its own words into deeds.

Thank you.

21 February 1990

The Legacy of the Past Regime and the Work Ahead

WHEN MY PREDECESSOR (whom we really can't feel too proud of) stepped out onto this balcony precisely forty-two years ago today, he announced to your fathers and grandfathers that there had just been a successful putsch. He called this putsch a "glorious victory of working people over reactionary forces"—and until recently this is what we all had to call it.

It is my pleasant duty to announce to you from this very same balcony that we're once again free to tell the truth about our modern history. And I won't be locked up if I state this fact: that what happened in February 1948 was a putsch, and *not* a "glorious victory of working people over reactionary forces." Just the opposite: it was an inglorious victory of reactionary forces over working people.

Nevertheless, the fact remains that a considerable number of our citizens believed this lie, and thought that this violation of democracy was a necessary step on the way to a socially just world. Some of them felt they had to carry rifles and organize manhunts against various levels of society, since a clean end justifies dirty means.

The majority of our two nations has been violated, the minority deceived. As in any country that has found itself in a similar situa-

---

This piece is from a speech delivered on Revolution Day on the Old Town Square in Prague, 5 February 1990.

tion, Czechoslovakia has had its share of criminals who wrapped themselves in a veil of noble ideals and were then willing to torture people in cold blood, killing them and scattering their ashes over frozen roads.

We mustn't forget any of those who were mistreated, tortured or executed. We mustn't forget anyone who was able to resist totalitarianism. And we mustn't forget the people who did the torturing and executing. If history's truth and justice are not allowed to emerge, then our nations' drawn-out illness will never have a chance to heal.

At the same time we mustn't mock those who really did believe the insidious official lie, but didn't personally or knowingly do anything cruel. They worked honestly, without noticing that what they were building had rotten foundations. One of the most beautiful human qualities is the ability to forgive. If we find it in ourselves to forgive our captors, then we should certainly learn to forgive our fellow prisoners, who were locked up not behind the fences of a prison camp, but behind the infernally elusive bars of dialectic ideology. Who wouldn't long for a world without masters and slaves, exploiters and exploited? Who wouldn't dream of a world in which a pampered industrialist's son doesn't insult his serving girl? Who wouldn't long for a world in which the workers have a say in the management of their factory? When people are offered such beautiful ideals, and when the ugly means to this end are given a purportedly scientific explanation, it's no surprise that some people swallow the bait.

Science has no conscience. It may be beautiful and important, it may be a great achievement in the history of human thought; but the human mind is more than intellect. It is also prudence. Reflection. Conscience. Decency. Choice. Love of someone near to you. Responsibility. Courage. Detachment from oneself. Doubt. And even humor. Had Mr. Marx been a peaceable and cheery fellow instead of an angry and vain man, his scientific discoveries might not have been so easily turned against humanity and the very basis of life.

I'm not a historian, and the Old Town Square is not the Great

Hall of Charles University. Uncovering the truth about our recent history is a matter for free debate among historians. Although February 1948 is an event that belongs to the past, to history, I mention it because it still affects us. It was then that everything started that is coming to an end today—what has been called the totalitarian system. We now face an urgent task, to set straight the unenviable legacy left us by that system. This is the main topic of my speech today.

What is the legacy we have inherited?

A very sad one. It's amazing how much can be done in a mere forty-two years.

We can't breathe our air. We can't drink our water. Children are born handicapped because their parents breath sulphur instead of oxygen and drink oil and chlorine instead of water. We've destroyed or let fall into disrepair beautiful cities and villages, the splendid cultural heirlooms of dozens of generations. In their place we've covered our country with rabbit-hatches where you can't really live, but just spend the night or watch some TV series. Our forests are dying. Tens of thousands of people work only to see their lives deteriorate. Our biggest machine tool industries earn debts, not money. Farmers work hard, and that's why we still have something to eat, but at what cost? Our agricultural produce is subsidized by the state, and in a couple of decades nothing is going to grow in our soil. Our obsolete economy heads the list of the world's energy wasters. Yet we keep on building appalling, megalomaniac power plants whose purpose is to destroy nature and supply energy to unprofitable industrial giants.

Our money isn't really money, since you can't use it to buy anything just a few kilometers beyond the Sumava mountains. Most of our hospitals can't do their job properly, and thousands of our splendid doctors spend half their time filling out forms that no one ever reads. A million people do senseless work, while we need another million to set up five small shops in every street to sell what can't be found elsewhere. Our students don't travel around Europe, as they do in other countries. As a result they speak no foreign languages. At school they don't learn who Shakespeare was, but find out that communism is the crowning achievement of world history. On television you can't choose from ten independent channels offering different programs—but you can comfort yourself with the fact that Czechoslovak Television probably holds the world record for the ratio of employees to broadcast time. TV personalities who both inform you and offer some cultural edification form a small minority. Why the others are on the TV payroll, and what they actually do—apart from reporting on each other and collecting their paychecks—no one knows.

I don't want to suggest that nothing decent has been built, or that nothing works. Here in Prague, for example, we have a metro system that works well—and the ridiculous names of some of its stations will surely be changed soon. Tens of thousands of people use this metro every day to commute from the South City to the capital,* and so occasionally have a chance to see a real city, not the bizarre thing in which they live. And on it goes: there are countless examples I could give. What is worst of all, though, is our spiritual state. It's hard to recover the ability to be kind to one another, to help each other unselfishly, to take care of our weaker fellow citizens.

We treat people of other nations or ethnic groups who are living in our country in a way that you would never catch a white New Yorker behaving towards his black fellow citizen, who not so long ago was his slave. Our two nations have lost their self-esteem, which has led them to look at each other with suspicion. Many Slovaks regard the Czechs as their colonizers, and many Czechs see the Slovaks as an appendage that does nothing but complicate their life.

Putting this situation straight will take years, and will require much self-denial. But there's no other way.

Today we have publicly commemorated Father Toufar's martyrdom and the warning that Jan Zajic gave through his sacrifice. May

---

* The South City is a concrete residential jungle south-east of Prague, famous for its identical apartment buildings and general unattractiveness.

these two, like thousands of others, from Milada Horáková to Jan Palach, from the tragic personality of Rudolf Slánsky to the legal heroics of Pavel Wonka,* always remind us that we have survived the destruction—although rarely with much honor—and that it is now up to us to do something for our country, and to make a few sacrifices.

Dear friends,

We have clearly inherited a joyless legacy. At first it seemed that here as in neighboring countries, public pressure might make the Communist party change its leadership, snap out of its decline and set about working with the rest of society to correct what had been committed in its name.

But history overtook us, leaving it up to us who are not now and never have been Communists to take up the task of renewal. With a couple of exceptions, none of us has ever held a political post. But now we must be a thousand times better and more professional at politics than the people we replaced, people who devoted their whole lives to politics—if you can call what they did politics.

As you understand, this is no easy task. Some people would like

---

* Father Toufar was a Catholic priest who was tortured to death during the anti-Church show trials of the early 1950s. Jan Zajíc was a high school student who followed the example of Jan Palach (see below) by burning himself to death in 1969 to protest the Soviet-led invasion of the year before. Milada Horáková was a hero of the Czech underground during World War II who subsequently became a member of parliament. She was tried and executed in 1950 on what were admitted in 1968 to be trumped up charges. Jan Palach was a Czech university student who committed suicide by self-immolation on 16 January 1969 to protest the Soviet occupation. Rudolf Slánsky was the general secretary of the Czechoslovak Communist Party until relieved of this post, tried and executed for "anti-state activities" in 1952. His show trial—involving fourteen codefendants, eleven of whom were Jewish—was one of Eastern Europe's most spectacular. It resulted in eleven executions, with the ashes of the dead being scattered over an icy road outside Prague. Pavel Wonka was a legal rights activist who died under police interrogation in 1988.

to see us solve the problems that have accrued so appallingly over the decades in the course of a single week. That, of course, is impossible. This does not mean that we can put up our feet: time is running out. To put it another way, we have to be both prudent and quick to act. If someone is not up to this task, he should step aside immediately and allow someone else to take over so that the functioning of his office or plant is not interrupted. If someone is asked to leave and feels hurt, or that he has been treated unjustly, this will only show that he values his position more than the interests of his country, and that he thus deserves no post at all. Of course nothing will happen to such people: they will simply have to make a living like any other citizen. As for myself, I swear that I shall resign as soon as I am told—or realize myself—that I am no longer capable of my job.

I know another, less exhausting way to help my country. I don't like to offer myself as an example, but in this one area I would like to call on people to share my approach. This is not the time to pursue one's ambitions; but the opposite holds true as well. If people agree that someone should be assigned to a post, but that someone would prefer not to take on the responsibility, I call on that person to set personal preferences aside and to accept the nomination in the public interest, at least for a while.

Shortly after the November massacre of our students, Civic Forum emerged in Bohemia and Moravia, along with Public Against Violence in Slovakia. Both of these movements grew rapidly to become the most significant political forces in the country. It was these movements that thrust us into high political posts. Notoriously, neither Civic Forum nor Public Against Violence are without their problems. Their centers suffer from a constant exodus of experienced leaders, who leave to take on state functions. On the other hand, their local and professional branches sometimes suffer from an influx of ambitious opportunists. Nevertheless, at least until the June 1990 election (and probably after it as well) these initiatives will remain an important safeguard for a peaceful transition to political pluralism, democracy and freedom. They are a safeguard for everyone—

even for Communists who want to help build a democratic and prosperous Czechoslovakia. Civic Forum and Public Against Violence don't want to inherit the Communist party's leading role. Their aim is to return the real leading role, not just some formula on paper, to where it belongs in a democracy: with the people . . .

My fellow citizens,

If I had to summarize the task that our government, parliament and I face, I would say that it is to professionalize ourselves immediately and completely. This is the task that all of us residents of this country face. We all need to turn ourselves into thorough professionals as soon as possible.

The totalitarian system has collapsed and its structures, if they still exist, are now either in the service of our new time, or have been paralyzed to a point where they can do no more harm than muddy the waters.

This is a fine thing, something that can serve as a full stop, an end, on the day when we remember the moment of that system's beginning.

But we should also put an end to the chaotic and rather amateurish festivities with which we have been celebrating this victory of freedom. Of course I'm not against such beautiful gatherings as today's. I'm not against singers singing everywhere. On the contrary, they should sing more and, for a change, make fun of us rulers, lest we become proud and gloomy-faced. I'm not even against 200 new parties emerging: that may also be appropriate. Our country has had a single party for too long, so we can afford to put up with 200 for a couple of months. Nor am I against the press writing all sorts of rubbish. This is a small price for the huge gift of free speech. The only pity is that this freedom cannot be exercised with greater responsibility to the public.

I've just one recommendation to make: that besides making merry and celebrating, we need to work methodically and professionally—or at least like those singers, who manage to spread irony, merriness, broad-mindedness, gentleness, spirituality and an atmosphere of friendly tolerance.

Winston Churchill once said that he could promise England nothing but blood and sweat. I can promise you more: the sweat may flow, but not the blood. My predecessors also used to say that our sweat needed to flow. Their words meant something different, however: that we would sweat for nothing. No longer will our sweat be for nought. It will drive the turbine that produces our freedom and prosperity.

Yesterday I read *Rudé Právo** for the first time in a while. I must say that I quite liked it: it certainly has improved since I studied it so closely in prison as my only source of information on the world outside. As I read it yesterday, I noticed something: from as many as 3,000 letters on our recent trip to the USA, *Rudé Právo* had chosen one saying that someone's personal opinion was that I am more a gentle, romantic and naïve dreamer than a real statesman. Perhaps I really am a dreamer, particularly if that means that I always bet on people's good qualities. And I never have considered myself a real statesman. But I would like to assure you of one thing: that no matter how great a dreamer I am, I'm nowhere near as preposterous as the people who dream of bringing tyranny back to our country through some new February revolution.

You may not believe me, but I'm really not afraid of anybody. Least of all do I fear the friends of the friends of the old regime. We've not had our freedom long, but should someone try to take it from us again, I guarantee that this time we shall defend it. We can't always use the excuse that we're outnumbered. Anyone who thinks like that has lost from the outset. After all, we have a better weapon than anything all the weapon designers in the world could develop. Our weapon is the knowledge that truth and justice are on our side. Should someone say that this is just another dreamer's illusion, then I will tell him that anyone armed with such a weapon fears nothing, not even the most sophisticated firearms.

It's no coincidence that our first president used to say both "Truth prevails" and "Don't be afraid and don't steal."

---

* The Czechoslovak Communist Party newspaper.

If we teach ourselves not to lie and steal, things will turn out all right. We won't live to see paradise on earth, but we will see a more dignified and peaceful life.

Dear friends,

From socialist realist paintings and poems, we know that Prague's weather in late February 1948 was overcast, and that freezing snow was lashing people's faces. Today the sun is shining.

Thank you for your attention.

"Bring me a complete list of all the idiocies we've managed to commit."

Presidential Politics After the Revolution

An Interview with Václav Havel

IN DECEMBER YOU *announced that you would remain in the office of president until free elections take place in June 1990, and that you would be their guarantor. Roughly two-thirds of your term has passed. During this time, several unavoidable complications have occurred. Faced with these problems, do you still feel that you can guarantee that the process of democratization will be irreversible?*

To begin with, I wasn't the first one to say that I'd be the guarantor of free elections. Rather I was talked into it by lots of people. I just wanted to make that small correction to your question, and now will get to its essence.

The elections will be somewhat different than I thought in December. Nevertheless they will be free and observable by all the world, and will clear our path into all the international institutions we want to join, and which have free elections as a requisite for membership.

In June we shall have a parliament that faces a difficult task: to prepare for truly democratic elections in two years' time—in other words, at a time when the political spectrum has crystallized and, we hope, some sort of political culture has developed. During these two years we'll introduce very severe economic measures, our new diplomats will make changes in our foreign relations, the federation of our two nations and the office of president will be defined, we'll establish new departments. . . In short, a lot of things are going to happen. From this perspective, I see today's elections as a sort of dress rehearsal for later, truly free elections. Who their guarantor will be I don't know. Most likely our society's last surviving remnants of democratic awareness.

On several occasions you've suggested that there's no turning back on the road we've been on since November. But in an interview for Le Monde, *you said: "If the Communists win the elections, I'm going to become a dissident again." Even allowing for a certain amount of jocular exaggeration, the contradiction between your first and second statement is clear. Do you think that if the Communists eventually win an election, they'd try to turn us off of the road to democracy?*

First of all I don't think the Communists will win any elections. And even if they did, I still think that the process we're going through is irreversible. Terrible things would have to happen, which, I hope, won't. But these things won't just be decided in Czechoslovakia. They are a matter of global developments, the unstoppable course of history, although of course we will do our best to avert such a turn of events.

We all know what catastrophic consequences forty-two years of Communist rule have had for this country. As a result, a large portion of our society thought that the Communist party would be either temporarily or permanently denied participation in politics. These hopes were not fulfilled. And while the principles and methods of the Party remain basically unchanged, none of our leaders—including yourself—have proposed that the Party in its current shape be made illegal. Are you really convinced that in order to rid this organization of its fascist elements, it's enough to see a few of the most compromised figures leave?

I do not recognize the principle of collective guilt. If the Communist party is branded a criminal organization, every one of its members since 1948—or even since its founding—would have to be branded criminals too. So I see no reason to label the Communist party a criminal organization and to abolish it as such. I believe that anyone who committed criminal acts ought to be tried as an individual by an independent judiciary. Justice must be allowed to prevail, but you can't try an organization.

In post-war Germany the Nazi party was banned without that meaning that its every member was automatically a criminal. It's now fashionable in Czechoslovakia to equate breaking down structures with collective guilt. But what we're talking about here is not a manhunt for rank and file Communists, but rather an attack on the property and propaganda capabilities of a mafia.

I feel that abolishing the Communist party basically means accusing it of collective guilt. But who's guilty? Every member. And what's more, why shouldn't this mafia build a new organization if the old one is destroyed? As I see it, the problem you're raising, abolishing the Party, can't be resolved. It's an enormously complex problem.

According to all the indicators, our society now finds itself in the deepest crisis it has faced since November of last year. There are many reasons for this, including the fact that a certain comfortable and familiar lifestyle provided by "real socialism" is more deeply engrained in people than we are willing to admit. The newly emergent political parties and movements are not yet capable of resolving this crisis. In some cases their arguments and lack of well-defined political concepts actually exacerbate it. The public has seized on several conspicuous figures, notably yourself. But you seem not to find the situation serious. At least that's the impression one gets*

* "Real socialism" was a term used by the Communist regime to describe an idealised version of Czechoslovak "socialist reality," and came to describe Communist domestic policy in general.

from your speeches (with their reassurances over our economic development), from your large number of trips abroad, and from what we see as a disproportionate emphasis on the politics of petty symbols. Is this impression fair? Do you really not see any crisis, or are you not speaking out about it in order not to unsettle our citizens?

If I see any crisis . . . How could I not see a crisis, when every day from early in the morning till late at night I'm flooded with it's countless effects? Yes, we're in a crisis, an extremely deep crisis, one that's perhaps deeper than even you think. But I knew that something like this would happen. It was unavoidable. But when I say that we'll survive it, I really mean it. We'll survive this crisis, but we have to go through it. Tomorrow won't save us from it: on the contrary, it will grow deeper. If I had to guess, then I'd say that in about seven years we'll have the worst of it behind us. By that stage people should have lost the worst habits that forty-two years of totalitarianism left them with. Our nations have survived worse things, so we shouldn't see this as too much of a tragedy. This is the conviction that leads to the surprisingly optimistic tone of some of my speeches and comments.

Now about those symbols. Look, an enormous part of the work I do is practically invisible. People occasionally see me on television as I'm rushing off somewhere, or making a speech on some square. But besides this I do countless other things that are far more significant. But at the same time these petty symbols are not unimportant. It's clear that given today's breakdown in morale, people long for some feeling of national identity, national pride, they long for symbols that somehow show that, for example, we're capable of defending ourselves.

And now my travels. Here and there I've heard gentle hints that I travel a lot. I've been in office 100 days, of which I've spent thirteen abroad. Right now it's important to see that not only Czechoslovakia, but all of Europe is going through enormous changes. This movement is so fast that most politicians don't understand it at all, they can't keep up with it. That's why my advisors and I planned a few short trips to certain countries, to take care of a few things that are important for Czechoslovakia. Our policies need to take a long-term view; we have to start getting ourselves involved in the structure of the new Europe. We're a small state, today we're on the level of a developing country, and next-door we've got the colossus of a unified Germany. We have to think ahead, about what Czechoslovakia will or won't be, about whether someone's going to gobble us up or not. To do this you need to know the lay of the land, who you can rely on, in economic affairs as well. You can't think it all out in your study. And I can say that thanks to these short trips, we have got to know something of the lay of the land.

Civic Forum's gradual loss of prestige is among the most dangerous aspects of our present crisis. The exodus of several leading figures to government posts is part of the problem. We're witnessing a strange phenomenon: Civic Forum's strength has to a certain extent been sacrificed to the temporary "government of national understanding." This would not necessarily have happened had not most of the new politicians severed links so astonishingly quickly with the popular movements that had nominated them. You're reproached for not trying to portray Civic Forum on your trips abroad as Czechoslovakia's authentic anti-totalitarian front. Does this spring from the fact that you already consider yourself the nonpartisan president of a normal democratic state, and that you feel it inadmissable to support only "one of the political forces"?

There are many causes and reasons for my behavior, which I didn't know, and couldn't know, beforehand. That is the beauty and drama of life, that we don't know everything beforehand. Society was and is inscrutable. We never know everything that lies hidden within it. Even though I get reports from all sections of society every day, and occasionally pay an unexpected visit to a housing block, or a miners' pub, or surprise citizens in their apartments, my "contact with the people" is limited. So I'm not surprised that society is somewhat different than I imagined. I'm not a Marxist, and don't share their arrogant conviction that society and history can be understood, explained, planned.

I also understand why Civic Forum developed the way it did, and why various ministers including myself "distanced" themselves from it. Neither Civic Forum nor those ministers are responsible. The responsibility lies only with the extraordinary pace of history, when at any moment you have to resolve a whole range of problems at once, when each of these problems is interconnected with all the others. We're all swamped with work from morning till evening. We all found ourselves in a situation whose complexity we had no idea of beforehand—after all, we're not clairvoyant. In short, what ended up happening was inevitable, but it's not necessarily a tragedy. I repeat: I believe that we'll outlive this crisis, and after our free elections we'll have a strong government, even if its tasks will be so terribly difficult that we'll probably end up calling it the "government of national sacrifice." During these two years—by comparison with which what we're going through now will seem child's play—we'll gradually establish some kind of stability in our turbulent corner of Europe. Of course I can't say that I'm absolutely certain it will all turn out so well. I don't know how things will go. But the hope that I feel is a state of the human mind, which is always independent of what happens.

When you took office in January, you chose from among your personal friends the advisors who would accompany you to the Castle. Given the qualitatively different type of life that you were beginning, this came as no surprise. Nevertheless the demands placed on the office of president are such that simple friendship may not be enough. Every person in high office needs above all a strong opposition. In a free society, specialists and public opinion perform this function. How do you address this problem in a country where nothing like this exists? How do you test your opinions?

As far as my fellow workers are concerned, I've relied on one particular piece of experience: that the people who work the best and the most professionally are those who aren't themselves professionals. And the people who fulfill their duties the best are those whom it took a long time to talk into accepting their posts. The present situation is so completely new that anyone who still bears traces of the old political stereotypes and behavior can contribute less than a newcomer from the outside. I know that some people call my fellow workers a prince's entourage. That doesn't sound too good. They're ridiculed and portrayed as some sort of parasites basking in the glow of the presidency. This is a great mistake. They work harder than I do, and under truly enormous pressure. Without them I would quite simply be unable to keep the situation under control.

You asked me how I test my opinions. The answer is simple: by what the Marxists call the process of cognition. I'm going through this process like everyone else in our republic. This constantly alters my behavior. Every day I receive a vast amount of information, and try to react where I feel there is a serious problem. I'm always talking to ministers and delegates, and once a month I get an analysis of how the "Castle" looks from the outside, on television, in the press and so on. And there are problems with the press. Just as I don't know how to be a president and have to learn the job, so the press has to learn how to be the press. Journalists often fail to ask a tricky question that I simply can't answer. We need to make it a bit more interesting.

I don't think we'd have any problem finding a couple of questions that you couldn't answer. That's not the point. When you just mentioned the future government, you called it the "government of national sacrifice." You yourself took office after much persuading and are also basically a "sacrifice." This state of affairs is far from ideal for sharpening the critical reflexes. How can you be hard on a sacrifice? How can you criticize someone who immediately reacts by thinking: if you know someone better, then I'll happily step aside . . .?

You have to learn how to get at even this type of politician. It's true that if someone does a bad job in a normal democracy, then someone else takes over who is already prepared, has an alternative program, government and so on. England's Labor Party has a shadow government assembled, and could take over the running of the country at any time. We've got nothing like that. So our comments about possible resignations can be seen as an attempt to spark the democratic understanding that everyone has to be replaceable. But could a mature alternative government come into being here? After all, our present government is to some extent adolescent, as you certainly will have noticed. It would have been difficult to expect that perfectly trained, mature figures could emerge from an infantile society, in a nation whose development was arrested. Take the French revolutionaries, for instance: what capricious children they were, with all those executions of one other. That's not something that we're facing in Czechoslovakia, at least I hope not. But mudslinging is in full swing in our papers now. It's a product of the revolution. A revolution spawns children and revels in their caprices.

We feel that whether the government is adolescent or not is not what's important. What strikes one about many of the new men is that by getting involved in politics, they've so far managed to destroy only the conventional formality of public life—protocol, if you will—because they haven't yet mastered it. But otherwise they've been very willing to take over some of the political features of the totalitarian regime. For example, a distaste for open information and its converse, a love of making decisions behind closed doors. Your thesis about newcomers always being better than old professionals apparently can't be 100 percent correct.

Of course nothing holds true in all places at all times. But I'd like to share a thought that seems appropriate here. Over the course of the revolution and my time as president, I've come to understand one of our situation's tens, thousands, perhaps millions of absurd aspects. A proverb sums it up: when a man takes over a job, the job takes over the man. It's as if the old totalitarian structures can only be crushed in a totalitarian way. . . As I see it, this all follows a general law. The new government inherited the vast, centralized tools of power, which it can't destroy immediately, because it needs them. It's a paradox: it's best to destroy these colossi from within, using their own strength against them. From the outside it looks as though ministers have taken over these structures, and that everything is continuing in the old style. But to begin with they have to find out who's who in their area, then decide on the *raison d'être* of their department, and then clean it out—keeping it all under control in the meantime. For the time being these powerful central departments will be needed for several tasks: economic reconstruction, shifting dozens of thousands of people into new fields, redrawing mining districts . . . This is the work that these central giants can do before they are destroyed. Their extinction will of course bring a more balanced climate. But in our predicament we can't begin with the climate, we're already in the thick of it. The time for preparing the climate was before the revolution. An observer passing by a gloomy ministry will see that the same officials are there as five years ago, that the ministry still makes announcements and behaves as it did before, that nothing has really changed. But that's not true, quite a lot has changed, and the deepest changes are just now beginning.

Fine, we'll grant that in this area you're right. But what about changes in the structure and programs of the pre-revolutionary political parties? Is that also a matter of cleansing processes that so far have remained invisible? As president you've spoken with the head of the Czechoslovak Communist Party, Vasil Mohorita. What's your opinion of this man?

Turn off your microphone . . .

24 April 1990
Interview conducted by Ivan Lamper, Jan Ruml and Zbynek Petracek for *Respekt*.

"I'd love to know what's going to happen to the poor devils who wrecked our lives."

Franz Kafka and My Presidency

FIRST, ALLOW ME to thank you for the great honor that your university bestows on me by conferring this honorary doctorate. This is not the first honorary degree that I have received, and I accept it with the same feeling with which I accepted my earlier degrees, one of deep shame. I fear that my incomplete education makes me unworthy of it. I accept it as a strange gift that brings me new embarrassments. I can easily imagine that any moment now some vaguely familiar man will walk up to me, snatch the diploma that I have only just received, grab me by the scruff of the neck and throw me out of the hall, saying that it was all a mistake, the result of my impertinence.

You doubtless see the direction my idiosyncratic thanks are taking. I would like to use this occasion to confess my deep and intimate affinity to the Jewish people's great son, the Prague author Franz Kafka. I am not a Kafka expert, and do not read writings on Kafka with much enthusiasm. I cannot even say that I have read every word that Kafka ever wrote. I have my own peculiar explanation for this apathetic approach to Kafka studies. It is the feeling that I am the only person who really understands Kafka, and that therefore no one else can do anything to make his works more accessible to me. My indolence springs from the vague sense that I do not have to read and reread all that Kafka wrote, since I already know what I can find in his work. I am even convinced in my heart of hearts that if Kafka had not lived, and if I could write a little better than I can, I would have written his complete works myself.

What I say sounds strange, but I am sure that you understand me. I am saying nothing more or less than that I have always found in Kafka a part of my own experience of the world, myself, and my way of being in this world.

I shall try to give a very brief, telegraphic description of the more easily described aspects of this experience. These are: a deep, basic and thus thoroughly undefined sense of personal guilt. As if it were my very existence that were a sin. Then there is the strong sense of both my not belonging and of the inappropriateness of everything that contributes to these feelings. An oppressive sense of unbearable claustrophobia, a constant need to explain and defend myself before someone. A longing for an unattainable order of things, a longing that grows stronger as the ground on which I stand becomes more unpredictable and indecipherable. Sometimes I feel the need to reaffirm my problematic identity by shouting at someone, by standing up for my rights. This shout is of course completely futile, the reply never finds the right audience, but vanishes into the black hole that surrounds me. Everything that I experience reveals to me first and foremost its absurdity. As if I were running after a group of strong, confident men whom I can never overtake or match. I am basically an aggravating person, and I feel that I am only worthy of mockery.

I can already hear what many of you would probably like to tell me: that I only style myself as a Kafkaesque character, for in reality I am someone quite different. A person who calmly and consistently fights for something. A person whose idealism has placed him at the head of his country.

Yes, I admit that from the outside I may seem the complete opposite of Josef K., the surveyor K., or of Franz K. himself. But I stand by what I have said. I shall only add that it is precisely this feeling of exclusion or non-inclusion, a sort of disinheritance and existential nonbelonging, that is the hidden motor of all my stubborn efforts. And it is my longing for that higher order that has dragged me again and again into the most incredible adventures. I would even go so far as to say that any good I have ever done was probably the result of my trying to conceal this metaphysical sense of guilt. It seems that I am constantly doing or arranging something only to defend my dubious right to exist.

You may well ask how a person who sees himself this way can be the president of a country. It is a paradox, but I must admit that if I am a better president than someone else might have been, then it is because somewhere deep in the well-springs of all my work is a constant doubting of myself and my right to execute my duties. I am a man who would not be at all surprised if while carrying out my presidential tasks, I were to be summoned before some obscure tribunal, or taken straight off to hard labor. Nor would I be astonished to hear a shout of "Rise and shine!" whereupon I would wake up in my cell and entertain my fellow inmates by recounting everything that had happened over the past six months.

The lower I fall, the more I feel that I belong. The higher I rise, the more I suspect that some mistake has been made. With every step I take, I realize that knowing that I may be removed from office for good cause is a great advantage in successfully executing the duties of president.

What I have said here was neither a lecture nor an essay, but rather a short commentary on the subject of "Franz Kafka and My Presidency." I find it fitting that a Czech should address this topic here at Hebrew University. Perhaps I have shown more of my cards than I would have liked, and perhaps my advisors will rebuke me afterwards. But even this will not disconcert me, for it is just what I expect and deserve. My preparedness for this rebuke can serve as further proof of how beneficial it is for my illusions that I am always prepared for the worst.

I thank you once again for the honor you bestow on me; and after what I have already said, I am ashamed to repeat that I accept it with shame.

26 April 1990
From an address at Hebrew University, Jerusalem.

Ján Carnogursky

BORN IN 1944, Carnogursky is a Slovak and an active Catholic. He received his law degree from Prague's Charles University. After earning his doctorate from Bratislava's Comenius University, he did his national service by specializing in military law. From 1970-81 he worked as a defense lawyer in Bratislava, where he took on political and religious cases. He lost the right to practice law after defending Drahomíra Sinoglová, who was being prosecuted for "incitement." (She had duplicated the works of Czech and Slovak writers who had been expelled from the Writers' Union in 1969.) From 1982-86 he worked as an enterprise lawyer in Bratislava, and continued to give legal advice to dissidents and religious activists. After 1987 he was unable to find work. He became a member of the Movement for Civil Liberties (HOS) in 1988, and was also involved in Czechoslovak-Polish Solidarity. At the time of the November 1989 revolution, Carnogursky was standing trial in Bratislava for his dissident activities, and was released from prison by (then) President Husák's decree on 25 November. He immediately became one of Public Against Violence's leaders. The opposition nominated him first deputy prime minister in the new federal "government of national understanding." In February 1990 he founded the Christian Democratic Movement, an independent political party based in Slovakia, and withdrew from Public Against Violence. In the June 1990 elections his party formed a coalition with Václav Benda's Christian Democratic Party (in the Czech Republic) and the Czechoslovak People's Party.

Following the June 1990 elections Ján Carnogursky became the first deputy prime minister of Slovakia [ed.].

Physics, Psychology and the Gentle Revolution

YEARS AGO I read an article about how the West's strongest suit is physics, while the East tends to specialize in psychology. When I see the quality of Western manufactured goods, I have to agree that physics really does seem to lie at the heart of your success. Then I start to wonder why psychology is our forté, and once again it is manufactured goods that provide the answer—only this time it's their lack of quality in Eastern Europe.

I doubt that we've only the Communists to blame. There are examples of our lagging behind the West in every century of our history. When the warriors of the Great Moravian Empire wanted a good sword, they bought one in the West (the going price was ten cows). I myself have an example from 1968, when I was coming back to Czecho-Slovakia from West Germany. I was on the night train from Nuremberg to Prague. It was the first time I'd made the trip, and it was dark. I didn't know when we were due to cross the border. But suddenly the train, which had been running smoothly, quietly and fast up till then, started to shudder and shake, and had to slow down. The train tracks in West Germany were welded together for fast, smooth travel, while in Czecho-Slovakia there were still gaps between the strips of track, so that the train was constantly lurching. There are hundreds and thousands of examples like this.

Anger at their perpetual backwardness makes East Europeans look for quick, dramatic solutions. The solution often has to be a psychological one, since we're not up to much technologically. This search for a dramatic way out of a situation—or at least a dramatic explanation of one's failings—is what characterizes the world of Dostoevsky's heroes, several works of Russian philosophy, and Polish or Hungarian sagas of personal sacrifice in the defense of Europe. It also creates fertile ground for hare-brained political schemes.

Of all the East European countries, Czecho-Slovakia has been the one most influenced by the West, and shows the greatest combination of physics with psychology. In times of crisis we seem to find psychological solutions very alluring, although they tend to mean a reduction in action more than a real solution. This is how I see the Communist victory in the Czech lands in the last free and democratic elections we had, in 1946. I can imagine how the Communist platform seemed at the time to present a coherent and theoretically consistent whole that could offer psychological release from the years of existential terror under Nazi Germany. The psychological weight of communism in Czecho-Slovakia was symbolized by the biggest statue of Stalin in the world, which was erected on the banks of the Vltava in Prague. The Stalinist model of communism collapsed under the pressure of revelations about the camps and under the pressure of the West's economic growth. The world's biggest statue of Stalin was taken down in 1956, two years after its unveiling.

There are many of us who still remember another example of a psychological solution. Alexander Dubcek's slogan "socialism with a human face" became the cliché of leftist intellectuals during the 1960s. It gave us hope that we'd find a way out of the technological and economic backwardness that—this time—communism had given us. In the 1960s it was obvious that communism was lagging behind the West. The students who were demonstrating in Western Europe may have thought otherwise, but we had no doubts. The slogan "socialism with a human face" gave us the illusion that we had found an original solution. Unfortunately, this originality didn't have

"Closing time, gentlemen."

time to develop fully before it was crushed by the Warsaw Pact tanks in August 1968.

In the interests of symmetry, I'd like to continue with my periodization of our history according to whether the basic feature of a given time was physics or psychology. I would categorize the twenty years of "normalization" under Gustáv Husák as a time when physics dominated. True, this was physics on a lower level than we see in Western technology. This was politics without any messianic goals. To use Milan Simecka's term, the order that had prevailed throughout the Soviet bloc was restored. It was restored at the price of political dissidents' and religious activists' freedom. Teachers who were Christian lost their jobs, and conformity became the norm.

I remember one document that epitomized this policy. It was part of the trials that took place at the beginning of the 1970s, which I was involved in through my work as a defense lawyer. In 1970, Bratislava radio fired an unusually intelligent and capable editor for supporting Dubcek in 1968. The legal reason given was that the editor had thereby broken the socialist peace. There was a law that dealt with this at the time. The editor took her case to court on principle. The court in Bratislava rejected her appeal. During the hearing, the court had a chance to convince itself that this editor really was an extremely capable woman whose reports were first-rate. There's a sentence in the court's rejection of her appeal that I think typifies the whole "normalization" period. The court wrote that the accused broke the socialist peace and, even more important, might break it in the future, since her intellectual level was above average.

Husák's regime based its economic policy on the quantitative distribution of goods and services through artificially set prices. The system seemed to work as long as people were isolated from the world outside and couldn't find out that a better system existed. The self-censored press concealed financial and political discrepancies in society. This was a closed system that could only function by being isolated. In an era of quantum physics, this was a social order derived from an extension of Newtonian mechanics.

The self-satisfaction of this regime is particularly interesting from a political-science point of view. The system that fell apart like a house of cards in November 1989 called itself, in the early 1980s, the most successful phase in the history of building socialism in Czecho-Slovakia. Václav Havel called this system entropic. What actually happened was that the parameters of the system deteriorated as people got to know it, as they learned its rules and how to get around them. Lord Acton's observation on power corrupting also played its part. Czecho-Slovakia had a policy of not changing personnel. As long as an official didn't make a major mistake, he could count on keeping his place in the *nomenklatura*.* But a slow, gradual increase in *nomenklatura* members' perks was never considered a major mistake. These tired and corrupt officials enjoyed less and less respect, and so had to put up with more and more lack of discipline in ordinary people. Economic statistics of the late 1970s show how correctly Havel had characterized the situation. Productivity fell as technological lag increased.

Communism's anachronistic nature was also reflected in the way technological progress became its mortal enemy. It was increasingly difficult in the age of the information revolution to sustain the Communist states' isolation. Western radio and television programs became the most listened-to in Czecho-Slovakia. Public phones that could be used for international calls meant that news on the internal situation which had been withheld officially could be sent abroad and then broadcast back into Czecho-Slovakia. In the last few years dissident circles started making plans for using computer disks for free publication of *samizdat* literature.** Underground printing presses could thus become quicker and more flexible, and by the same token more difficult for the police to detect.

All the Communist system's shortcomings were clearly visible from within. We learned with a certain astonishment that it was our visit-

---

* The *nomenklatura* system ensured Communist party approval of staffing decisions.

** Underground literature (from the Russian: literally, "self-published").

ors from the West who showed the greatest sympathy for this system. When we met, they used to go into great detail about the disadvantages of their own societies and pointed to the superiority of the East European system at least as a theoretical model. As I remember it, doubts about the rationality of the Western system and the irrationality of the East European led in the mid-1970s to articles questioning the ability of the West to win its competition with the East. Such articles seem comical in 1990. But then, when we read them, we were astonished. Jumping ahead in time, one might imagine that the spiritual climate of, say, the mid-1970s might find a new home in Eastern Europe sometime in the future. It could return in the form of nostalgia for a time when the East could make the West quake with fear. This sort of longing for the past could come about if at some later date the rapprochement of East and West proves to be less than beneficial to the East.

But to return to the recent past: In the closed system of communism, which was ostensibly quite effective, there had always existed groups of free-thinking people. They got together on the basis of cultural interests or religious faith, and together they would dream their dreams of a free society. They rarely formulated political programs, for this was the most dangerous activity of all. The drafting of plans for political opposition was an offense punishable by death in the 1950s, and still warranted imprisonment last year. There were groups of free-thinking people everywhere, in cities, towns and villages. Few of them were well-known, and those who were lived mostly in the big cities. When they met in people's apartments, they discussed more or less abstract topics, more out of the sheer joy of feeling free than because they thought that the conclusions of their discussions might soon be put into practice. We also met with professors from Oxford and other British universities, who proved that the world hadn't forgotten about us. Without their knowing it, these dissident groups were discussing the changes that Eastern Europe brought about last year.

One of the problems these groups had was one of numbers. Meetings in people's apartments were attended by ten, twenty, at the most thirty people. More people would go to religious events, but at these gatherings political topics weren't discussed, and political demands weren't made. But when the situation allowed it at the end of last year, hundreds of thousands of people coalesced around these little groups and overthrew the Communist regime. Numbers were also a problem when we met with visitors from the West. Accustomed to precise election results, they tended to ask how many people there were attending various dissident events—and then probably compared these figures with the massive, and official, May Day demonstrations. We weren't too successful when we tried to convince them that the number of participants in official and unofficial gatherings was relative, and couldn't offer any absolute conclusions . . .

• • •

ONE OF THE legacies we've had to confront since the revolution is an underestimation of the role of nationalism. This is something that is an issue in Czecho-Slovakia, and has also made its presence felt in the Soviet Union. Our own nationality problems emerged when we tried to rename our state. President Havel had originally intended only to eliminate the word "socialist" from "Czechoslovak Socialist Republic." He proposed a law to this effect in the Federal Assembly, but called the law a "law on the name of the state."

At this point problems that had lain just below the surface for seventy years exploded. Czecho-Slovakia was founded at the end of World War I by agreement of the victorious allies, and according to talks between Czech and Slovak representatives. Final agreement between Czechs and Slovaks was reached in May 1918 in the United States in Pittsburgh, Pennsylvania. Slovak autonomy was defined within the framework of a republic which was called "Czecho-Slovakia," with a hyphen. This is the name that appears in the international accords and treaties that were signed in Paris at the close of World War I.

When the 1990 debate on the republic's new name began, some

of the Slovak deputies pointed to the fact that in the original French and English treaties the country's name appeared with a hyphen. Czech deputies responded with two main arguments. The hyphenated name became the country's legal name in October 1938, after the Munich agreement, and lasted only until March 1939, when Czecho-Slovakia ceased to exist.* For Czechs, the hyphenated name was strongly reminiscent of the Munich agreement and everything that followed it. This version also makes the word "*Cesko*" ("Czech") a separate word, though there's no region called "*Cesko*" in the Czech language. There are the "Czech lands"—Bohemia and Moravia, and perhaps Silesia—but there's nothing by the name of "*Cesko.*"

The arguments about our country's name were unexpected, and revealed wounds in both nations that people had not realized were there. For Slovaks there was the sense of Slovakia's not being well enough known, especially abroad, where the word "Czechoslovak," without a hyphen, is often abbreviated (particularly in English) to "Czech." For Czechs these wounds were the memory of Munich. A compromise was finally reached, and Czecho-Slovakia's official name is now "the Czech and Slovak Federative Republic" . . .

• • •

IT WAS OUR citizens' unanimous desire for freedom and democracy that brought about the overthrow of communism in Czecho-Slovakia during November and December 1989. The public's main demands in the very first days of the revolution were to abolish the Communist party's leading role and to hold free elections. Even as time passed, there continued to be consensus on political freedom and the shape

---

* In the Munich agreement of 30 September 1938, Britain and France (and Mussolini's Italy) appeased Hitler by granting his territorial demands in the Czechoslovak Sudetenland, prefering to abandon Czechoslovakia than risk another world war. Germany annexed the Sudetenland; in March 1939 Hitler invaded the rest of the Czech lands (Bohemia and Moravia), which became a German "protectorate." An "independent" puppet fascist state was set up in Slovakia.

of our political system, so that the government had no serious problems preparing laws on political parties, elections, assembly, association, freedom of the press and other legislation affecting civil rights. The first free elections in forty-four years will take place on June 8 and 9, 1990.

These elections ought to stabilize our democratic system and produce a government and parliament with a clear-cut mandate. One of the new parliament's first and most important tasks will be to elect a president. President Václav Havel's term in office ends by law forty days after the elections. Civic Forum, Public Against Violence and of course other parties are putting him forward to continue his work as president. The new parliament, the new government and the new—most likely, the same—president will immediately begin their two-year terms in office. They will set about accomplishing a task for which there is no precedent in history: the return from communism to capitalism. As they rule, they will need the help of both physics and psychology. What else? Perhaps I'll be able to tell you in two years' time.

May 1990

Jirí Dienstbier

BORN IN 1937, Dienstbier is a Czech. He graduated from the Philosophical Faculty of Prague's Charles University, and in 1958 became a member of the Communist party. He then began work as a foreign affairs reporter for Czechoslovak Radio and Television, spending time in both the Far East and the United States. In 1968 he was among the group of journalists who continued to broadcast "illegally" after the Soviet-led invasion. In 1970 he lost his job and Party membership. In 1977 he signed Charter 77, and in 1978 became a member of the Committee for the Defense of the Unjustly Prosecuted (VONS). He subsequently could work only as a nightwatchman and stoker. In 1979 he became a Charter 77 spokesman, but was arrested in May of that year and, along with other VONS activists, found guilty of "incitement."

He served his full three-year sentence; offered the opportunity to emigrate, he refused. He published extensively on international relations (and particularly European unity) in the underground press and edited an unofficial foreign affairs journal, *Ctverec* ("Square"). In 1985 he was once again a Charter 77 spokesman and published a book of essays on international relations in both the underground and foreign press: *Dreaming About Europe.* He maintained extensive ties with representatives of both foreign governments and independent peace groups. He was a founding member of Civic Forum during the November 1989 revolution; the opposition nominated him foreign minister and deputy prime minister in the new "government of national understanding." One of his first acts as minister was to quit his job as stoker and find a replacement, apologizing for the short notice.

Central and Eastern Europe and a New European Order

. . . CENTRAL AND EASTERN Europe has been the rest of Europe's biggest problem for forty years. It still is today. As previous regional structures cease to exist, the unsettled situation in Eastern Europe and the Soviet Union is generally seen as a potential source of destabilization. New structures are taking shape in the midst of profound economic imbalance, while new political arrangements are still uncertain, and ethnic and historic rivalries are reemerging. All this is happening in a region beset by shortages. . . .

It is generally recognized that the Cold War is over; but certain stereotypes from that era still survive and are reflected in the anachronistic preservation of blocs in Europe. This can be seen in efforts to restructure NATO, or attempts to institutionalize the Warsaw Pact by establishing a permanent secretariat and representatives. But there is no longer a balance of power in Europe. There is, in fact, profound *imbalance* between the two blocs. The Soviet Union is no longer the monolithic force it once was: its whole military and political bloc is in a state of crisis and decay. Although the Soviet Union still possesses powerful means of deterrence, these cannot be used unless there is absolutely no other choice. Thus the assertion that peace in Europe is guaranteed by the two blocs—the old idea of "peace through strength"—cannot be true.

These two politico-military blocs are now in a state of serious imbalance, and can guarantee neither security nor a balance of power. This will only be aggravated by the emergence of a unified and economically strong Germany. Unless we start looking for new, all-European notions of security, this imbalance may lead to unpredictable and destabilizing developments. The conclusion we have to draw is that we need to strive for peace not through "strength," but through "law." The new European order should be based on democracy and pluralism, and should incorporate the existing blocs into new structures based on a common commitment to the rule of law, treaties and human rights.

I feel that the Council of Europe can become the first truly pan-European institution. This is very important. The Council of Europe focuses on strict respect for human rights, establishment and support of the rule of law, and the basic principles of European political culture. A state that wishes to join the Council has to meet these conditions. At the moment, most of the former Soviet bloc countries have special guest status. With membership of all European states in the Council of Europe, the ideological and political division of Europe over the past four decades would be ended. In this respect, the United States and Canada are also considered part of Europe.

Various groups of countries are already making agreements on cooperation in economic, environmental, transportation, telecommunications, energy and other fields. Czechoslovakia is currently joining a group of countries that share many interests and traditions. Czechoslovakia, Italy and Hungary have belonged, and still do belong, to different political, military and economic alliances; Austria and Yugoslavia are neutral or non-aligned. Thus this group stands as an example of regional cooperation across bloc borders . . .

The world has seen a growing tendency to integrate as the economic strength of the wealthiest countries increases and international relations move away from the competition of two ideological systems. Despite this, international stability remains fragile as the end of the century approaches. Europe is sensitive to the effects of the Middle East conflict, for since the twelfth- and thirteenth-century crusades, the civilization of that region has been close to Europe. European politics are also affected by the deteriorating situation in the developing world, which is looking less and less like an ideological competition and more like a simple struggle for survival. Despite the fact that this problem has been pushed to one side by the sweeping changes in the former Soviet bloc, it may yet turn into a time bomb. Third World countries are voicing their fears that the developed world's cooperation with Central and Eastern Europe will entail cuts in development assistance. Unless new aid programs for these regions are established—and this will be difficult given current circumstances—the gulf between the North and the South will only widen.

I mention all this to remind you of the pressures affecting developments in Europe, and to stress the need for all of Europe to eliminate the causes of its own instability . . .

Politically, economically and militarily there is an undefined space —what is often called a vacuum—developing to the east of Germany. This space may soon be filled by the economy of a strong and unified Germany. Given the marked economic disadvantages of the East European countries, this could well take on distinctly neo-colonial features. Renewed Soviet pressure might also be felt in this vacuum, particularly given economic failure, social strife and unsuccessful political reform, i.e., the defeat of Gorbachev's policies. Such a turn of events will only be accelerated if European politics continue to be defined in terms of blocs and not a pan-European security concept. This all-European alternative has an important advantage: it would help to link positive forces in Eastern Europe, including the Soviet Union, with the rest of Europe, and could strengthen these forces in their domestic struggles against conservative and authoritarian tendencies. If we want to weaken the political power of military elites, this can best be done through arms reduction, including cuts in troop levels and an abandonment of the "enemy image."

Just as the Americans filled a power vacuum in 1947 through

"How many times do I have to tell you?!
Central! Not Eastern! *Central* Europe!!"

the Marshall Plan, so they should now support the establishment of a pan-European security system. This could help fill the political vacuum that is left by the disintegration of Central and Eastern Europe's current defense arrangement. The old system was based on the military power of the Soviet Union; but it was also based on that superpower's previous claims to hegemony, which the current Soviet leadership has renounced. Support for the creation of an all-European security system could also help allay the fears of Germany's neighbors over the possible future of that state.

Beginning in 1948, the Marshall plan helped West European states reconstruct their economies and thus take the edge off of social strife. Today's wealthiest states—the members of OECD—could help East European countries in a similar way, particularly as they move from a centralized, command economy to a market economy. If economic reform fails in the former socialist countries, the effects could destabilize the rest of Europe as well . . .

We are putting forward two proposals that correspond to what I have said so far . . .

The search for a new security structure is a fundamental problem in European politics. It is also one that the United States is clearly reluctant to tackle. Security can no longer be based on a balance of power or fear, for we hope that Europe will be neither divided nor balanced. The countries of Europe need to find a new system of security safeguards within the framework of the Helsinki process . . . At a March 1990 Warsaw Pact meeting in Prague, we proposed the establishment of a European Security Commission, involving consultation and coordination at the ministerial level. The Commission would have a small executive secretariat, along with a military council subordinate to a consultative committee of foreign ministers.* The Security Commission would work parallel to the two military alliances, which would continue to exist until they become irrelevant. If the Commission is successfully founded, we could then estab-

* The Czechoslovak government has since suggested Prague as the permanent seat of this secretariat.

lish an Organization of European States. This would be grounded on a pan-European treaty, which would contain the commitments of the Helsinki "Decalogue" as well a pledge to cooperate in joint defense of a member country under attack. Eventually—perhaps this can be a target for the next millennium—we could establish a confederated Europe.

It is clear that an idea like this depends on cooperation by the peoples of both North America and the Soviet Union.

We submit this proposal realizing that it will be greeted with both approval and criticism. But rejection needs to be substantiated, and once arguments are presented, discussion will be generated, which can only lead to a better proposal . . . One objection we've heard is that NATO must be preserved at all costs. We have nothing against NATO. It has played a successful role, and will continue to play it for some time to come. We simply feel that security is not enhanced by maintaining a powerful alliance of sixteen privileged states, around which various atomized entities move on the international stage. Against whom will this NATO be defending itself? Against Havel's Czechoslovakia, Mazowiecki's Poland, free Lithuania? Our experience of Munich and Yalta warns us that security can also be based on sacrificing others. The question is, how long does such security last? In the case of Munich, World War II provided the answer; the Yalta agreements led to the Cold War. We should not make the same mistake.

Another objection to replacing blocs with cooperative structures is that this would involve the departure of American troops from Europe. But how long do we want the American people to pay for our freedom and inability to provide stability in Europe? How long are American boys going to have to serve in the place of Europeans? Let there be no mistake: just as long as America and Europe need them to. We don't want to jeopardize or destabilize security. Mistakes like this have already led to Europeans and Americans sending their boys to die in two world wars. We simply want to create the conditions in Europe so that a foreign military presence is not indispensable.

This does not mean an American withdrawal from Europe. America is and will remain in Europe, with its economic strength, its culture, its liberal-mindedness and democratic traditions. In the information age it couldn't be any other way.

Related to this is my second proposal, which I shall lay out in more detail. If it is acted upon, it could help create a pan-European economy. As you know, President Havel said in his address to the joint session of Congress that the best way for the United States to help us is by helping the Soviet Union. Both Central Europeans as well as Americans want to see an orderly and peaceful transformation of the USSR into a democratic society and a community of free and equal nations, whether they are federated, confederated or independent. I believe that this would be encouraged by improving the Soviet market and investments in the Soviet economy.

In my country, too, the transition to a market economy will entail the abolition and restructuring of enterprises as well as the liberalization of foreign trade and prices. This may produce a temporary deceleration, or even stagnation in our development, and will involve a decline in production. To be realistic, we have to assume that for several years the economic gap between Czechoslovakia and its West European neighbors will increase, and that it will take some time to halt and reverse this trend. Our entry into the European economy may thus take place at a time when the discrepancies between Czechoslovakia and the advanced countries will be even greater than they are today.

This gap is a barrier to our gradual integration in Europe. Eliminating it will depend among other things on Czechoslovakia's maintaining relative economic and political stability. This stability will depend on the influx of foreign investors, without whose resources and experience the transition to a market economy is inconceivable. The elimination of this gap will also depend on economic and political developments in three parts of Europe:

- in Eastern Europe (what have until now been the Council for Mutual Economic Assistance (CMEA) countries), where most countries face similar problems to Czechoslovakia's;

• in Western Europe, where much will depend on the progress of political and economic integration, and on the willingness of these countries (and their institutions) to assist Eastern Europe in overcoming the difficulties of the transition period;

• in the region surrounding the unified Germany, which will not only be our neighbor and apparently our biggest economic partner, but also the most important economic actor in the new Europe.

As we move towards a unified Europe, there may be certain rivalries between East European states that cannot be ignored. At the same time, there is bound to be a reduction in the volume of trade between East European countries, which, in the long run, is desirable. But to begin with, this reduction will deprive many of our enterprises of uncompetitive and therefore attractive markets, and will force them to adapt to more demanding trade partners. This will necessarily bring some disruption and uncertainty.

This disruption and uncertainty are of concern to us because they may produce tensions and political consequences that we would rather avoid. I estimate that this critical transition period may last two or three years, during which time our enterprises and economy will need a stabilizing and supportive program.

The success of the Marshall Plan was based on two conditions:

• beneficiaries were obliged to cooperate with one another;

• beneficiaries were obliged to reinvest profits generated by Marshall Plan aid.

Our proposal draws on these two principles, and is outlined as follows:

(a) The world's wealthiest states will extend credit to the Soviet Union through the European Bank for Reconstruction and Development. This will amount to $16 billion, spread over three years and repayable within ten years.

(b) This credit will not be transferred to a Soviet bank. Instead, the European Bank will use it to pay for deliveries of industrial goods from Czechoslovakia, Poland and Hungary to the USSR. Each year $4-5 billion will be divided between these three states, which will supply goods based on Soviet orders. The industrial enterprises of these three states will thus win production orders for a crucial three years, which would mean less unemployment and diminished social tension.

(c) The USSR will repay the dollar credit in rubles, over ten years, by investing these rubles in its own industries according to guidelines established by the European Bank. If the Soviet Union does not invest the entire amount within ten years, the remainder will become a dollar debt owed by the USSR to the European Bank.

(d) The sums paid by the European Bank to Czechoslovak, Hungarian and Polish enterprises will have to be used for modernization under the supervision of European Bank officials. In practice, this means that the money will be spent in Western markets.

Does this sound too fanciful? Unfeasible? It would be a shame to reject it out of hand. I believe that this $16 billion (less than 0.1 percent of the annual GNP of the USA, European Community and Japan) would be an investment in better security and would save much larger sums in armaments and forces. The proposal may be imperfect as it stands and may need further elaboration, but that is what I am here to ask for.

I've long been intrigued by a sentence in a well-known letter that Einstein wrote in 1946. There he says that the unharnessed power of the atom has changed everything except our way of thinking. He then adds: "We shall require a substantially new manner of thinking if mankind is to survive." At that time, this appeal was aimed at policies of strength. Today, it relates to a policy of reason and cooperation. If we want to raise our international relations to the level of modern civilization, we must focus "new thinking" on the morality of politics, and on finding ways to reduce the economic discrepancies that exist between different societies . . .

Five years ago I wrote a book entitled *Dreaming About Europe*. Many found it naïve. I see it as proof that we need to think about politics in a way that seems unsophisticated to politicians and political scientists. We're too often influenced by ideas and structures that only make sense because we've not yet come up with an alternative that corresponds to new developments. Trapped in the logic of the past, many people are incapable of seeing politics as an expression of free will.

It would of course be unquestionably naïve to think that we can have everything just as we want it. Many have thought they could: their failures caused millions to suffer before their systems collapsed. For our dreams of the future to be realistic, they need to be based on our aspirations, traditions, culture and potential. If this potential remains unrealized, or if a barrier is set in its way, what we need to do is pull down the barrier, and not despair that someone set it up in the first place. I'm heartened to see that there are so many Americans who are helping to pull down the barriers of the past.

15 May 1990
From an address at Harvard University.

Redesigning Czechoslovak Foreign Policy

An Interview with Jirí Dienstbier

YOU ONCE WROTE *a book called "Dreaming About Europe." You've been foreign minister for a few months, which isn't too long. I'd like to ask you whether the initial outlines of the Europe of your dreams are beginning to take shape.*

If it were just a matter of dreams, then there probably wouldn't be any outlines of anything. But some things are beginning to take shape, mostly because we've tried to come to grips with the contemporary situation and the way it's developing. The problem, of course, is that lots of people don't want to risk any sort of transition or change. They're satisfied with the fact that things more or less worked: for example, that there wasn't a war. They don't want to lose a bird in the hand for two in the bush. But we have to try to change things, otherwise history would simply stand still.

Some critics of Czechoslovakia's new initiatives on European security say that there's only one bloc in Europe, the Warsaw Pact, which faces an assortment of democratic states wishing to protect themselves from potential aggressors. What do you think of this?

I feel that my criticism of the so-called bloc concept holds just as true today as it did five years ago, when we drafted the Prague

Appeal.* Everyone in Eastern Europe is now beginning to realize this. The only problem is that not everyone wants to build a new order as quickly as we do.

Some people say that Czechoslovakia's foreign policy assumes positive developments in the USSR. What if a conservative military faction seizes power there? Wouldn't it be simpler for the East European states to join NATO, and then work within its framework to transform Europe?

You've asked about fifty questions at once. We think we're suggesting the best option given a continuation of favorable international circumstances, and a successful transition by the USSR to being a democracy and federation, or confederation. If that changes, then we need to have various alternatives and options. It's not as though we propose something and think that's the way it has to be, without any changes. There's basic agreement about the need for a relaxation in confrontational attitudes as part of the Helsinki process. There's also consensus that existing structures don't correspond to the new political situation in central and eastern Europe. I do think that if we manage to push our proposals through—and here I mean the European Security Commission, followed by a permanent council of foreign ministers, and ultimately a confederation of European states—petty quarrels and conflicts will become less important. Movement in this direction (and this movement is already happening) will be strengthened by progressive forces in the USSR, since it will be accompanied by significant arms reductions. There's already agreement at the Vienna talks that there should be no more than 5,000 foreign troops in any country. This is the first phase of a very substantial reduction, and will limit military and police power throughout the continent.

* The Prague Appeal was a letter sent by Charter 77 signatories to the fourth Amsterdam conference on disarmament in 1985. It identified the division of Europe as the greatest threat to peace, and proposed dissolution of NATO and the Warsaw Pact, denuclearization of Europe, and the withdrawal of all U.S. and Soviet troops. It also looked to the Helsinki Final Act and the Madrid concluding document for a possible framework of European cooperation.

There's a specter leaving Europe...

Our plan has several phases and aspects. We think that the Council of Europe should become the first pan-European institution. If every country accepts its basic precepts—that is, respect for human rights, the principles of a legal state and of European culture in general—then the break with the past forty years will be complete. Nationalist frictions may arise, but the Council of Europe should be able to resolve these if all members pledge to recognize the rights of minorities. The Council of Europe could thus provide a philosophical framework. As I see it, this organization would contain sixteen rich states, while around them would be a sort of atomized space of less predictable developments.

Your whole plan is based on the anti-bloc concept, but at the same time the government supports at least initial membership in NATO for a unified Germany. Isn't there a certain contradiction here?

No. The unification of Germany is an accomplished fact. Five years ago, in the Prague Appeal, we spoke of how it was necessary to support German unification. We ought to use this process to accelerate the unification of Europe. If Germany were neutral, it would exist in a vacuum. Until new structures can be created, it makes more sense for it to belong to the Atlantic pact.

In parts of Western Europe people are saying that our initiatives are often provocative, but that they haven't been worked out well enough technically. What's your response?

We're not offering the world some sort of established truths. This is why we don't want to work out all the details, which in fact need to be discussed by about thirty states. We're putting forward ideas that correspond to our perceptions and notions of what could change for the common good. Details will be worked out collectively. We're just suggesting what we see as the right direction.

Did you ever think that you'd be foreign minister?

Yes, when I was ten. I went off to Skalicky's bookstore in Kladno, bought myself the three-volume *History of Diplomacy,* and began to study. But I understood that there was more to it than that. Later, when I looked at our foreign ministers, I reckoned that this wasn't what I wanted to be. I gave up the idea when I was about fifteen. But foreign policy was of course a great interest of mine when I worked as a journalist.

We'd thought that the changes in the government after November 17 would take place more slowly. But it all happened terribly quickly. Of course we didn't expect that our proposals at the round-table talks would be accepted immediately. We had to show our cards and publish some proposals, naturally, since Adamec had brought in that government of his that only lasted a few days,* which was a sort of ultimatum for us. The public was saying that if you're going to criticize, then you've got to put something forward yourself. We had a Civic Forum meeting and I was asked if there was any other ministry I'd prefer. I answered: not on your life. I really shouldn't be a minister, but a journalist. The Foreign Ministry or nothing.

I know you as a journalist. Don't you miss it a bit?

I've been missing it for about twenty years . . .

You worked for three years at Lidové noviny** . . .

Sure, and it was great, but that wasn't really journalism. You've got to "hustle," go to conferences, speak freely with people, and that's something we couldn't do. Now I can do that again, but I don't even have enough time to write myself notes.

---

* See "From 1968 to 1989: A Chronological Commentary," 3-7 December 1989.

** Before becoming the leading independent newspaper after the November revolution, *Lidové noviny* had been an underground newspaper since January 1988.

When something happens in diplomacy, journalists are allowed to be around at the beginning, but then the doors close and we have to guess what goes on behind them. You used to go through the same thing. But when the doors slam now, you're on the other side. Does what happens inside correspond to what you used to imagine?

Meetings that journalists can attend aren't very important, most of them are pretty much a waste of time. There are a lot of protocol rules, and what's achieved could be done in much less time. International conferences are a good example. When a minister speaks at one of these conferences, he talks to his deputies and the camera. But when the film crews leave, it gets more interesting, since that's when the experts go to work. After all, a minister can't be a jack of 250 trades. That's the technical side of things. Until the ministers sign all the documents, nothing happens on the political level. It all has both technical and diplomatic aspects. The bureaucracies work things through, and the ministers have a cup of coffee and talk face to face about major political problems. At that point it's a matter of being able to establish human contact. You can get months of work done in an armchair by the window.

When a president is a famous personality, or when a country has a presidential system, foreign policy is often the head of state's domain, with the minister working more as an executive secretary. You've known our president for many years through your political activity. Could you tell us something about who has what share in formulating our foreign policy?

I think Czechoslovakia has quite a broad consensus regarding foreign policy. Any differences of opinion that exist are slight. The president and I are of the same generation, we worked together in Charter 77, we did time in prison together. We've often discussed foreign policy over the years. The two of us seem to agree so much that sometimes it verges on the comical. When we were in the U.S. recently, I spoke with Secretary of State Baker while Václav Havel had a separate conversation with President Bush. Then we went to the White

House and discovered that both our questions and answers had been practically identical. Baker jokingly asked me if we'd arranged it beforehand. Of course there are meetings between the president's advisors and mine. Then, when we've come up with something, the president and I get together and chat. There have never been any problems.

There's no doubt that Czechoslovakia's foreign policy has changed. But what about the Foreign Ministry itself? How has it changed?

I've been here five months. This ministry has a few peculiar features. It never used to make foreign policy: that was the responsibility of the International Department of the Central Committee of the Czechoslovak Communist Party. The rank-and-file people who work here are specialists and speak several languages. They always had some sort of contact with the outside world. On the political spectrum of the old regime's institutions, they were among the most progressive. Alongside them were of course people who had won positions as a reward for faithful service to the Communist party, as well as employees of other ministries. We're giving the genuine professionals a chance to retire normally if they can't adapt to the new situation. But consider the fact that it costs on average 30,000 hard-currency crowns to recall an officer. Where can we get that kind of money? We're overstaffed by sixty people, but they had to be given five months' notice. We've got to do everything in accordance with the law.

Our readers abroad complain that our diplomatic service is changing too slowly. What's your response?

We shall have our basic personnel problems solved in about two years. It will of course take a lot longer to create a truly first-rate diplomatic service . . .

18 May 1990
Interview conducted by Jaroslav Jiru for *Lidové noviny.*

Alexander Dubcek

BORN IN 1921, Dubcek became a member of the Slovak Communist Party in 1939. Working as a blacksmith during World War II, he took part in the 1944 Slovak national uprising against the fascist government. In 1955 he received a law degree from Bratislava's Comenius University. He was then selected for training at the elite Party Institute of the Communist Party of the Soviet Union's Central Committee. Graduating in 1958, he returned to Bratislava and became a regional Party chief. In 1963 he was named first secretary of the Central Committee of the Slovak Communist Party. In January 1968 he became first secretary of the Czechoslovak (i.e., federal) Communist Party, and started to expand the reform program that had been developing since the mid-1960s.

This was the beginning of the "Prague Spring" of 1968. Dubcek's government responded to increasing popular pressure by declaring a policy of "socialism with a human face." With censorship and police harassment virtually abolished, an increasingly activist populace began to demand more than what Dubcek was offering: "socialist pluralism," meaning limited pluralism and reform within the framework of state socialism. Public enthusiasm swayed Dubcek's sympathies, much to the consternation of Communist hardliners. Despite Dubcek's assurances that Czechoslovakia would not leave the Warsaw Pact or abandon the leading role of the Communist party, the Brezhnev leadership decided to nip the reform flower in the bud. On the night of 20-21 August 1968 the armies of the Soviet Union, Bulgaria, Poland, Hungary and East Germany invaded Czechoslovakia to combat "counterrevolution." No military resistance was met. Dubcek remained in office until April 1969, when he resigned and was demoted first to chairing the Federal Assembly, and then to an ambassadorial post in Turkey. In June 1970, he was expelled from the Communist party and returned to Slovakia to work as a mechanic in a forestry enterprise.

Dubcek was mostly silent in the ensuing years and was never active in the dissident movement. In 1974 he wrote his first annual letter to the Husák leadership that had replaced him, demanding an apology for the way he and the country had been treated. His tentative reemergence began in 1987, when he granted an interview to the Italian Communist Party newspaper *l'Unitá*, which had long been critical of Soviet-style "socialism." When the revolution started in November 1989, Dubcek became immediately involved in Civic Forum and Public Against Violence. His return to political life was welcomed as a symbolic link with the earlier reforms of 1968, but Dubcek has remained more a public relations figure than a formulator of policy. On 28 December 1989 he was elected chairman of the Federal Assembly, and thus regained one of the posts he had held twenty years before.

1968 Revisited

An Interview with Alexander Dubcek

WHY DID YOU *sign the "Moscow Protocols"?* Weren't they de facto political agreements by Czechoslovakia's leaders to the August 1968 occupation?*

Not at all. By signing the "Protocols" we never agreed that the military intervention was justified, and certainly not that what had been happening in Czechoslovakia was a counter-revolution. We never abandoned democracy, and we didn't succumb to the earlier pressure of the so-called "Warsaw Letter."** On the contrary. What we announced on the night of 20-21 August 1968 still holds true: that the intervention in Czechoslovakia was illegal, and contradicted not only international agreements but the Warsaw Pact as well. Any chang-

---

* See "From 1968 to 1989: A Chronological Commentary" (August 1968).

** As Soviet concern over Czechoslovakia's increasingly radical reform grew, a Warsaw Pact meeting was called in July 1968. The five members who were to invade a month later—the USSR, Poland, Hungary, Bulgaria and East Germany—sent a letter to the Dubcek government from Warsaw. Accusing Czechoslovakia of abandoning the leading role of the Communist party and subverting the socialist system, it was part of an escalating program of pressure that included troop movements and KGB subversion operations.

es that were made to this announcement were carried out after 1970 by the "normalizing" government of Gustáv Husák.*

*What about the so-called "letter of invitation"?** Didn't you have a hand in its writing?*

I could never sign anything like that. But you're quite right that a story like this did circulate for a while. At the bottom of it all was Vasil Bil'ak's† lie in *Der Spiegel*: "At the meeting in Bratislava on August 3, 1968, Dubcek, Smrkovsky†† and I, among others, signed a document saying that Czechoslovakia was threatened by a counter-revolutionary coup." As I remember, this story was published throughout the Czechoslovak press.

I complained to Vasil Bil'ak, but wasn't given a hearing. Why? Not even totalitarian regimes can take care of everything. Forging a document is tricky work. This was a falsification that I managed to deny in the international press.

I'm going to press you even harder. Because of your mistakes—your silence both during the invasion and afterwards—people have come to feel that the tragedy of 1968 is directly linked to your character, and particularly your "softness."

What softness? Even now there are all sorts of things that emotion

---

* Gustáv Husák became general secretary of the Czechoslovak Communist Party after the Soviet-led invasion.

** The pretext for the invasion was a supposed "letter of invitation" by Czechoslovak Communists, asking for Soviet protection from anti-socialist "counter-revolutionary" forces.

† Vasil Bil'ak was a Slovak hard-liner who supported the Soviet-led invasion, and who subsequently rose to the number two position in the Czechoslovak Communist Party.

†† Josef Smrkovsky was chairman of the Federal Assembly during the Prague Spring of 1968.

keeps me from saying. When the intervention took place, I didn't give up. Most of us completely rejected the occupation without any hesitation whatsoever. At the same time, I had to find the strength to join Cerník and Svoboda* in giving instructions that the advancing army of occupation not be opposed militarily.

That's right! Yet again in the history of modern Czechoslovakia, its people fail to put up any resistance! You're to blame more than anyone else!

Does the public blame me? I don't think so. Certain individuals do. But they judge the past through the prism of the present. We—and I'm speaking about myself here—had to make decisions at a particular moment, in a particular situation, immediately. Lives, many lives were at stake. And the international situation was different from the one we're in today. The current situation favors us. But it didn't then. There was sympathy, but nothing more.

I'm not so naïve a politician that I couldn't see what calling for military opposition would have meant for the people of Czechoslovakia. The Hungarians would have torn off the southern part off Slovakia, the Poles would have occupied the Ostrava region, and the Bansko-Bystricky area would have become the Bulgarian zone. The East Germans and the Soviets? A gigantic army, about 700,000 strong. An operation of unprecedented size against a country as small as ours, bigger than the Allied landings in France during World War II. And our army? It was almost completely concentrated on our western border.

What would have happened if we had fought? They would have literally steam-rollered us, and our nations would have drowned in blood. I couldn't bring myself to take that sort of gamble. There are many people who may now feel that this was wrong from a moral standpoint. But back then it was a matter of fighting tanks with your bare hands. You have to take that into account.

What does a military machine look for when it's given the task

* Oldrich Cernik was prime minister in 1968; Ludvík Svoboda was president.

"What do you mean, you don't recognize me?!
I'm your dream of 1968!"

of liquidating a peace-loving, reformist policy and not some armed, aggressive enemy? A pretext. For what? For unleashing a massacre. I couldn't make the chess-player's mistake of doing what the other side was expecting. Just the opposite—I had to find a political solution.

But we were crushed!

Fine, I grant you that. Yes, we were militarily subjugated. But we didn't lose. Morally. The idea of democracy and healthy reform lived on, even if it was repressed. But there was far more to lose if we'd acted differently. It wouldn't have ended with hundreds of thousands of people losing their jobs, as they did; there would have been hundreds of thousands of corpses as well. There were revolutionary tribunals ready to be set up.

I'll put it a different way. Given the international situation, and particularly the consolidation of neo-Stalinism in the USSR, wasn't our policy naïve? Didn't you see the sword of Damocles hanging over your head?

Yes. Our policy could have taken a different course. We could have been like the Poles, the Germans, the Hungarians and all the rest, who were forced under the yoke of the inhumane East European system.

But this isn't the core of the problem. Even before 1968, Czechoslovakia was increasingly unsettled as it compared itself with what might have been. Its internal capabilities, for instance, versus the way things had turned out. And that's not even comparing it with the developed world. Out of all the countries in the East bloc, it was Czechoslovakia that needed to reform the earliest, for both subjective and objective reasons. I'm thinking here of the 1960s. These changes were coming from below as well as from above. I was wholeheartedly convinced of all this, which is why I presented the reform program in October 1967. It was just beginning to be put into practice in 1968.

There either is or there isn't democracy. The Warsaw Pact armies came to cut off not only our road to progress, but that of the other East bloc states as well.

I'm hypothesizing. Could the occupation have been avoided through a violent internal crackdown, like the one in Poland in 1981?

Our situation was completely different. In the first place, people were united on basic issues. In the second place, I could never have done that. First, initiate reform, and then use my authority to crush it. That's completely immoral!

You were never warned of the possibility of Moscow's deciding to occupy us?

No. There was no warning. Never.

Our intelligence had no indications? That can't be true!

Well, no. We knew where the forces were, we knew that there were exercises going on and all that. But should we then have gone out and mobilized the army and security forces, and started pumping people up for war? Don't forget, it was 1968, and given the way the world was shaped at that point, we were all alone. Were we meant to give into Moscow's aggressive wishes by taking these steps? That was the problem.

Why didn't you resign from your political position until the spring of 1969?

I had originally wanted to resign when they took us off to Moscow like a bunch of convicts. But the Czechoslovak leadership wouldn't accept my resignation. I also felt responsible. I couldn't leave my friends in the lurch. We carried on working together against more confrontational types, who wanted to make what was already a bad situation worse.

Of course, I had my limit. When Husák and his followers said we should change the Czechoslovak position on the military intervention, and we upheld our original statement, that was as much as I could take. The situation was becoming impossible. It was my own personal decision. I couldn't go against what I had previously supported. I resigned.

What about communism? How strongly did you support it before, and what is your attitude today?

Fate made me understand sooner than most of my colleagues that everything needed to be reformed. The Party, ideology, propaganda, the economy, everything. I realized that the world had changed. It wasn't witnessing "the dictatorship of the proletariat" and "the decline of capitalism." My thinking first started to change when I saw the way politics and the law were deformed in the Soviet Union of 1938. I then went through the same thing in the Czechoslovakia of the '50s. Just as I finished my university studies in the USSR, I was completely bowled over by the Khrushchev period. This gradually helped me realize that what we proclaimed to be socialism had nothing to do with a humane and prosperous society, and that not only the word itself but its whole meaning had been discredited. This helped me escape the dogmatism of the circles I'd lived in for several years before that.

What do we want today? A republic that's socially just, freedom of the press, adherence to human rights, economic and trade freedom, a pluralist system . . . We want a democratic society that is humane, tolerant and everything that flows from this. We wanted the same things twenty-one years ago—within the limits of what was then possible . . .

March 1990
Interview conducted by Jaroslav Hanzel for *Evokace.*

"I apologize for my reticence, Miss. I belong to the generation that never said boo."

A Conversation about Communism

THE "REAL SOCIALIST"* *regimes of what we used to call the East bloc disintegrated in the course of a few short months . . . The political vacuum created by communism's collapse raises some important questions that directly affect the Left and its future prospects. How can this vacuum be filled? By whom?*

These questions have to be asked, for there's no doubt that the Left is going through a crisis. But I would like to stress that this is mostly a crisis of Communist parties and communism, and less one of the Left in general. This is true because the world didn't develop the way the Marxist-Leninist classics described . . . While capitalism changed shape and improved, the East European "socialist movement"—I have to put that in quotation marks—gradually degenerated under undemocratic and militaristic regimes. This was the Stalinist political system, and the neo-Stalinist version of the Brezhnev era. What we saw was certainly not socialism, much less communism. On the contrary, what emerged was so far divorced from its original goals that there's no point in even discussing it today. What we now need to talk about are completely different things . . .

What East European socialists are talking about is modern demo-

* "Real socialism" was a term used by Communist regimes to describe an idealized version of "socialist reality."

cratic socialism, which is precisely what Italian and Western socialists are after as well. We're talking about a democratic socialism that can incorporate individual values and social justice. This would be a movement that can measure up to the challenges of the market and, more importantly, its political framework—democracy. This is one of the basic elements uniting the democratic reform movement throughout Europe. The name we give this movement is irrelevant. Its importance lies in its ability to rise to the challenge of social justice and a market economy, in order to encourage real development in society.

The values you mention are directly opposed to those that dominated this part of Europe for forty years. They are mostly the values of Western societies: democracy, the market, prosperity. Is capitalism the model for your reforms?

Your question referred not to one, but many "Western societies." What we're dealing with are different realities. But if you must have a model, mine—or ours—is that of a modern society that wants to keep its identity without overlooking the broad range of European experience.

You mention the victory of capitalism, but I have to ask, which capitalism do you mean? The original version, like the type we had in Czechoslovakia between the wars, has certainly not withstood the test of time. That kind of capitalism no longer exists. The democratic systems of developed countries show how deep the changes have been. How did all this happen? New political systems were produced by democracy and pressure from the Left. There are now new blends of democracy and social concerns. What has happened is something that Marxism couldn't foresee.

As far as Czechoslovakia is concerned, the biggest problem we face today is the transition from totalitarianism to democracy, and from economic centralism to the market. This is a difficult process for which there's no precedent. Countries have been able to move in the other direction, from democracy to totalitarianism, since they already had a working market economy. At the moment, I find it difficult to imagine what our future holds, or what sort of political or economic structure we're going to have. We do have a few clear ideas. We want to establish a market economy, but we also realize that this is not a cure in itself. We want to cooperate with other countries more developed than ourselves, but we don't want to leave huge debts to our grandchildren. We want the social effects of the changes we have to make to be held to a minimum. The democratic state we're building after totalitarianism's collapse has to succeed in creating the right conditions for free enterprise at the right time. We're working on a series of laws in parliament that will help allow this in the future.

. . . In these times of convulsion, it's hard to see any "leftist values" coming to the fore—apart from people like you, who represent the Left because of their past . . .

Every movement has personalities who symbolize it and express its ideas. I've already mentioned what I think the values of the new Left are. I could add some more: respect for the individual, the right of even the weakest social groups to a decent life, tolerance of others' opinions, the ability to grasp the common interests of humanity. I'd like to emphasize the precedence of individual over class interests, which means democracy for all, with the greatest number of people possible participating in the running of their country and the decision-making process. I also stress the standards of a modern society, which in fact correspond to as many rights, beginning with the right to property (individual, cooperative or state). The means of maintaining these standards are standards in themselves: tolerance, cooperation, understanding, nonviolence, solidarity, conformance with the Helsinki Final Act, protection of our planet and the people who inhabit it . . . Standards which I consider to be socialist are often part of other progressive movements as well.

There's one change I want to emphasize. East European social democracy has to divorce itself once and for all from the ideological and organizational legacy of Stalinism and Brezhnevism. It has to free itself of residual dogma, and give up any of the precepts of the Marxist-Leninist "classics" that time and history have proven wrong . . .

. . . The countries that led the wave of revolutions in 1989 have started the process of building new political structures . . . What is their starting point?

I can tell you what the situation is in Czechoslovakia. Democracy and social justice are ideas that are deeply rooted in the minds of our people. These ideas haven't been imported, but are drawn from our own history. This is particularly true of democracy, as we've seen over the past few months. This idea didn't die during the decades of totalitarianism, but survived and will continue to shape our evolution. I'm convinced that the process that has been set in motion is irreversible.

What will democratization consist of?

I believe that it ought to consist of what should be the norm everywhere: the defense of human and social rights. Looking at the work of the Federal Assembly—our parliament—I see that there is still much work to be done if we're to establish the Helsinki Final Act in legislative form (as well as the other agreements that were reached there after 1976). In Czechoslovakia the question of human rights is particularly important; I don't think I need to explain why. This is another legislative area in which we need to raise ourselves to the level of developed Western democracies. I'll suggest a succinct definition of democracy: a striving for the respect and development of human rights, together with the principles of social justice. These conditions represent an individual's right to civic participation. . .

Will the mere introduction of market mechanisms be enough for reform to succeed? Will this open the way to true prosperity?

No. Personally, I don't believe that the market is a solution in itself. There needs to be a fundamental affirmation of human rights as regards the market as well. There are also issues of environmental protection and preservation. Ecological problems are enormously important today in both your country and mine.

Does the East have a Left that can assert itself after the collapse of "real socialism"? A Left that can keep watch on a market economy and help develop the rules of democracy?

Looking at our present situation, I'd have to say that nothing like this yet exists. Market policies are only just being adopted. As the market grows and develops, it will certainly allow—even provoke—the crystallization of movements, tendencies and political forces that will act as counter-balances or regulatory mechanisms. There's no doubt that the union movement has a bright future. It's currently reforming itself, and will no longer defend only limited interests, or be the "transmission belt" for a certain party.

A seventy-year-old system has collapsed. (In Czechoslovakia it was forty years old, with a brief interlude in 1968.) Does this imply the collapse of leftist ideals as well? Has socialism lost the battle, or will new left-wing forces appear?

I'd put it this way. Many of the ideas that original socialism, or Marxism, came up with have fallen by the wayside. The theory of violent acquisition of power, for example, or the dictatorship of the proletariat, or complete centralization of the economy, culture and society. The theory that capitalism would collapse (because of "gradual pauperization," ending in revolution) has failed. As we've said, capitalism developed differently.

Let's not forget the Third International. The Communists' rejection of gradually working towards socialism was one of the main causes for the split in the labor movement after World War I. Socialist parties continued to exist and grow because they renounced these dogmas, and recognized the value of democracy and social justice. These concepts are still far from fully developed in the capitalist countries of Western Europe. But this also means that the Left can spread and take on new forms. Did anyone foresee the emergence of the Green movement? What's its place on the political spectrum? What about the youth movements that are moving in the same direction? True, we can't point to a new Left that is well defined and clear-cut. What we're seeing is a movement that is growing and that can be effective in general humanitarian terms by helping defend people's interests in any given country. As I see it, the Left has good prospects—as long as it can react to changes quickly enough, and modify its positions to attract broader-based support.

There's another question facing the East that adds strain to international relations: nationalism's emergence in the vacuum of Eastern Europe. What dangers do you see in this regard?

Every movement has its positive and negative aspects. National consciousness, patriotism, pride in the tradition of a particular culture—these are the things that make a people a nation, with all that the word "nation" implies: national sentiment, a way of thinking, a certain sensibility, cultural achievements. This is what distinguishes one people from another, and is something that I see as positive.

Nationalist movements tend to appear during particular phases in history. There are examples of this in several countries today. They're the legacy of intolerant and destructive tendencies. In various countries—including Czechoslovakia—this can give rise to separatist aspirations, and involve a weakened sense of belonging in the larger state. These tendencies can also make the process of democratization and integration even more difficult on the international level, particularly when what we aspire to is a sense of common membership in what we might call the society of friendly European peoples.

Nationalism is certainly part of today's European scene. But it can also make a positive contribution to the development of various nations. Let me give you an example. In 1968, we decided to make our Czechoslovak republic a federation of two nations, the Czechs and Slovaks. Raising the national consciousness of both these peoples was seen as a positive achievement: it was intended to, and did increase their sense of belonging in a shared, federal state. But this is not always the way it turns out. There are times when extreme nationalist tendencies emerge, usually when there are changes and upheavals in the political system. This is generally the result of an unfortunate tradition, and the fact that these negative developments haven't been dealt with quickly or effectively enough. We can see this happening today in Gorbachev's Soviet Union, where the long-standing grievances of certain republics are erupting. These feelings are the result of a time when individual peoples and nations were denied the possibility of an autonomous existence. In these cases, changes for the better have been blocked by the accumulation and explosion of unwanted problems.

One last question. Can the victory of individual rights mean a new beginning for the Left?

I'd say that this victory is the result of human rights, civil liberties and social justice being trampled on for so many years. This is why I feel that today's leftist movements need to adopt these causes as their own, and draw from them a permanent impulse to act.

21 April 1990
Interview conducted by Renzo Foa for *l'Unitá*, the Italian Communist Party newspaper. Translated from the Italian by Clare Brooks.

Václav Klaus

BORN IN 1941, Klaus is a Czech, and graduated from the Prague School of Economics in 1963 with a specialization in foreign commerce. In 1966 he spent six months doing post-graduate study in Naples, Italy, where he was introduced to the work of F.A. Hayek et al. On his return he worked in the Academy of Sciences' Economic Institute. During 1968 he was openly critical of the so-called "third way" ("socialist market") economics being pursued at the time, and worked in a department of the Economics Ministry responsible for digesting and criticizing non-Marxist economic theories. In 1969 he spent a term studying and lecturing at Cornell University in the United States. On his return Klaus wrote entries for the first Czechoslovak *Encyclopedia of Economics,* but was fired from his position in the Economics Institute because of his political views. He subsequently worked his way up from menial jobs in the State Bank, and in 1988 joined the Institute for Economic Forecasting in the Academy of Sciences, a prominent center of informed criticism of the Communist regime's economic policy. Klaus was involved in Civic Forum from the first days of the revolution, and served on its strategy council. The opposition nominated him finance minister in the new "government of national understanding" in December 1989.

Václav Klaus was elected chairman of Civic Forum in early October 1990 [ed.].

Creating a Capitalist Czechoslovakia

An Interview with Václav Klaus

DR. KLAUS, WHAT *is the message you want to bring Americans about the new Czechoslovakia?*

The message is the same for whatever group. We want a market economy without any adjectives. Any compromises with that will only fuzzy up the problems we have. To pursue a so-called Third Way is foolish. We had our experience with this in the 1960s when we looked for a socialism with a human face. It did not work, and we must be explicit that we are not aiming for a more efficient version of a system that has failed. The market is indivisible; it cannot be an instrument in the hands of central planners.

At a Council on Foreign Relations breakfast, you were asked about what kind of economic system you planned for Czechoslovakia.

Yes. I told the questioner that he did not fully understand what a market economy is. I often use the line by F.A. Hayek that the world is run by human action, not by human design. To talk about planning an economic system is to talk in old terms, and I find myself sometimes having to teach Westerners about what the market really means. They often don't realize that they often might need a little of a market revolution in their own countries. You cannot predict the outcome of the market process; you can only set the conditions for a challenging competition. What we want is to establish the rules of a market economy—not to plan its outcome.

How will you bring about the transition to a market economy?

This is the key question. It is what makes the reform process an art, not just a science. You have to develop a strategy that tells you what reform measures you should follow and in what sequence.

The sequence of reforms is a legitimate question for debate, but not, I think, the speed and direction they take. I fear that our neighbors—Hungary and Poland—may be falling into what I call a "reform trap," in which partial reforms can turn out to be worse than none at all.

But you have also indicated that you think it is wise to wait on cutting subsidies for such things as rent until the June elections bring a government with a popular mandate. Is that slipping into the reform trap?

My budget* will be very tough. Subsidies will be cut at least 15 percent everywhere. This government realizes that when you are dealing with the daily expenses of people, you need some kind of mandate. Remember, no one has elected us. This is a government that was called in to fill a vacuum.

You and President Václav Havel were quoted as telling President Bush that you wanted lower barriers to trade and investments in Czechoslovakia, but not foreign aid. Why are you the only Eastern European country that is not asking for foreign aid?

Well, of course we are applying for admission to the International

---

* Released 8 March 1990.

Monetary Fund.* I think there are some problems with their economic prescriptions for developing countries, but it is important for us to have the kind of credit rating that IMF membership would indicate. But as for classical foreign aid, this is the last thing on our agenda. I know what it has done to other countries. For us, it would bring inflation and a certain timidity in the making of economic policy. It could allow us to delay needed economic treatments and send us into the reform trap.

*Your colleague Valtr Komárek** recently said that "If a market economy were imposed immediately on Czechoslovakia, economic agony would result." He claimed at least a third of the country's production would be destroyed. This sounds like there is a real disagreement within your government about how much of a market economy the country should have.*

It is true that the move to a market economy has sometimes to be tempered by considerations of power. I share with my colleagues a broad consensus on what needs to be done, although there are issues where I want to move faster than they. We all agree on what things should be done, but there is the political problem of selling it to the public.

Privatization of the state-owned economy is not yet on the agenda. We cannot do it immediately; my colleagues would not agree to it. But we must put all forms of ownership on an equal footing immediately and let different types of ownership compete with the state firms.

Will Czechoslovaks welcome foreign investment in their country, or will they resist it?

I had a long interview with a trade union paper on this issue a few days ago. They asked me whether I would allow a money-losing

---

* Czechoslovakia was granted membership in the IMF in the autumn of 1990 [ed.].

** One of Czechoslovakia's first deputy prime ministers.

old plant in Slovakia to be sold to foreigners. I laughed and said, "Do you know what you are saying? A money-losing, run-down plant and a foreigner wants to buy it? We should be lucky if we find a fool in the West who wants to buy it and try to make it profitable. Everyone will benefit from that, except perhaps the Western investor." They had to agree.

Are you getting a lot of enquiries from potential Western investors?

We are flooded with hundreds and hundreds of requests and ideas from Western investors. The problem is that we have no rules set up for them to follow yet. We must have the time to create strict rules so that property is not sold by Communist managers for a low price. They often get payments under the table to sell to the first bidder. This does not build public support for a market economy.

You mention that Westerners have some common misconceptions about Czechoslovakia. What are they?

First, there was this belief that Czechoslovaks were satisfied with communism and would not rise up as the East Germans and Poles did. What is not known is that there was a quiet revolution going on for months before the end of November 1989. Civil disobedience, bureaucrats ignoring orders, soldiers resolving not to shoot at demonstrators—the Communists had lost control before November.

New thinking was going on in many places. The Western press concentrated on the brutality of the police, which was important, but it missed the changes from below. People like me, who were engaging in brinkmanship with the Party economic bosses, and the open dissidents, who were being arrested, were pursuing a common goal in different ways.

Are you getting what you consider bad advice from some Western economists?

Some, but only because they misunderstand the Czechoslovak economy. They think we had a classic centrally planned economy and therefore must decentralize economic decision-making within the government. But a centrally planned economy implies very powerful central planners and weak state managers of enterprises. This is perhaps how the country started in 1948 when the Communists took over, but now we have giant, powerful state monopolies and very weak central planners. These economic giants were almost totally independent. The task is not to give them more power, but to break them up. Our philosophy can be summed up as demonopolization. That means following a very restrictive fiscal and monetary policy which will squeeze the monopolies and cut their subsidies. On the micro level we will allow other economic agents, both domestic and foreign, to compete with them.

How did you first become interested in the ideas of classical liberalism?

I was twenty-five years old and pursuing my doctorate in economics when I was allowed to spend six months of post-graduate studies in Naples, Italy. I read the Western economic text books and also the more general work of people like Hayek. By the time I returned to Czechoslovakia, I had an understanding of the principles of the market. In 1968 I was glad at the political liberalism of the Dubcek Prague Spring, but I was very critical of the Third Way they pursued in economics.

I worked in a department of the Economics Ministry that was meant to criticize non-Marxist economic theories. I was paid to read Western economic texts. In a way, the regime paid for their own undermining.

Then, in 1969, I spent spring term at Cornell University in New York. The invasion of August 1968 had already happened, but the hardline regime took several months to crack down on dissidents.

Did you remain quiet and hope that the regime would not punish you?

No, I remember very much enjoying the entries I wrote for the first Czechoslovak *Encyclopedia of Economics* in 1969 and 1970. I prepared an entry on John Kenneth Galbraith that dismissed him as a social critic rather than a serious economist. I was criticized for that. I also wrote the entry on "economic liberalism," and I enjoyed making that a dramatic and stirring attack of the role of government.

Eventually, they found me. In 1970 I was identified as the leading counterrevolutionary in the ministry and fired. They took special pains at my hearing to point out that I was the worst one in the whole place.

What did you do then?

I worked in very menial jobs for a while at the state bank. Gradually the climate changed, and by the 1980s I was the unofficial advisor to the chairman of the state bank.

How did you come to know Václav Havel?

We served on the editorial board of a literary monthly called *Tvár* ("Face") in 1968 and 1969. He was a young writer, and I was also interested in broad cultural issues. We agreed on all major issues and became friends.

What was your role in the revolution of November 1989? How did you become involved?

On November 17 the revolution began when the police beat demonstrators in Wenceslas Square. It galvanized the nation. I had been in Austria that day, giving lectures attacking government economic policy. You see, the regime already could not control its critics. I returned to the train station in Prague about 11:00 that night, unaware of what the police had done. As I walked up to my house, I met my twenty-year-old son, Václav Jr., coming from the other direction. He had been a victim of the evening's events and had barely escaped. He was white with fright.

We had a discussion right outside the house. "I saw you on Austrian television," he told me. "You make very good sense as a literary playboy, talking about what needs to change. But we students were beaten in the square tonight. We children did our job, and now it's the role of the parents to do something." The events in the square, of course, made a deep impression on me and many other parents. Two days later, Civic Forum was started.

Were you active from the beginning?

Oh yes. I worked with Havel twenty hours a day. I spoke at the main rallies. I was on the strategy committee for Civic Forum.

Offering economic advice?

No, political advice. I also helped write the five-page statement of principles that Civic Forum issued in late November. That was the first public expression of what the new government wanted to do.

How did you become finance minister?

I wanted instead to be head of the state bank, but I was told there was no one else who could do the job of finance minister. There is, sadly, a real shortage of human capital in the country. I have to run both the finance ministry and also serve as the ministry's chief economist. It is an impossible situation.

What are your chances of remaining as finance minister or holding another post in government?

I never intended to be a politician or office-seeker. But the Civic Forum has put me in a very visible position, and I expect that I will be in parliament after the June elections. Whether I will be in my current job, I cannot say.

February 1990
Interview conducted by John Fund for *Reason.*

Radical, Realistic Economics

An Interview with Václav Klaus

DO YOU KNOW *exactly how much money you have in your pocket right now?*

About two hundred and fifty crowns . . . (Pulls a roll of banknotes out of his pocket).

You don't carry a wallet?

I forgot it in my other suit . . . But I have to admit that, paradoxical as it may seem for a finance minister, I don't use money as such. Every morning I tell the children what groceries we need. My secretary pays for my lunches once a month. I drive to the ministry, and the papers are waiting for me here in my office, so I don't need to stop by a kiosk. And I don't get out of here until all the shops are closed.

Do you know how much money we have in circulation?

Yes and no. One of the basic obscurities about our economy is that we don't have just one type of money. Wholesale prices have been completely divorced from retail prices. As a result, we have two spheres that can't be joined, since we don't have any exchange rate between them. We're working to give the country a single form of money. It would be more or less meaningless to give the total amount of money circulating in our economy today, since we'd be adding apples and oranges.

The amount of cash in use—that is, money used by our citizens to buy from stores—is probably around 70 billion crowns.*

How do you intend to link these two spheres?

You start with taxes and prices. In the past, our wholesale and retail prices were simply irrational . . . At the moment, our wholesale prices plus turn-over tax do not equal our retail prices. These different price levels function independently, and the result is chaos. Some taxes actually work in reverse: the state subsidizes manufacturers instead of collecting any money from them. This is particularly true of basic foodstuffs. Our goal is of course to introduce a uniform tax system, which will involve a significant rise in relative prices. As soon as we achieve this, we'll have a single form of money.

How will this affect us? Are all our prices going to go up?

I'd like people to understand the difference between two terms: relative prices and absolute prices. Or price structure and price level. *Ideally,* what we just spoke of affects *only* the price structure. As an example, let's take the removal of negative turn-over taxes, that is, subsidies. In basic foodstuffs this is probably about 35 billion crowns a year. If we stop giving this money to the producers and give it to the consumers, the state doesn't make a penny out of the whole operation. Since these subsidies were established on an individual basis, and not according to some set system, and since people's

* The official tourist exchange rate in May 1990 was approximately $1 = 16.40 crowns. The black market rate was about 40 crowns to the dollar.

consumption patterns are not always the same, you can't come up with a plan that leaves everyone feeling the same effects. If the highest subsidy was for meat, and meat is all you eat, then you lose. If you're a vegetarian, you gain.

An economy with an irrational price structure behaves irrationally, and no one can really be sure of what will help it or harm it the most. Our first step needs to be adjusting all our prices. Wholesale and retail prices, interest rates, wage structures, exchange rates—these are all prices . . . And we've got to do it in such a way that the resolution of these microeconomic problems doesn't create macroeconomic difficulties, such as inflation and unemployment. The slower we are, the more hesitantly and indecisively we set about repairing our microeconomic system, the more serious the macroeconomic problems that threaten us.

Once we complete this one-time price adjustment, we'll be ready to shift to a completely new tax system, including a value-added tax that is completely normal in Western Europe. We'd like to be able to do this in about two or three years.

What should we be most afraid of—inflation or unemployment?

I can't help remembering my first popular article, which came out in *Kulturní tvorba* ("Cultural Creation") in 1966. It was called "Fear of Inflation." It caused a small scandal, with the international press saying that it was the first time the word "inflation" had appeared in a socialist country. Fear of inflation is one of my lifelong interests. But as far as your question goes, there's no choosing between inflation and unemployment. Both are bad, and it's a mistake to think that one's better than the other.

To what extent can economic processes be kept under control? At what point could the helmsman lose control of his ship?

There's much that's unique about our situation, but also lots that's not. As it happens, the vice-president of the International Monetary

Fund, Professor Frenkel, is currently on a visit to Prague. The IMF has had a lot of experience with this, since they've been giving advice on transformation and stabilization programs in about 150 different countries. Universal laws don't only exist in physics, but in economics as well—although people trained in our School of Economics wouldn't think so, since they never had the chance to learn about them.

We're going to put the greatest emphasis on restrictive exchange and fiscal policy to keep the economy from running out of control. We can't allow a state budget deficit, or have excess money in our economy. This would create a vicious circle that would then start to spin faster and faster. Speaking for Tosovsky, the chairman of the State Bank, and myself—and we're the ones responsible for money and finances—this is an absolutely fundamental starting point. As long as parliament doesn't force us to print more money, we're going to stick to this principle.

As specialists are you given free rein in your work?

We keep emphasizing that the economic has to prevail over the uneconomic, which is what the old system was. And now we're seeing a few breakthroughs, even though (understandably, but unfortunately) we're working, and will continue to work, under certain pressures. But if it's not economics as a science that determines the decisions we take about our economy, then it would simply be a lie to speak of economic reform. We'd be back where we started.

Can you give an example of what you call a "breakthrough"?

My assistant Kocárník made a nice comment in a television interview not long ago. The chairman of the State Planning Commission, Dlouhy, had just announced that they had made the state plan responsive to the state budget. Kocárník noted, "Look, this is a revolution: for the first time we can remember, the plan will react to the budget and not the other way around." Perhaps lay people won't grasp this, but for people who understand a little about economics, this is a truly fundamental shift, quite literally a breakthrough.

One of the words that people in your department use most frequently, and with the greatest longing, is "convertibility," or "free exchange." When will we achieve this? In ten years? Five years? Fifteen?

No, if it takes more than a year or two then I'm not sitting here and chatting with you . .

Be careful now, Mr. Minister, we're taping everything you say!

Yes, I know. Of course it's possible that after the elections there will be someone new, with a completely different economic policy, so I can't guarantee anything with absolute certainty. I may have to step down along with other reformers. But speaking for myself, if we can continue down the road that I consider sensible and possible, then I think it should take less than five years.

What exchange rate should a convertible crown have? Something close to today's black market rate?

This is something else that people don't have much idea about. This also has to do with price structures. Listen: if two countries operate completely on world prices, then their exchange rate only reflects the amount of money either of them has printed. If the original rate is 1:15 and the first country raises prices and wages fifteenfold, nothing changes except the exchange rate. The bottom line is that relative prices stay in proportion. In reality, this ideal situation between two countries doesn't exist, and as a result Belgians living on the border find it cheaper to nip across to Germany to buy certain goods. The differences between countries like this are minimal, which is why I can speak of border areas—but it wouldn't make economic sense for people living further away, since petrol and time are also costs.

In a country with a price structure like Czechoslovakia's, this system falls apart. To think that a kilo of butter costs so much in Czechoslovakia, while in Austria it costs so much, and therefore the exchange rate ought to be such-and-such, is to misunderstand the problem completely. The truth is that when differences aren't minimal or negligible, as they are with Belgium and Germany, and when the system is absolutely illogical and upside-down, the worst rate will control the marketplace. When there's an item that one of our citizens finds worthwhile buying in Austria despite the present bad exchange rate, he has to hoard shillings to buy it.

*Are there any reasons to fear the sort of currency reforms that the older generation saw in the 1950s?**

My answer is unambiguous: no. It would be a huge mistake to introduce such reforms, and there's no reason to do so. What I can't say with the same certainty is whether next year's inflation will be 2 percent or 5 percent. This depends on a lot of factors, some of which we can control, some of which we can't. If someone stops delivering our crude oil tomorrow, or if there's a bad harvest, or if German currency unification significantly alters the flow of goods we're used to, or if there are strikes . . . If things like this happen, there could be a situation that we can't foresee today. And then we ourselves might make mistakes. But there is absolutely no threat of currency reform. We'd have to make some really huge mistakes before that could happen.

You have spoken less than flatteringly about our economics graduates. On the other hand, you've also been heard to say that we have economists who understand "real economics." Where did they come from?

---

* In 1953, the Communist government initiated drastic currency reform and commodity price rises in an effort to combat the inflation that high capital investment in heavy industry had brought. This contributed to mass demonstrations by industrial workers in Pilsen and strikes throughout the country, which were harshly suppressed by the security police.

Setting aside individuals like my colleague Dlouhy—people who will succeed under any circumstances, albeit in a haphazard and unplanned way, since they are and were lucky—the last forty years has left us with two groups of economists.

The first comes from my generation, and was lucky enough to join the Czechoslovak Academy of Sciences in the mid-1960s, when our famous economic reforms were being set up. As soon as we finished school, we started graduate or specialist work. Czechoslovakia was a relatively liberal and popular country: we pored over foreign text books, and practically all of us got a chance to go somewhere. I did a six-month post-graduate course in Italy, and spent another half year studying and teaching at Cornell University in the U.S. Half these people were later thrown out of the Academy, as I was, and for many long years we had no chance of doing any (official) research.

The second, better-rounded group of economists began to emerge in the late 1980s. This was another generation that coincided with gradual relaxation of controls, when more and more could be written about real economics in economic journals, when it again became possible to study foreign textbooks. This younger generation came to realize that our earlier group had also been able to study these works . . .

Do you consider yourself an optimist, a pessimist or a realist?

Someone once called me a radical realist, or a realistic radical, I can't remember which it was now. It doesn't matter, though: however you arrange them, I do see myself in the combination of these two words.

How do you like your work? Is it better or worse than you imagined?

I had a fairly good idea of what the work itself would be like. But I didn't expect the flip side of the coin, the political role that I see in the thousands of letters that I receive, and which show how many people are behind me, trusting me, relying on me . . . This sometimes brings me up short. I hadn't imagined the enormous sense of responsibility.

Everyone is raving about what a wonderful younger generation we have. This sort of opinion can't be completely true. Do you agree?

Last week I got really annoyed in Ostrava. People sometimes think that I do nothing but smile, but unfortunately that's not the case. I had just come up out of the Fucík mine: I had never been so far underground in my life, and it had a very, very strong effect on me. Two young lads came up to me and said that they were with some northern Moravian student paper, and then asked me to answer a question. They were studying education. They asked if, when they left school, they could count on getting the same pay as their counterparts in West Germany. I have to admit that together with what I had just seen, this was too much for me, and I started telling them off. Had they asked if they'd be able to teach according to their training and conscience, unfettered by ridiculous syllabi and Party decrees, I'd have been happy to answer their question. But when the first thing that interests them is something like that . . . I don't consider this unpleasant episode something that defines my attitude towards younger people in general. But I do agree with what you said.

Let's finish the way we started, with a personal financial question. If we gave you a million crowns, what would you do with it? Put it in a savings account? Spend it? Invest it in your own firm? Or do you have some other idea?

Well . . . I really wouldn't have any time to do anything with it, I'd have to start by leaving all this behind . . .

You have to imagine that you're relieved of all responsibilities. We don't really have the million crowns, either.

Then my first step would be to look for alternatives to simply depositing the money in a savings account and getting the usual 2 percent or 4 percent interest. There's a whole swarm of other possibilities opening up today. As it happens, I've just been to a publishing factory where they were running off bonds for a company in Bratislava. You buy a 10,000 crown bond, and then for each of eight years you can go to the company cashier for an eighth of the purchase price plus a share of the annual profit. This is something that's already possible, not something that will happen in the future. And not only enterprises are doing this: the Commercial Bank needs more capital at its disposal, and so it's issuing a billion crowns in bonds. New firms will be established. The savings bank is going to have to react to this, since soon no one's going to deposit money at a paltry 2 percent interest rate. Maybe it will issue its own bonds as well . . . That's the approach I'd take right now if I had a million crowns . . .

28 April 1990
Interview conducted by Lubos Beniak and Rudolf Krestan for *Mlady Svet.*

"Dear children, our country is a source of hard currency for our economy."

Why Am I Optimistic?

AFTER THE INITIAL euphoria, Czechoslovaks are coming back down to earth. People are beginning to realize that political liberalization does not bring automatic improvements in other areas, least of all in economics. The transformation of our economy into an effective market system will not be painless. We shall need to change many of our habits, and to sign what specialists call a new "social contract" that will be very different from what we knew in the past. It does not help to say that we (or at least some of us) did not want this past, or that it was forced on us by external force—as well as by our passivity, delusions and rashness. The establishment of new economic, social and political relations will give individuals greater responsibility, freedom and power; but it will also bring more individual risk, meaning both losses and gains, as well as greater discrepancies in income and wealth. I believe that radical economic reform is threatened less by the bureaucratic sabotage people are always talking about than by our lack of courage, ability and decisiveness in undoing the comfortable old social contract that left very little room for individuals either to lose or gain.

Nevertheless I am optimistic. This optimism springs from my belief in the wealth of our country: the wisdom, skill, capacity for action and adaptability of 15 million Czechoslovak citizens.

I do not intend to play with paradoxes. But as a liberal economist I base my hearty optimism on something much more fundamental than whether politicians or bureaucrats can or cannot come up with some solution to our problems. I base it on a deep distrust of the "centralist" thinking of politicians (or intellectuals in their role of advisors). I feel that there is no wise minister, ministry, government, party or parliament—no matter how great their intellectual capabilities, and even with the support of the most powerful computers—that can ever substitute for the functioning of the impersonal market. I believe that there is very little that a government can do, although on the other hand this is quite a lot. The government should only concern itself with the circumstances in which the market can function, maintaining a stable currency and a healthy state budget. The government should not want to know what individual companies and organizations are doing, and certainly ought not advise them on what they should produce and to whom they should sell.

What we have lived in for the past forty years has been nothing but a gigantic experiment, in which society ceased to be governed by the general laws that hold true for all people, that is, for both governments and citizens. Instead, our society placed its fate in the hands of people who gradually lost any sense of restraint. We abandoned our most precious civic values, the product of a thousand-year evolution, embodied in institutions, rules of behavior, the market framework, language, morality, and community structures.

When I use the first person plural, I exaggerate. It was not "we" who did this. None of "us" would ever have had the audacity, for we do not know this type of ambition. Behind every arrogant attempt to draw up completely new social institutions, there lurks the cerebral and sometimes physical violence of a handful of self-important intellectuals. This involves a deep contempt for the thoughts and feelings of others. The attempt at socialism could only mean that those who raised their own theory on high did so by seriously assaulting the dignity of their fellow citizens. This was not some "mob rebellion" (in Ortega y Gasset's terminology), but rather a revolt by a group of leftist intellectuals.

I am optimistic because I believe that no future government will accrue so much power that it takes on a greater role in decision-making than it can handle. I am optimistic because I believe in people's healthy and creative pragmatism, and in the power of the market's impersonal mechanisms. As long as I am finance minister, I shall (parliament permitting) continue to cut state budget expenditures; for I believe that the market can allot limited resources far better than the most democratically elected parliament—even if that parliament follows the proposals of the most brilliant finance minister in the world.

26 March 1990
Literární noviny

Petr Pithart

BORN IN 1941, Pithart is Czech and earned his law degree from Prague's Charles University. He then became an assistant professor on the law faculty, and worked as an editor of various periodicals, including *Univerzita Karlova* ("Charles University"), *Literární listy* ("Literary Notes") and *Listy* ("Notes"). An active supporter of political reform during the Prague Spring, he lost his positions after the Soviet-led invasion in August 1968. The only work he could subsequently find was manual or clerical; this was only aggravated when he became a signatory of Charter 77. Pithart wrote a series of underground political science and historical studies in the years that followed, including a critical book on the Prague Spring, *Sixty-Eight*. He was one of Civic Forum's leading strategists and legal experts during the "velvet revolution," and headed the Civic Forum Coordination Center until he was nominated president of the Czech Republic in February 1990.

The Political Culture of the New Czechoslovakia

FOR POLITICAL SCIENTISTS, sociologists and social psychologists, today's Czechoslovakia is the ideal laboratory. After fifty years, this country has embraced political freedom—but without any sort of transition period. The episodes of 1945-48 and 1968-69 were just that. The first one turned increasingly obviously into the slippery slope that ended, in February 1948, on the plateau of totalitarianism. 1968 never managed to step out of its own shadow. The Prague Spring was always defined as a political "renaissance": it was to be led by intellectuals associated with the Czechoslovak Communist Party, many of whom had a place in its power structure. There were few political forces that were not affiliated with the Party, and as a rule their programs were underdeveloped. The question to ask about today's situation is clear. Are traditional European models of political behavior being reborn, or is something completely different happening in contemporary Czechoslovakia? Will the system that is developing here ultimately become a version of what the rest of Europe considers normal and rational?

There is no easy answer to this question, in part because it is still too early to say for sure. The legacy that has been handed down to today's Czechoslovakia has been passed on in a way that resembles a game of "Consequences." One person tells another person what a third person told him, and so on, until we end up with some muddled information about how our fathers—or rather today, our grandfathers—engaged in politics.

Soon after November 17, several political parties emerged that had existed in Czechoslovakia between the two world wars. These parties often kept the same name. Their advantage has been that they can use their party's original program, adapting it where necessary to the current situation. They often seek continuity by merging with representatives of their parties in exile, thus emphasizing their legitimacy. This is particularly true of those parties whose programs still contain the word "socialist": the Czechoslovak Social Democratic Party and the Czechoslovak (National) Socialist Party. But what on the one hand seems an advantage can also become a handicap if there is not enough adaptation to the present situation. Are these parties really alive and well? If they appeal to the past, can they absorb what is vital in today's Europe? There are many social democrats and Christian democrats who operate outside these two established parties. The Socialist and People's* parties existed throughout the forty years of totalitarianism, and were thus tainted by collaboration with the Communist party.

The right is also trying to find its feet: the Republican party, for example, or the intriguing liberal conservatives known as the Civic Democratic Alliance (ODA).** These two parties are a novelty in Czechoslovak political culture. During the First Republic (1918-38), the fairly weak right was dispersed among the right wings of explicitly professional interest groups, particularly the Agrarian party. A right wing in the Western European sense is weak in Czechoslovakia, and tends to appear mostly in denominational or traditionally Christian parties.

Being the president of the Czech Republic's government, I am speaking mostly of the Czech, and not Slovak political scene. Al-

* The People's Party is Christian democratic in nature (see "After the Velvet Revolution: the First Six Months" for a discussion of this and other parties).

** See interviews with Pavel Bratinka, leader of ODA.

though it is only three months since our revolution, I would say that our political parties are not going to have an easy time of it. Young and old people are joining, but for the moment the middle generation is showing no interest. These parties have scarcely any chance of getting more than the 5 percent minimum in the June 1990 elections;* if they do win any seats in parliament, it will only be under the protective umbrella of the "non-party-members' party," Civic Forum, or as part of some coalition. It may be true that most of these parties would never receive the minimum number of votes, even if the election were to take place in six months or a year. This problem is least likely to face two of the parties mentioned above, the Social Democrats and the Christian Democrats. One reason for this is that the "young" parties' programs are vague, and their political goals are not clearly elaborated. They all know what they don't want, but have yet to formulate programs of their own.

At the moment, the dominant feature of public political opinion is distrust and an unwillingness to participate in political parties. This is true even among people who are politically active. This is the reflection of an instinctive distaste for political parties in general, and for everything that is associated with party apparatuses, discipline, leaders' privileges, perks and so on. These are vague, overgeneralized dislikes, and spring from the experience of Communist party rule. Vague they may be, but they still remain strong. Historians are reminded of the overpoliticization of the otherwise democratic First Republic. In 1925, for example, as many as twenty-nine parties ran candidates (and sixteen of them won seats). All these parties represented professional or ethnic interests, and their delegates were quite literally the vassals of party secretariats.

Traditional, civic-oriented, European parties—like the Social Democrats, Christian Democrats, Christian Socialists and Republicans — are developing more slowly than they would like. This is partly the result of the distaste for party activity described above, and partly

---

* A party must win 5 percent of the overall vote in one of the two republics to be assured representation in the Federal Assembly.

due to the stereotypes that interest parties are once again propagating. The rhetoric of these groups now contains a strong element of protectionism, and appeals to various fears about the uncertain future (business and agricultural concerns, for example). But the most important reason for this slow development is the destruction or, more precisely, the flattening of our social structure. Traditional models of political and party behavior have somehow slipped away. Political parties cannot find a foot-hold. Until recently, after all, all Czechoslovak citizens were state employees, so that the spectrum of economic and social interests remained limited, latent, invisible on the political plane.

Without socio-economic differentiation, the new political parties are an attempt at planting islands of painstakingly nurtured greenery on an intellectually arid hillside. At the bottom of this hill there lies the dangerous terrain of demagoguery, ploughed by professional, ethnic and local interests. Political life on a level with Western Europe finds this terrain uninhabitable. Even our professional athletes have formed their own political party! This is a post-totalitarian landscape, which does not mean that it cannot also be fertile ground. The distaste for political parties is basically a distaste for political thinking and for political dialogue. There are many people today who want just one thing: to want, to demand, to side vehemently and exclusively with particularist interests.

The strength of Civic Forum, the avowedly nonpartisan initiative, is somewhat linked to this. Civic Forum is our original Czechoslovak invention. It is a broad-based, politically active, democratic movement. Its members are all those who want to be involved in politics but who insist on remaining nonpartisan. There is often a vast difference between Civic Forum the parent organization (in Prague), which is political, and the Civic Forums that exist locally, and which are more or less particularist, that is nonpolitical. Hence Civic Forum's immense problems. It is now gathering around itself the greater part of the politically active public, but still exists without individual membership . . .

Civic Forum is also as politically diversified as it could be, and contains both extreme rightists and leftists. Only the first steps from totalitarianism to democracy can be taken collectively. By the time you reach the fifth, or certainly the seventh step, disagreements break out that cannot be solved by common hatred of the old order. Can Civic Forum, which took such dazzling control of the political stage during the revolution's first months, survive until the elections? Or will it disintegrate before then? How will Civic Forum stand up to the pressures created by the approaching elections to behave like a political party? For Civic Forum finally did decide to run its own candidates in the election. How will a group that doesn't want to be a political party behave when that really is *de facto* what it is? The June elections will use the proportional representation system in large voting districts. Civic Forum is promising to include on its candidate list representatives from the new and emerging political parties that for the moment support Civic Forum. But how can Civic Forum include them if it does not want to lose the elections—but also wants to keep its promise of opening the way to political pluralism by helping new political parties get established? Some of the new political parties are now considering electoral coalitions with other parties, and are leaving the Civic Forum that until recently was so dominant. These problems seem insoluble. I say "seem" because Civic Forum has faced insoluble problems from the very outset, and so far has found decent, even elegant solutions for them all.

For all of Czechoslovakia's lack of a traditional European political culture, President Havel's friends and advisors—centered around Civic Forum—have shown notable judgement and sense of proportion. In this they have drawn not only on Czechoslovakia's democratic traditions, but also on fifteen years' experience in the political subculture of dissent. The rich, often controversial, shadow politics of Charter 77 and other similar initiatives have provided thousands of people with healthy political habits. The most important of these is the ability to communicate with people who hold completely different political views. The level of tolerance and willingness to act together is still exceptionally high. Hence Civic Forum's reputation for making quick decisions, precise formulations, and—most importantly—for dealing effectively with the old power structures (now mostly reconfigured). It is no coincidence that Civic Forum is called "a movement of decent people."

The political culture of contemporary Czechoslovakia is still untraditional. There are people in Civic Forum who are specialists in various fields. The result of their specialization is that they have their own particular view of the world, their own political opinion. This is excellent for attracting people to the Civic Forum platform. The word "amateur" means "lover" or "admirer." In other words, political amateurism need not mean lack of specialist training or political naïveté. Our new political leaders are amateurs in this sense. They still feel a certain contempt for professional politicians, and this fact explains a lot. These determined amateurs find great support in Václav Havel, who is their spokesman and intellectual leader.

Traditional political structures have not proven themselves all that well in Czechoslovakia. If they do reemerge, it will not be soon. From the upper reaches of Civic Forum to citizens on the street, the loudest voice is saying: make room for independent candidates, limit the influence and power of the new parties! It is more instinctive fear than considered opinion that produces this attitude, which ignores the fact that pluralism without political parties is an empty slogan. There can be no doubt that political parties will develop, just as it is certain that even after the elections, Civic Forum will still exist in some form—most likely as its own type of guarantee that particularist politics will not take over the whole political scene.

Perhaps one can see a bit of impractical political vision in this, something that has found expression in Havel's maxim "nonpolitical politics." We cannot rule out the possibility that there is a new political style, a new political culture being born. Czechoslovakia has been through so many bitter experiences with traditional politics—both conventional democratic politics and what amounted to the negation of politics by totalitarianism—that it would be surprising were it not to come up with some alternative suggestions. Something interesting had to emerge from the intellectual capacity of a cultured

Central European country that has also had the unprecedented experience of two types of totalitarianism. We should avoid any hint of messianism, but we should not passively adopt models simply because they have been successful elsewhere. This is where we differ from the GDR. Perhaps we will have to pay for this arrogance one day; on the other hand, perhaps we won't.

It was students, artists and particularly actors who started the revolution of November 17. The fundamental imprint of their liberal-mindedness, creativity, sense of humor and rejection of ideology will not disappear overnight. Economic realities will certainly pin us to the ground. But our load will be lightened by the improvisations of these amateur-democrats. I dare not guess what the resulting synthesis will be. But I believe it will be something that Europe will find interesting.

22 March 1990
Tydeník vlády Ceske Republiky

Rudolf Battek

BORN IN 1924, Battek is Czech. He trained and worked as a skilled mechanic until late in World War II, when he joined the resistance. After the war he studied social science and then worked in various managerial positions. From 1965-69 he was a sociologist at the Academy of Sciences. In 1968 he founded the Club for Committed Non-party Members (KAN) and served as a member of the Czech National Council (parliament). He was dismissed from these positions after writing a letter to parliament calling for discussion of the Soviet invasion. He then worked in a variety of manual jobs and spent 1969-70, 1971-74, 1979 and 1980-85 in prison. He was among the first to sign Charter 77, and was one of its spokesmen in 1980. He cofounded both the Committee for the Defense of the Unjustly Prosecuted (VONS) (1977) and the Movement for Civil Liberties (HOS) (1988). From 1977-80 he helped publish *Dialogy* ("Dialogues"), an underground journal for independent socialists. In 1978 he helped establish a group of independent social democrats, the first open political opposition movement since 1968. In November 1989 he helped set up Civic Forum. In January 1990 he became a member of its Council, and was co-opted into the Federal Assembly. His Social Democratic Club is part of Civic Forum.

Following the June 1990 elections, Rudolf Battek became deputy chairman of the Federal Assembly [ed.].

From Totalitarianism to Democracy

An Interview with Rudolf Batteck

IN THE MONTHS *preceding November 1989, Czechoslovakia was one of Central and Eastern Europe's most conservative and repressive Communist regimes. There was a certain amount of civic unrest, but not enough for people to think that things would change as quickly and completely as they did. What snapped in November 1989? How could a totalitarian system collapse so quickly?*

The November revolution wasn't the result of some instantaneous transformation. In fact, there were many events leading up to the break, as is always the case with any radical change. Social pressure in Czechslovakia grew in waves over the two decades following the August 1968 invasion. This was certainly influenced by social movements in neighboring East European countries.

A schematic description of the milestones in this progression would look something like this:

(1) Arrests without trial for political reasons, political trials and sentencing: 1969-72.

(2) The creation of Charter 77 and the Committee for the Defense of the Unjustly Prosecuted (VONS): 1977-78.

(3) Founding of the first openly proclaimed independent political group: the Independent Socialists, registered with the Socialist International (Rudolf Battek, Jaroslav Mezník, Jirí Müller, 1978).

(4) Political trials of Charter 77 and VONS signatories: 1979, 1981.

(5) Establishment of Charter 77's collective of spokespersons, an attempt to create a new structure better able to withstand police repression (January 1, 1980).

(6) Founding of several independent civic initiatives: the Democratic Initiative (1987), the Movement for Civil Liberties (HOS) (1988), and the Independent Peace Association (NMS) (1988).

(7) Massive street protests to commemorate various anniversaries: August 21, 1988,* October 28, 1988,** December 10, 1988,† Palach Week in 1989,†† August 21 and October 28, 1989.

All this eroded the Communists' previously stable and centralized control over society. This of course was influenced by social and political developments in the Soviet Union, including Gorbachev and his new policies of *perestroika* and *glasnost*.

By 17 November 1989, the Czechoslovak Communist Party leadership was deeply shaken and disunited. Despite this, their reaction was to use brutal violence—but they were already incapable of a decisive response, and couldn't crush the ensuing demonstrations by force. With the establishment of Civic Forum on November 19, 1989, the Communist leadership went on the defensive, and couldn't use its overwhelming armed strength the way the Chinese did. Could it be that Czech national characteristics—like the traditional unwillingness to gamble or take risks—played a part in

---

* Twentieth anniversary of the Soviet invasion.

** Czechoslovakia became an independent republic on 28 October 1918.

† 10 December is International Human Rights Day.

†† Jan Palach, a Charles University student, committed suicide by self-immolation on 16 January 1969 to protest the Soviet invasion.

all this? Or were the Communists afraid of history condemning them?

The opposition's demands gradually increased as the massive demonstrations during that first week put an end to the last fears of an armed intervention by militants in the Communist Party, the Ministry of Internal Affairs or the army.

By brutally attacking demonstrators in the streets, the power elite lost its power. They switched to political negotiations. Their strategy was one of deception, and aimed to keep them as many of their former powerful positions as possible. (The first post-November 17 government, headed by Ladislav Adamec, was an example of this.)* The opposition, headed by Havel, opted for a rational course in the negotiations, one that didn't attempt to exclude the Communists altogether. This is part of the explanation for the Communist party's continued existence today.

Was what happened really a "revolution"?

The changes we've seen in society, the government and our legislative assemblies can only be called a revolution. Totalitarian power has been destroyed, the Communist party has begun to disintegrate, and the opposition, despite its amateurness, has started to be less equivocal in directing further developments. Without agreement in its ranks, nothing could be achieved.

What threatens Czechoslovakia's transition to democracy?

I'd like to be able to say that we're now at a turning point in history when nothing stands in the way of a basic trend towards democracy. Everything will of course depend on our ability to give political life a stable shape, so that people can identify with it and see it as supporting their economic and social rights.

---

* See "From 1968 to 1989: A Chronological Commentary," 3 December 1989.

What are the basic reactions of Czechs and Slovaks to greater freedom and pluralism?

I'm not surprised that our society is experiencing something like a hangover, and that our behavior sometimes seems schizophrenic. This is probably part of the transitions and social changes we're undergoing. When a totalitarian society is opened up, you can't be surprised that people's reactions are a little unrestrained or undisciplined. I think it won't be long until we see a certain reaction against some of the negative features of a pluralist society. I only hope that through our political work we manage to preserve this basic feature of democracy.

Since the November revolution, a plethora of political parties and movements has sprung up in Czechoslovakia. You have twenty-three parties, movements or coalitions competing in your June 1990 elections. Does today's Czechoslovakia really need all these political parties? Aren't Civic Forum and Public Against Violence enough at this stage to beat the Communists in the elections?

I consider Civic Forum and Public Against Violence to be the main, legitimate guarantee of our transition from totalitarianism to democracy. They've brought a modern element to politics: a nonpartisan understanding of public work. Of course it would be impossible to stop other political parties from functioning; their establishment is simply the expression of political pluralism. Our society clearly objects to the idea of a unified anti-Communist movement that could beat the Communists by itself. People would most likely see that as threatening to become a new totalitarianism, which is something they're already talking about as it is.

Until March 1990, you yourself were active in the Social Democratic Party. You've since founded the Social Democratic Club of Civic Forum, a separate organization. What happened?

After the 24th Congress of the Social Democratic Party, a wing led by Horák and Janyr took over the party leadership, along with a group of people who had originally worked with Klaban.* I found it impossible, for many reasons, to work with this leadership, since our group had chosen a different approach.** I'm a member of the party's executive committee, but I no longer take part in its work. Instead we've created the Social Democratic Club of Civic Forum, which will pursue its own intellectual, political and organizational line. I feel that I'm an integral member of Civic Forum, which I helped create, and believe that social democrats can play an important role within Civic Forum, attracting other former supporters and members of the Social Democratic Party.

What are the basic outlines of your Club's program? What can it do to advance social and democratic renewal in Czechoslovakia?

---

* The Czechoslovak Social Democratic Party—one of the country's most prominent political forces between the world wars—was forcibly incorporated into the Communist party in 1948. The party was reestablished in November 1989 under the leadership of Slavomír Klaban. He was replaced at the 24th Congress (March 1990) by Jirí Horák, an exile who, like Premysl Janyr, had returned to Czechoslovakia after the November revolution. These and other exiles had preserved the party in the West after 1948, and for the most part belong to the generation that emigrated after the Communist takeover. The financial and logistical aid they provided after November 1989, together with the continuity with the past they represent, have given their group control of the party leadership. The congress withdrew the party from its previous alliance with Civic Forum for the June elections.

** In the "Declaration of the Social Democrats' Club of Civic Forum," Battek et al. state: "The sad state of social democratic renewal is due, among other factors, to the fact that a group of people with no political identity or understanding has taken control of the party. This group is completely dependent on a few individuals abroad . . . Its leadership consists of people who have no history of opposition activity, and who for the most part did not personally work in Civic Forum." Battek's Club ran in the 1990 elections under the Civic Forum umbrella, although supporters have also retained their membership in the Social Democratic Party. They have not ruled out merging with the party at a later date—and under a new leadership.

It seems that party programs aren't playing a particularly important role in the development of either the old or new parties. This is mostly because there's not much difference between these programs: the left has moved somewhat to the right, and the conservatives have yet to show themselves in all their colors. Social democrats emphasize their traditional position as a workers', wage-earners' party, stressing the social aspects of these groups' interests. As a traditionally prominent party, it can play an important role on the "left" side of the scales, contributing to the political equilibrium we need.

You've been a deputy in the Federal Assembly since late January 1990. What do you see as your role in parliament?

Before the June elections, parliament needs to make legislative changes, including reform of the constitution and legal system, so that the new government will have the groundwork laid for its work after the elections.

What do you see as the greatest difference between your pre-revolutionary activity and your present political role? Do you sense any conflict between the moral stance of a dissident and the everyday compromises of a politician?

A dissident's position is in a way much simpler. What was at stake wasn't one's position, but rather of one's willingness to take risks. We were all under police surveillance and pressure. As dissidents, people judged one another as moral individuals. Today, when there's nothing at risk, the most important thing is finding yourself a place in the structure of power. The moral aspects of political behavior fall by the wayside.

Forty years of Communist rule has had catastrophic consequences for Czechoslovakia. Many people—both here and in the West—expected the Party to be denied participation in politics. But that never happened. What is your opinion on this?

"Fine. I'll take my lies and go to hell.
But I warn you, you're going to miss me!"

I'm not a supporter of fighting totalitarianism with totalitarianism. But nor am I sure that we did the right thing in letting the Communist party keep the form it still has today. Perhaps we should have pressured it into dissolving itself, at which point the Communists could have set up some new party. I think it was a mistake not to do this; it would have simplified things a lot. Nevertheless, I do see that a democratic politician can't rid himself of his opposition by administrative fiat. In terms of political culture, we've done quite well. In terms of power politics, what we've done is of course enormously naïve. But that, unfortunately, is the way it goes in politics. Since we've started on this road, we've got to try to defend our gains and win.

The Communist party has relinquished some of its property since November 1989, but still has assets estimated at billions of crowns. What do you think should become of these assets?

Any assets the Communist party has, including what the Party chiefs gained illegally, should be transferred to a rehabilitation fund, which could then be used to compensate for the Communist party's crimes over the past forty years.

One of the most urgent tasks you face is to "detotalitarianize" your political structures and society in general. Do you think that the resignation of only those figures who were most compromised by their activity under the past regime will be enough to achieve this?

I certainly don't think that the country can be democratized by having a few compromised people resign. There needs to be a thorough purge, or whatever one calls it, that will take some time. The struggle for just such a purge in the Ministry of Internal Affairs shows how difficult this will be. Anything connected with State Security (StB) should be abolished. This should happen in all our organizations, but particularly in the Communist party, our ministries and so on. I feel that after the elections our elected bodies—the Federal

Assembly, the Czech and Slovak National Councils—ought to contain no one who was a member before November 1989.

What reforms would you like to see in the army, the Ministry of Internal Affairs and the security services?

I'm a pacifist, and consider the army to be a hold-over from a pre-civilized stage of social development. Minister Vacek* knows this, and dislikes me. But of course I support a decent army with a year's required service, reduction in the overall size of the armed services, and perhaps even the gradual introduction of a professional army.

The Ministry of Internal Affairs should be placed under the control of trustworthy people, democrats, who have been tried and tested in the opposition to the former Communist regime. There should also be a system of control mechanisms set up, to keep this section of the government's power from swelling and turning into a state within a state.

You have spoken of how democratic structures and systems ought to work. What's your idea of life in the free world based on? Have you been able to travel? Where?

My own practical experience of how political structures function in the West is limited and brief. I have visited Italy, Switzerland and West Germany. My personal experience has drawn more on our own democracy before 1948, though I also remember the prewar period. I was fifteen in 1939, and my father was very involved politically.

Do you see any Western country offering a model for improving Czechoslovakia's current situation?

Western countries can only serve as indirect models for today's

---

* Colonel General Miroslav Vacek was Czechoslovakia's defense minister until late October 1990. Lubos Dobrovsky, who replaced Vacek, is the first civilian to hold the position in over fifty years [ed.].

Czechoslovakia. Because of what we experienced under totalitarianism, we can't simply adopt a whole Western-style system. We often talk of the Swedish model. The example of West Germany will clearly be very influential in Czechoslovakia, and our "search" will doubtless find some inspiration across the ocean.

Do you think people here in Czechoslovakia are willing to risk their stable, familiar world to transform their economic system?

There are certainly people who were satisfied with the deadening facade of "real socialism":* they'll probably look back on the past with nostalgia. But these people are mostly members of the elite. Normal citizens who feel like this are for the most part unenterprising, and are satisfied with the certainty of receiving their perpetually guaranteed income at no risk or trouble to themselves. It all depends on the make-up of people's characters.

What sort of dangers do you think total abandonment of "real socialism" may bring to Czechoslovak society? According to several hints in Rudé právo,** *Czechoslovak citizens can expect to lose their subsidies, pensions and benefits, and they'll then have to go out and beg on the street . . .*

Our society's abandoning "real socialism" can bring no evil. Only we must be prepared for the problems that accompany every democracy, as well as the social questions that an effective economy must raise. No one is going to have to beg in our future society, but nor will anyone be well-off without reason. No one should collect money for not working, or for not bothering to work.

---

* "Real socialism" was the term used by the communist regime to describe an idealised version of Czechoslovak "socialist" reality, and came to describe Communist domestic policy in general.

** The Communist party newspaper.

If you were to become prime minister after the elections, what would be your first step in the sphere of economic reform?

As prime minister I would choose one of the possible models for economic reform, which I would then hand over to a team of co-workers who supported the choice I had made. I would leave opponents of the plan—in fact I would challenge them—to keep working on their own models, in order to catch and eliminate any shortcomings in the adopted policy as soon as possible. I don't hold to the theory that as devastated an economy as ours can be cured by abandoning it to an ocean of market economics prowled by sharks. We need to evaluate our negative experience and find the best way forward.

The Czechoslovak press is constantly talking about the problems Czechs, Slovaks, Moravians, Poles, Germans, Hungarians, Gypsies and Ruthenians have living together in one country. Do you see a solution to these various problems? What effect will they have on the future development of Czechoslovakia?

Our nationality problems, which totalitarianism basically suppressed, are beginning to take on their natural shape. Given this, the only option available is balanced analysis of the situation and of course politically mature handling of those nationalist groups that contain separatist tendencies. Minorities must of course be guaranteed all basic rights. Slovak-Czech relations must crystallize into a stable federative form, with full equality of rights as well as constitutional and national sovereignty. I'm optimistic about prospects in this area.

What changes would you like to see in Czechoslovakia's foreign policy? Do you agree with the efforts of the "government of national understanding" in this area?

Our foreign policy is just getting under way. It currently consists mostly of testing the various tools and options it has. Sometimes

I think that we needlessly adopt the stance of a major player when more modesty might be in order. I don't think there have been many serious mistakes. I hope that we'll join the group of states that adheres to the established principle of respect for the rights of others in both domestic and foreign policy. Our policy will of course be to support European integration.

Where do you think the Soviet empire's collapse is headed, and what effect might this have on the future of Czechoslovakia?

Several years ago I argued that the Soviet empire had to disintegrate, and that it would take on the new, modern shape of a confederation that was held together by the same old czarist methods of isolation and the knout. Whole sections of the USSR will become independent: the Baltic states and the Caucasus, for example. Belorussia and the Ukraine's futures are still unclear. Otherwise, the Russians ought to pull back in the Far East: their treatment of Japanese territorial claims is the outright rudeness of typical imperialists. The USSR's influence on Czechoslovakia will continue to decline—as it should. At this stage in our history, they've got nothing to offer us.

Do you think that a revolution like yours could take place in the Soviet Union?

The Soviet Union will develop into a democracy, although it probably won't follow our example. The pressure to democratize is completely unrelenting, and if Gorbachev understands things at all, he must see that the Communists have already played out their role as any sort of leading force.

Much of the world has been discussing what it should do to help Central and Eastern Europe's new democracies. How can the West help you? And what does Czechoslovakia have to offer in return?

No one has more experience than the West of the democracy that the world seems to be moving towards today. As a result, it has something to offer a country like ours in practically every area. This of course is particularly true when it comes to finding the best way to integrate these new democracies in the world economy. At the moment, Czechoslovakia is in the process of establishing itself, and will need some help from the West. But I've no doubt that in a short while we'll be able to offer cooperation to a number of countries less developed than our own. I'm convinced that bilateral arrangements won't be enough, however, and that we'll need to find global solutions to all these problems.

9 May 1990
Interview conducted by Tim Whipple.

Václav Benda

BORN IN 1946, Benda is Czech. He received degrees in both mathematics and philosophy from Prague's Charles University, where he was chairman of the students' council in 1968. He was awarded a doctorate in philosophy, but lost his subsequent teaching position because of his Catholic views. After further study of mathematics and physics, he worked as a computer programmer. Upon signing Charter 77 in 1977, he lost this job and became a stoker. In 1978 he was a cofounder of the Committee for the Unjustly Prosecuted (VONS). In 1979 he was one of the Charter 77 spokesmen until his arrest and sentencing for "collusion with foreign agents" along with several other VONS members. Having refused offers of release on condition that he leave the country, Benda was finally let out in 1983. In 1985 he started the journal *Paraf,* and in 1988 was a cofounder of the Movement for Civil Liberties (HOS). His essays on philosophy, politics and mathematics appeared in the underground press; he has also written a novel, "Black Girl," and several children's stories. After involvement in Civic Forum in the early days of the "velvet revolution," he founded the Christian Democratic Party (based in the Czech Republic) in December 1989. This party subsequently split away from Civic Forum to form a coalition with the Czechoslovak People's Party and the Christian Democratic Movement in Slovakia. In December 1989 he was co-opted into the Federal Assembly, where he has been a member of the presidium and committee for constitutional law.

Dissident Turned Politician

An Interview with Václav Benda

YOU HAVE TWO *university degrees, in philosophy and mathematics. After fifteen years of being active in dissident circles, stoking furnaces and spending time in prison, you could finally get yourself a normal job. Instead, you take another risk: you found a political party. But does Czechoslovakia really need parties right now? Isn't Civic Forum sufficient for beating the Communists in the elections?*

What you said about the risk I run in cofounding the Christian Democratic Party is problematic. I participated in our "gentle revolution" from the very beginning, in various positions and functions. Having spent twelve years working to prepare the conditions for these democratic changes, I consider it my responsibility and duty to be involved, regardless of personal or professional preferences.

The revolution is far from over, and much remains to be achieved, including *renewal*. This will be a very tricky task. It involves both the peaceful dismantling of the totalitarian system and the renewal of society. Once these structures are dismantled, we'll be left with what will be more or less a wilderness. We need to renew our social and political life; and to renew our political life, to let democracy really start working, we need to renew pluralism and learn to develop different political opinions. This is why it's necessary to form different political parties.

"If all you're going to be is velvet and gentle,
we're never going to have any kids..."

Independent boards of specialists can suggest courses of economic reform. Do political parties have anything to contribute in this area?

I believe that a functioning democracy and government by specialist officials are diametrically opposed. If we want democracy, then we need to have full political life, and we need the people, the majority to govern in accordance with set legal rules, with full respect for pluralism and minorities. When I say this I'm not of course attacking specialists. On the contrary, democratically elected politicians need to have specialists to consult, and ought to use them as much as possible. But politics itself is a matter for democratically elected politicians.

Don't political parties present a danger of our letting the moral aspect of our changes slip away? People who have collaborated, or at least kept quiet for twenty or forty years can easily make their way up these parties' ladders . . .

This completely depends on what's meant by a political party. If, in the spirit of totalitarianism, we take a party to be a single, unified expression of political will, to which individual members have to subjugate their own wills, then we've gone astray. If this happens we either build a totalitarian party, or else political life disintegrates into hundreds and thousands of individual political wills, meaning tiny groups and parties of every kind.

There's another danger that's appeared in several democratic countries. Ruthless careerists can infiltrate a party's apparatus, and thus move into positions where they can define and control political life.

Of course, if we see a political party as an association of individuals in which each member has his own will and responsibility—a group of people who, in order to advance their political beliefs more effectively, have decided to join forces with like-minded people—then not only does this sort of party *not* present any threat, but it's the natural cornerstone of healthy political life. It's a natural basis for the transition from a plurality of individuals to the creation of a political grouping with a unified political direction.

What do you think threatens our road to democracy?

I think there are two threats, or rather one threat and one problem. The threat is that totalitarianism is far from defeated. You could say that we've managed to cripple a few of its brain centers, but its apparatus has survived and is still functioning. I don't think I'm an unrealistic optimist when I say that I don't believe in a violent upheaval, although of course the path of peaceful, gradual dismantling of the totalitarian system brings numerous problems. I'll mention two of them.

Even though we've been able to put our people in positions of leadership, there's a danger of the old structures swallowing them up before we manage to destroy them. These new people could begin to see things through the eyes of the old structures, and might feel, for instance, that a few personnel changes are enough for the old system to start working in a new way.

The second danger lies in the fact that we've taken on enormous responsibility in interests of continuity. We've got a president, ministers . . . but this apparent responsibility is only held together by a negligible share of real power. Our strength lies only in the public's support. This support can of course be threatened: it would be enough for people to tell us in two or three months, "So, now you've got everything in hand, but have things got any better?" If something like this happens, then that will be the moment for the totalitarian forces to start their counter-offensive.

The problem I started with consists of believing that democracy can be reestablished by waving a magic wand (i.e., free elections). But it's far from being that simple. Democracy and the legal state need more than good intentions. There are two preconditions for democracy: the establishment of constitutional and legal structures and institutions, and citizens feeling a certain sense of political and civic responsibility. Democracy also requires the diversification of society: there need to be various organizations, associations, formal and informal groups, which can steady the course of social life. This whole process will be painstaking and time-consuming, but if people throw themselves into it with gusto, then we'll have a functioning democracy and legal state in three or four years. But if the majority of people stop being interested in public and political life after the June 1990 elections, this public and political life will correspondingly decline. I don't mean to say that there would be a return to totalitarianism. But we would have a very imperfect, poorly functioning democratic system.

What can the Christian Democratic Party do about this?

There are two phases of what the Christian Democratic Party can and must do. The first will be the period leading up to the free elections in June 1990. This will be the time to join the public in fighting the forces of totalitarianism. The second phase will consist of reforming everything that can be reformed. This will involve reconstruction in various areas (from the reestablishment of respect for basic moral values, to the addressing of cultural, economic, ecological and many other problems). This reconstruction will be enormously difficult, and is unprecedented in history. It's not just that we'll be building on ruins, for this has happened throughout history, when people have to make a fresh start after some enormous catastrophe. But we're going to have to build on ruins fifty years old, on ground that's been devastated for half a century. It wasn't just buildings or the economic infrastructure that was abused; it was also people's souls. The foundations of education, traditionally well-respected in Czechoslovakia, were shattered. People's health was ruined, people's memory and conscience were deformed.

This will be enormously difficult work. I feel that the Christian Democratic Party can do a lot by being clear-headed, devoted to the upright and unequivocal Christian ideals and values that have stood the test of centuries. It can try to move up into political life from among the people and their needs, in the understanding of politics as service. Our party will serve as a corrective for utopias and phantasies of any size or shape. Their appearance threatens our shattered land, be they those of the socialists or the nationalists. In this context we're going to have to avert many dangers. I feel that a strong Christian Democratic Party can make a great contribution to limiting the effects of these dangers to a minimum.

What do you think is the most important feature of nonsocialist alternatives for our country's future?

All socialists make social justice the responsibility of the state. As a Christian Democrat I acknowledge the enormous importance of social security: as a Catholic I accept the church's social teachings, and social justice means something concrete to me. And apart from this, as a politician I realize that a society that's not built on principles of social justice is threatened by injustice, and thus is unstable.

On the other hand it's precisely because I'm a Christian Democrat that I reject the idea of the state being entrusted with ensuring social justice. This implies giving the state the sort of power and authority that sooner or later would necessarily be perverted into a kind of totalitarianism. We emphasize that social justice depends first and foremost on society itself, from individual morality to social cooperation, from specialized and other associations to charity in the broadest sense of the word. Charity is far from just giving alms; it's the purposeful, well-intentioned and solid cooperation of all with everyone.

Nonsocialist alternatives mean emphasizing the individual as the ultimate basis of all other structures, whether the family, other social groups, or the state, which should be responsible for serving these groups, concerning itself with their safety and equal development.

I'd like to ask you to be a bit more precise. As you know, Rudé právo*

* The Czechoslovak Communist Party newspaper.

has been making allegations that by the time the elections come, newspapers will be rivaling each other in their gloomy descriptions of a Dickensian Czechoslovakia. Citizens who have lost their government subsidies for childcare, health and pension support will have to scour the streets and beg for alms . . .

There are some papers that have been exaggerating for forty years, and that still don't care for the details of what's been said or done. All the same, what I said about limiting the state's role does not affect the social security items you mention. By the end of the twentieth century, it ought to be a given that a developed state (which after all we still are) should have a decent social security system.

Can totalitarianism be overcome in the former Soviet satellites?

The totalitarian systems of the former Soviet bloc are in decline, and will be overcome. As far as the Soviet Union itself goes, that's a separate question which I won't address here. It's impossible to foresee how it will develop, and I'd only guess that what happens will be dramatic.

I don't believe that any totalitarian ideas that might appear here could be based on communism or socialism. These notions have been so thoroughly discredited that their defeat is assured in advance.

But the victory of democracy in these former satellites is still far from being a foregone conclusion. Democracy is the result of a certain development, certain traditions, it's the result of the attitudes of individual citizens and all of society. If even the most perfect democratic institutions and mechanisms are artificially transplanted, they won't be strong enough to ensure society's continued development. I'm afraid that in years to come, the former satellite countries will be a battleground between the democratic trends whose value we've come to appreciate, and new totalitarian ideas based on different concerns (nationalism, etc.).

Don't you think that abandoning socialism involves certain dangers?

Yes, of course it does. There are several. But there are even more dangers in democracy itself, and most of all in life in general. A person who wants to live responsibly as a Christian is bound to take certain risks. This is the only way—in Christian terms—to achieve salvation, or—in lay terms—to become full-fledged people or a full-fledged society.

You talk of how people live in a democracy, and how democratic structures work. Excuse my asking a slightly personal question. For twenty years you've been denied the right to travel. Do you think your idea of life in the free world is realistic?

I don't think anything like the "free world" exists—except for the kingdom of Christ. If you mean my understanding of democratic countries, either in Western Europe or elsewhere, then I feel that my realism is established by what I said at the beginning of my answer. I realize that these countries have a whole series of failings and problems. In the final analysis, the whole world is undergoing some sort of crisis, or rather a combination of crises. But over the last few decades I've had the advantage of having been able to study various material and, most importantly, to talk to lots of people with various views and social backgrounds. I dare say that my understanding of Western society is probably more precise than any impressions I could have got from a few tourist trips.

What can the West do to help Czechoslovakia?

My answer to this question also falls into two phases.

In the next few months, the West can help with concrete information, solidarity, technical and financial aid for (what was) the opposition, which is still locked in bitter battle with the old system. In the longer-run, we understandably expect some economic aid from the West. Not just direct financial aid, but a willingness for true cooperation. This won't come through a desire for easy profits from quick investments in the East. It will depend on wanting to have us as a truly equal trade partner, so that we can rebuild our economy and repair the damage inflicted by decades of totalitarianism. Parallel efforts will be needed in education and culture, where for at least some time to come we won't be able to get by without some help from the West.

But we must realize that we'll need to offer some help in return. It's not only the West that can help us; once we've crossed the first hurdles of democracy, we shall be able to offer the West help as well. I've already mentioned the West's deep crisis. I'd like to add that our experience of totalitarianism, and the sense we've developed over many long years of where danger lies, and of what values cannot be safely abandoned—all this could be of use to the West, and could help it out of its present crisis.

Do you see any particular Western country offering a concrete model for rectifying our situation?

No, I don't. Not because I'm over-critical, but because this doesn't work in principle. This has to do with the basic tenets of Christian democracy and its view of the world. Every country's situation is different, so you can't use someone else's model. The solution to a given problem depends on the nature of the problem itself. Any use of a model to overcome reality spells danger for the future.

14 January 1990
Interview conducted by Michaela Freiová for *The Christian Democratic Party Bulletin.*

Já osobně proti lustracím nejsem, ale varuji vás, pánové: bez tajemství nebude ani poezie!

"Personally, I've nothing against screening people's pasts. But I warn you gentlemen: There's no poetry without mystery!"

An Open Letter on Screening People's Pasts

. . . I WOULD LIKE to begin by dispelling the belief that is currently being put forward so vehemently: that screening people's pasts consists of investigating and interrogating government and other officials. This would of course be illegal. Rather, it is simply a statement of whether the Ministry of Internal Affairs has a person's file, and what that file contains. Until recently, these dossiers were available to any senior representatives who worked in the totalitarian regime's forces of repression. The question is now whether these files should be made available to other people as well; or whether, alternatively, they ought to be rapidly destroyed. The latter alternative runs the risk of the original (what we are talking about here are copies in the central archives) being freely used by other individuals, who could then manipulate it in various ways and use it for blackmail.

I feel that it would be neither wise nor realistic to launch a witch-hunt. There were several hundred thousand people in Czechoslovakia who cooperated with State Security either willingly or under duress. I also think that we can never rid ourselves of the burden of collective guilt and falsehood; that we shall never be able to rule out the possibility of manipulation by blackmail; and that we'll never summon the courage for a sufficiently radical slice of the surgeon's knife.

We can forgive those who were only the unwitting or naïve agents of totalitarianism. But there still remains a vast number of people who made a lucrative trade of performing these services, working as paid informers or professional agents with all the trappings of the trade: promises of cooperation, false names, directions from the center, etc. Perhaps we could forget those who at least had the good judgement to retire after November 1989, and who have been trying ever since to atone for their guilt, or at least let it be forgotten. But tolerance of the shameless people who still plan to be active in public life—influencing it through their shady ties with the past—would place our country at enormous risk. This would effectively amount to our nurturing a cancerous tumor, which could then end up devouring us all. History reveals how the Russian Bolsheviks occupied the *Okhrana*'s* archives and carried out a lightning purge of their contents. This was a major contribution to that terrible phenomenon we call Stalinism, since we're still shy about using the word Leninism.

This is why I think that before we hold elections, it is essential that we screen the pasts of at least all candidates for legislative bodies.** The results would not necessarily have to be made public; the person in question could decide before a responsible commission whether they want to defend their honor before the public or leave political life quietly.

All the political parties have officially supported a thorough purge of the security forces from all areas of our political system. But now that the screening of politicians is becoming a real possibility, and now that it is no longer a matter of pandering to the public, the parties are all trying to block the process and distance themselves from it. They say that it could destabilize the political situation if a quarter of the main parties' candidates suddenly disappeared from

* The *Okhrana* was the tsarist secret police.

** This process did in fact take place before the June 1990 elections, and resulted in a number of candidates dropping out of the race for more or less obvious reasons.

their tickets with no explanation. I'm afraid that if a quarter of our next parliament consists of secret police agents, the effects could be incomparably worse. The Christian Democratic Party is convinced that truth should prevail, and that it all will come out in the end anyway. We request that the appropriate departments start an immediate and unconditional screening of all our candidates. We also call on the other parties to undertake the same procedure, or to announce that they do not intend to do so. These shows of artificial staying power are becoming tiresome, and threaten to create a political situation after the elections that is beyond all resolution.

2 May 1990
Lidové noviny

Pavel Bratinka

BORN IN 1946, Bratinka, a Czech, received his university degree in atomic and applied physics. From 1970-74 he did graduate work in the Academy of Sciences' solid state physics department. He was refused his advanced degree for not being "politically engaged" (i.e., Communist), and worked as a clerk in the Technical Development and Information Department. He was given one hour's notice to leave this job after being caught distributing materials about Charter 77, of which he was a signatory. From 1981-89 he worked first as a janitor, then as a stoker in the Prague metro system. During the same period he gave underground lectures and translated works on politics, economics and history. From 1981-83 he ran the underground "publishing house" *Expedice* ("Dispatch," founded by Václav Havel). In 1988 he cofounded the Movement for Civil Liberties (HOS). Continuing his involvement in Civic Forum since the early days of the revolution, Bratinka also founded the right-wing Civic Democratic Alliance (ODA) in December 1989. In 1990 he worked on the Civic Forum Coordinating Center's Foreign Affairs Committee, and was elected a deputy to the Federal Assembly in June 1990.

Conservative Reflections on Czechoslovak Politics

An Interview with Pavel Bratinka

AS A SIGNATORY *of Charter 77 and a cofounder of the Movement for Civil Liberties, you were active in the pre-revolutionary "underground." There you wrote, lectured, translated . . . How did the tone of those dissident meetings change over the past ten years? Was there ever any sense of progress?*

Anyone who worked in dissident circles had a feeling of zero progress as far as weeks and months were concerned. But looking back over a number of years, I could see that things were gradually moving forward. Someone looking back at 1977 from 1989 had to see that year as a breakthrough. The number of people involved, their political maturity, the range of their work, its impact on society—all of this was a huge leap forward.

Did the dissident movement in Czechoslovakia produce the defined programs of a political opposition? Were there people waiting for the right moment to put those programs into action—or was it more a matter of unstructured discussion and the intellectual "dreams" of individual, independent idealists?

No one who worked in the dissident movement was a secluded idealist dreaming his dreams. We all belonged to some group. There were only a few people who consciously hoped for ultimate victory, but there were many of us who did on a subconscious level. Political programs were an important factor after the autumn of 1988, when the Movement for Civil Liberties (HOS) was founded.*

Why did the toalitarian system collapse so quickly in November 1989? What was the situation in late 1989?

People's patience ran out, but only partly on the conscious level I just spoke of. You can't simply say that people decided: "Enough!" It was more that something *inside* people snapped, and made them say that enough was finally enough.

As for totalitarianism: The regime wasn't 100 percent in control, since it had to take Western states into account, which allowed Charter 77 and other dissident groups to survive. And more generally, future totalitarianisms are also certain to collapse this suddenly, even if they get closer to the much-longed-for 100 percent control. Why? Because they can only sustain themselves through universal lying, and it's this lying that keeps the regime from keeping up with changes in the population's attitudes and subconscious, or from taking the public seriously at all. The situation in November isn't important. If the regime hadn't disintegrated in November, then it would have collapsed in December or January.

What role did you play in the revolution?

I was one of the people demonstrating on November 17. I then worked at the Civic Forum headquarters in the Magic Lantern Theatre, where I gave interviews to foreign television and radio reporters from morning till night.

---

* See "From 1968 to 1989: A Chronological Commentary" (1988) for a description of HOS.

"I can't tell anymore if I'm a comrade, non-aligned or just an idiot."

"Must be the Communist party apologizing for the last forty years."

Just after the revolution you cofounded the political party Civic Democratic Alliance (ODA), which characterizes itself as being on the "democratic right." In Czechoslovakia, a name like this sounds a little polemical, as if the combination of these two words wasn't normal. What do you mean by "democratic right"?

True, this combination is unusual, since communism equated the right with fascism and naziism. The word "rightist" ought to mean anti-utopian and imply the equation "a free society = freedom of the individual + freedom of reciprocity." By reciprocity we mean all forms of dialogue and cooperation, including "cooperation" with past generations in the sense of respect for tradition. To make this freedom of reciprocity possible, a legal state is necessary to create a framework for the responsibility by which people's acts are judged in terms of preserving other people's freedom.

How and where did you learn about ideas and theories like this? What philosopher or politician had the greatest influence on you?

I read good books and looked for bright people. I was most influenced philosophically by G.K. Chesterton, E. Voegelin, F.A. Hayek and a whole series of others, including Michael Novak at the American Enterprise Institute.

During the First Republic, there was never a very strong rightist tradition. Do you feel a shift of today's political center to the right by comparison with that time? What sort of future do you think the right has in Czechoslovak politics?

The right has good prospects on condition that it manages to neutralize the pseudo-right, and if it manages to create the sort of institutions that would correspond to the United States' Freedom House, American Enterprise Institute and others, which could then continue to generate new ideas.

"Conservatism" is an unambiguously negative word in Czechoslovakia. It means dogmatic insistence on something bad or discredited—an unwillingness, for example, to change for the better. In the days when history was wiping out the past and marching towards a "bright future," calling a brave democrat who refused to renounce his principles a "conservative democrat" would have been taken as a bad joke . . . Some people claim that the term "conservative" won't be useful in Czechoslovakia, since there's nothing left to conserve. There's a grain of truth in what they say. Czechoslovak conservatism has to dig more than forty-one years into the past to find a time when parliamentary democracy, the legal state, market economics and civil society were established features of this country. Bringing these things back to life will indeed be an extremely "conservative" undertaking.

What about socialism? This is another much-abused word, but after forty-two years of totalitarianism people are used to "socialist" guarantees of pensions, wages, social security . . . Will socialism play a large part in Czechoslovak politics and, if so, in what form?

Pensions, wages and all the rest are best guaranteed by nonsocialism. Of course there are jealous and lazy people in every society. It suits these people to have everyone be as miserable as they are, even at the cost of their own wretchedness. These people don't care about improving their own situation, if it means that other people's situations improve even more. I don't think that the "forces of envy" will get more support here in Czechoslovakia than they do in other countries that haven't been subjected to socialism.

You and ODA have worked with Civic Forum for half a year. Civic Forum—a broad movement that stretches from ex-Communists to the extreme right—has just won the elections, proving that at least for the moment it enjoys immense popularity. But how can Civic Forum continue in such a broad form? Will it collapse? What would be the best thing for Czechoslovakia? Are you and ODA, for instance, intending to continue working under Civic Forum's umbrella?

The best thing for Czechoslovakia would be a normal spectrum of political parties, including the left, right and loony fringe. For the moment we intend to stay with Civic Forum for political reasons —there are the local elections coming up in November 1990—as well as practical considerations—we don't have enough money to function on our own.

If Civic Forum doesn't manage to organize itself into clearly defined leftist and rightist camps—the center right would then be dominant—then it will be the former Bolsheviks who dominate things. They're unusually skillful manipulators. These people gravitate towards what you in America call "statism." Their influence could bog down economic reform, with all the unfortunate consequences that implies.

Havel's slogan "nonpolitical politics" is one of the intellectual cornerstones of Civic Forum and Public Against Violence. This is clearly a reaction to the last forty years, when "politics" was immoral and unjust. What's your opinion of this slogan? Can it still hold true if you want a healthy democracy? What do you think it means?

I regard politics as the noblest human activity, for it allows people to live together and still not lose their freedom. Politics is more sublime than poetry or science. I hope that I'll manage to persuade many of my fellow citizens that this true. The scholastics used to say: "*Corruptio optimi pessima est*" ("There is nothing worse than the corruption of the highest good"). You can see why the Tempter works hardest in politics.

What do you think of the government's economic reform program, and the speed of its application? Komárek says that there will be "economic agony" if the market is freed too quickly; Klaus thinks things need to start as soon as possible . . . Where do you stand? What would you like to see done?

Rapid reform will be painful, but there will be light at the end of the tunnel, so that people can feel that they're taking part in a struggle for the future. The reform goals—enterprise accountability to the market and rational behaviour—will also be clearly defined during all phases of the transition. Less painful reforms wouldn't have this advantage, and sticking to them would involve asking more of people's morale than is reasonable. That's why I'm a Klausian.

Are the people of Czechoslovakia willing to risk their stable, familiar world in order to transform the economic system?

The question of whether they are or not will depend purely on the ability of our political leadership.

Is there any particular country you see as a model for setting Czechoslovakia straight?

Basically all the Western countries could serve as models. Our country's specific characteristics will still survive, but the principles of the system will be the same as in the West.

Forty-two years of Communist party rule has had disastrous consequences for Czechoslovakia. Many people—both here in Czechoslovakia and in the West—expected the Party to be denied participation in politics. But this never happened during the "velvet revolution." Since then there have been demonstrations and even hunger strikes calling for the abolition of the Communist party. Procurator-General Rychetsky has also announced that he is investigating charges that the Party stole from the state. Is the "gentle" or "velvet" atmosphere changing? Or is all this just part of pre-election campaigning?

There's been a fatal confusion of two things: the right of demagogic parties to exist, and the right to proceed with the transmogrification of a particular mafia organization called the Communist party. The difference between these two things needs to be clear . . . At the very least, Party archives should be confiscated. I feel that the Communist party should be abolished, and that its assets should be confiscated as symbolic recompense for wrongs committed. Its elected members of parliament could then form some sort of new party to represent the preposterous left.

You've been working in Civic Forum's foreign affairs committee. How would you evaluate the "government of national understanding's" foreign policy? What have been its greatest successes and shortcomings? What would you like to have seen happen that didn't?

The government has managed to achieve some changes in the Warsaw Pact, and has established good relations with the countries we previously called "enemies." But these successes basically fell into its lap thanks to the international situation. One shortcoming is the absolute lack of change in our embassy personnel, where former or current Bolsheviks still dominate. I consider it unfortunate that we've taken a stand against NATO, and that we haven't even started to get involved in the European Parliament.

The government's initiative on establishing a collective European security system strikes me as rather shallow, since it doesn't really correspond to reality. It's another case of our president's penchant for symbolic gestures. The continued existence of NATO is simply a *sine qua non* for continued democratization and the general "defanging" of the Soviet Union.

There's a feeling today that the democratic processes in your country are a part of a world-wide phenomenon. Not only central and eastern Europe, but other areas of the world that have been ruled by dictatorial regimes are experiencing a wave of democratization. Has history reached a democratic phase?

G.K. Chesterton once wrote that if we want a white pillar to turn mossy, then the best thing is not to worry about it, and over the years it will turn mossy by itself. But if we want it to stay pristine and white, we need to take good care of it all the time. I agree that at the moment there's a wave of democracy; but it's not a natural process, but rather the result of innumerable conflicts and sacrifices. Which is why it's clear that more sacrifices, or at least readiness for sacrifice, will be needed if this trend is not to be reversed.

How can the West help you, and what do you have to offer in return?

Eastern Europe is falling apart as a bloc, and old frictions are threatening to reappear. The West ought to make it clear that states or forces that provoke conflicts in the style of the nineteenth, or ninth centuries—chauvinist and separatist tendencies, for example—will be given the cold shoulder and won't get a cent in aid. The West could also help by supporting institutions like the ones I mentioned before—Freedom House and American Enterprise Institute—and by giving financial support to respectable political parties.

As far as reciprocity is concerned, then I think we can offer our experience of totalitarianism—and our determined support of Western values, which are the only ones "worthy of man's obeisance."

15 June 1990
Interview conducted by Tim Whipple.

Martin Bútora

BORN IN 1944, Bútora is a Slovak, and received his doctorate in sociology from Bratislava's Comenius University. In 1966-67, he worked as an editor on the Bratislava student newspaper *Echo,* and was assistant to the editor-in-chief of *Reflex,* another student publication. Both of these periodicals were closed down after the 1968 invasion. He then became a researcher in the Institute for Labor and Social Affairs. In 1977 he started work in an alcoholism outreach center at Bratislava's National Health Institute, where he served as resident sociologist. He has published dozens of articles on alcoholism, some of which have been collected into a volume under the title *It Couldn't Happen to Me.* In 1988 he went freelance, continuing his work with self-help groups and writing literary and journalistic prose. In the late 1980s he was increasingly involved in the Slovak environmental movement, and published several articles on the subject. He was one of the leaders of the November 1989 revolution in Slovakia, and is one of the major strategists in the Public Against Violence Coordination Center.

Following the June 1990 elections, Martin Bútora became advisor for Human Rights to the president [ed.].

The Roots of the Revolution in Slovakia

FOR MANY LONG years, the world's commentators said that nothing was happening in the heart of Europe. At best there were a few defiant dissidents: people who lamented that this heart was diseased, saying that the longer its beat remained irregular, the greater the chance of a heart attack. The national trauma that followed the 1968 invasion paralyzed all attempts at reform. People were frozen with fear. Other East European countries reacted to Gorbachev's *perestroika* and started their own democratic reforms: of Budapest's goulash socialism, Poland's empty-store socialism, the Berlin wall and even Sophia's Turkish economy. But the old masters in Prague and Bratislava recoiled from these new concepts. Their stubbornness and arrogance produced monumental disgust with their rule, and their representatives became legendary symbols of stupidity.

When this idiocy, deafness and apathy combined with the fascist brutality of November 17, anger drove hundreds of thousands of citizens out onto the streets. People were no longer willing to let themselves be beaten about the head. With staggering speed, the public united against physical massacre, the massacre of truth, and violence of any kind. The public acted as a society of citizens who want the right to decide how their lives should be. People always used to say that apart from the candle-lit demonstration of September 1988, and a few small islands of opposition, Slovakia was noth-

"I don't understand. We had reports that everyone was terrified..."

ing but "peace and quiet." So how did this public action get started? How was it that thousands of people suddenly joined Public Against Violence, whose name, posters and activity in general would have struck us as science fiction just a month before?

The most important reason is that in the past people had been denied any real right to an independent political life. The republic —that is, *res publica,* public affairs—had become the territory of a political mafia, supported by state security and refined into an organized system of corruption, dependence and mutual benefit. When the foundations of this power began to shake, people were quick to see that they could step into the vacuum in order to defend their interests.

Slovakia was not in fact as moribund as it might have seemed at first glance. Several more or less "underground" networks existed, and they struggled for independence and truth. Among these were the ecological groups led by *"Bratislava nahlas"* ("Bratislava Aloud").* But there were also the independent artists, actors, writers, sociologists, forecasters and other scientists. Various Christian groups played an important role, especially among young people. The intellectual framework for reform was laid by human rights activists. Over the past decade, more and more islands of defiance began to appear. New groups formed to fight a defunct regime for at least some of the conditions they saw necessary for decent work and a dignified life. Sometimes these cultural and spiritual activities had an impact on official organizations; they certainly influenced our most progressive group, the students, who had already begun to demand a voice. At the critical moment, these students, actors, artists and scientists turned to the factory workers and wage-earners, where they found sympathy and the courage to act. Social learning accelerated to a previously unimaginable speed.

Unlike 1968, the basis of this revolution is not gradual reform from above, but a popular revolutionary movement from below. Initiative no longer comes from the offices of politicians, but from

* See "From 1968 to 1989: A Chronological Commentary," 1987.

universities, factories, companies, and from the mood of society as a whole. This is one of the broadest national coalitions of social and political forces in history. Their common background is democracy; that is, rejection of Stalinism and the entire totalitarian system that it was responsible for producing. Improving the general quality of life is the goal that unites this coalition . . .

Over the past three weeks, the revolution has cracked the power of a monopoly political party that for decades annexed each and every one of us. The Party has been cracked, but not broken. We shall have to fight for every position and every concrete application of our legislative reforms. The level of this struggle and the effects it has will depend on the reactions people have to the freedom they have won.

The worst thing would be for people to remain occasional citizens. If the rights and duties of citizenship do not become a part of every person's life, then everything is lost in advance. Citizenship begins with an interest in unsubstantial, everyday, petty problems. Citizenship means learning about these things, discussing them in public and then finding ways to resolve them. It means interest in one's community, and in politics. And politics is the ability to vote, to choose and to change. It's a way of achieving the goals that we set ourselves. Citizenship means opposing totalitarianism and supporting a plurality of opinions and interests. It means trying to achieve the peaceful coexistence of different, even incompatible, attitudes. Citizenship means not only delegating responsibility to someone else, but also taking it on oneself. Citizenship means being sensitive to situations where people's interests clash. It means having the courage to stand up against any power that seems to be developing to the detriment of others. It means expressing one's opinion, even when this opinion provokes disagreement, lack of interest or rejection.

Citizenship is not a single act. It is a state of permanent sensitivity and vigilance. To be a citizen is to have the opportunity to create a society of citizens, a society that is truly civil.

15 December 1989

Breaking the Spell

OUR PAST NOT only devastated our country, but defiled our language as well. Public affairs was an area that was particularly hard-hit. When we lagged behind the standards of the developed world, it was called "intensification of the scientific-technical revolution." Our economic reforms never made the slightest bit of difference, despite the length of their name: "The Set of Measures for Perfecting the Operation of the National Economy." In the good old days, *perestroika* couldn't be called *perestroika,* so we had to call it "perfecting" instead.* By the time the term *perestroika* was finally accepted, it had long since been emptied of all meaning. Thank God: if it hadn't we might still be fighting a revitalized hammer and sickle, and not just a couple of cherries.**

The two hundred days that separate November 17 from the June 1990 elections have given rise to a slew of new words. There's one

---

* For reasons why the Czechoslovak Communist regime was less than enthusiastic about Gorbachev's reforms, see "From 1968 to 1989: A Chronological Commentary," 1986.

** The Czechoslovak Communist Party's new symbol is a pair of cherries connected by their stems.

expression that has swept through Slovakia with the speed and force of an avalanche. But "breaking the spell" is more than an expression: it's an attitude, collective psychotherapy, even action. There's a reason for the popularity of this phrase. "Breaking the spell" means more than identifying something, or uncovering something evil or hidden. It also implies drama, and the opening up of a new dimension in time. In Slovak the phrase brings fairytales to mind. Perhaps the word caught on because it appeals to our subconscious. Fairytales, after all, have happy endings.

There are other new words that are foreign in origin and, consequently, less well-known: "articulate," "generate" or "algorithm." They all involve coming to terms with a new reality or solving a complex problem. The fact that they're used is a call for society constantly to seek new solutions.

A successful career has also been had by the catchy new word "software." In its standard, everyday usage it means the program and capabilities, or "culture," of a computer. In November 1989 the word suddenly caught on in a figurative sense: it began to mean a plan, approach, matrix, solution, idea, or the intellectual apparatus to deal with a given problem. The question "Got any software on this?" has been on everyone's lips during the two hundred days since November. It's not just students or people who work in Public Against Violence who use it, although they're the ones responsible for inventing it. "Software" has begun to spread quite quickly, and is widely used elsewhere as well. Even foreigners have been quick to pick up on the new meaning that the word has now acquired.

You don't have to take me at my word, but I feel that the age of "software" has begun. This has five important implications.

The *first* is that there can be no central, universal solution to our present and future problems. Instead, there's a whole spectrum of alternative approaches, of different ideas or "softwares." Not much can be said about most of them until we give them a try . . . *Second*, the future we're facing will be a permanent state of crisis. More precisely and less elegantly put, this will be a state of permanent problematics. This needn't be a turn for the worse: many Western societies have lived like this for decades and don't seem to be doing too badly today. But we mustn't let these problems appear to slip out of our control. We need mechanisms for controlling the crisis. Then every crisis becomes an opportunity: for changing systems, replacing leaders, and other more or less fundamental improvements. One of the reasons that communism collapsed was its inability to solve certain problems and crises.

The *third* implication is that we need a well-defined schedule. Very few issues can be tackled quickly and easily; for the most part we'll have to be patient . . . *Fourth,* Consensus, agreement and cooperation will also be crucial to success. Nothing is possible without them. Practically all our political groups have a single goal in common: a democratic society and healthy economy that doesn't ignore individuals. We're going to need vast stores of "software" to achieve this, and to find creative, nontraditional solutions to our convoluted problems. The approaches we'll need can only be developed right here in Czechoslovakia. There's no "big book" in the outside world that can answer all of our questions. No omniscient source of experience will mercifully come to our aid.

Fifth and finally: the age of "software" should gradually lessen our reliance on an all-determining, paternalistic state that solves all our problems for us. In the past, people have been subjected to a sort of subconscious Sovietization, with everything being nationalized and placed in the care of the state. This dependency was recently epitomized by some budding entrepreneurs who were demonstrating outside our government buildings. They were protesting imprecise information from the government, which had led them to lose their investments in bacon and sausages to sell during the Pope's visit. This curious event fascinated the foreign correspondents with whom I discussed it. But it ought to shock us even more, although this inability to stand on one's own two feet has a number of historical causes. We're going to have a hard time getting used to the fact that of the 4,500 West German firms that are established every year, 2,000 go bankrupt; or that in the U.S. seven out of eight new companies fail, so that every American entrepreneur has to invest several times before finally achieving success . . .

An old piece of wisdom may stand us in good stead: the best way to help a hungry man is to give him not fish, but a net.

Elections can't solve everything. They're just one of the "softwares" we can use for coming to terms with our future . . . But forty years' experience of communism and five years' flirtation with fascism* should have proven beyond all doubt that the alternative "software" doesn't work.

June 1990

* Between 1939 and 1944, Slovakia was an "independent" fascist state tolerated by Nazi Germany.

Fedor Gál

GÁL WAS BORN in 1945 in the Nazi concentration camp at Terezín. He is a Slovak. He worked as a laborer, foreman and production manager in various chemical factories. At the same time he studied chemistry at Bratislava's Technical Institute. His graduate work was in sociology, and in 1972 he started to work in this field. He is the author of several books on sociological forecasting as well as hundreds of articles in specialist publications. At the very beginning of the "velvet revolution" he became a member of the Public Against Violence Coordination Center, where he has been chairman since February 1990.

Slovakia's Problems and Prospects

An Interview with Fedor Gál

YOU'RE THE LEADING *representative of Public Against Violence, the Slovak movement that sprang up as a spontaneous reaction to the events of November 17, 1989 and the social situation that preceded them . . . Is this your first taste of politics, or did you have some experience in this area before November?*

I'm a sociologist and a sociological forecaster. I've made my living this way for more than fifteen years. I was never the sort of researcher who spends his time in the office. I think sociology needs the sort of research they call "participational" in the West. I've always liked being active and I knew the state our society was in. I'm convinced that sociologists shouldn't just observe what's happening in society, but should immerse themselves in events. It's the best schooling, the best way to recognize social problems. I've also come to believe that if we don't all get involved, then it's all over . . . As for the path my own life has followed, my friends and I have always had problems when we've offered the public some research that happened to be critical. I've never considered these problems to be catastrophes, and I haven't grown bitter as a result. I was always eager to find out if something was happening, and what it meant. So, to answer your question, this is my debut on the political scene.

How deep are the effects of the destruction that the previous political system wrought on our society?

Our society was basically destroyed. I'm not just referring to our devastated environment, the low productivity of our economy, or the fact that the old system was unjust. I'm talking about the human costs. Sociological research has conclusively shown that people are unmotivated and apathetic. You can see this just by looking at people on the street. People take refuge in internal emigration, consumption becomes the alpha and the omega of their lives, only what bears on their own privacy interests them. What started on November 17th came at just the right moment. Had it happened three, four or five years earlier, we wouldn't have been up to taking our place among the normal and developed countries of the world.

What are our prospects for improvement?

What we've seen in the past few weeks and months is radical reform of our political system. Before we see any results, and before this reform can really start to rectify the situation, there need to be radical economic and social changes as well. This won't be simple. People aren't used to having to fight or compete for their jobs and reputations. They're not used to being productive, or to being evaluated by their productivity. I believe that we can adapt to all this, and that we'll even get used to paying for our economic prosperity with a little social uncertainty. But I don't dare guess when our distorted values will change, or when we'll achieve that radical break within each of ourselves.

What are your impressions of the ethical relations between young people?

There's no reason to think that children are at all different from their parents, or that they're fundamentally different from the way we were when we were their age. Since November we've been in very close contact with the representatives of student movements, and with the movements themselves. Personally, I've got a very good impression of our young friends. That's one side of the coin. The other is that we can see the same thing happening among them as we see among ourselves, the middle and older generation. An ambitious type suddenly appears and exploits the situation to advance his own interests . . .

History's maxim that "revolutions devour their own children" has been borne out time and time again. You're one of the revolution's "children." Do you fear for the future?

The fact that "revolutions devour their children" doesn't alarm me. I'd be more worried if revolutions didn't only devour their "children," but other people as well. There's a simple way to guard against this: the revolutionaries of today have to learn from the past, and relinquish the power that they gained in the revolution at the right time. As far as I'm concerned, there's only one thing I fear: that I'll remain one of the revolution's "children" too long. I'm very much looking forward to getting back to my work, which I find fascinating and exciting. The fact that I'm still in the Public Against Violence headquarters is probably a sign of the responsibility I feel for what we started, and what can't be handed over to just anyone.

Do you think that the situation will require your working in the Public Against Violence headquarters for a long time to come?

I firmly believe that it only will until we hold our free elections in June 1990.

Is it possible to keep the "gentle revolution" from losing its velvet sheen, or from having its appearance spoiled?

You need to realize that the "gentle revolution" only lasted about a month. Whatever appearance it had at that point is now part of history. There will be legends told about it. But what we're now seeing is not the "gentle revolution," but normal political competition and an effort to get our everyday political life back on track. We'll remember the "gentle revolution" the way it really was: beautiful and velvet. The harsh things we're seeing today are part of everyday post-revolutionary life. Life among the ruins of the old regime.

We all remember the pamphlet that circulated during the first days of the revolution, announcing that the economic forecasters thought that Czecho-Slovakia could achieve Austria's standard of living in about five to seven years. What did the forecasters have to base this optimistic forecast on, and what are the basic measures that need to be taken to bring it about?

I won't describe in detail all the methods and approaches that forecasters use. Briefly and simply put, these conclusions are based on international comparisons, analysis of our society's development over the past forty years, analysis of our human, material and technical potential, and so on. The guess that it will take us five to seven years to take our place among the most developed countries in Europe was based on several large assumptions. We assumed, for instance, that we'll manage to make our currency convertible, open our society to the outside world, introduce true market mechanisms, dismantle irrational centralization, establish freedom for individuals and businesses, allow all types of property, and so on. But when I think about all this, the question keeps cropping up of whether we really have to imitate the type of prosperity that we see in developed, Western economies, or whether we couldn't enter the twenty-first century in our own particular way. Do we really have to whip our economy on to greater and greater productivity? Do we really have to stuff our apartments full of more and more consumer goods? Do we really need to have newer and bigger cars, and fancier houses? This often brings to mind the tone of the unofficial environmentalists in Bratislava, and particularly one of them—Marek Huba—who has long been battling for some sort of a new way of living that is both fuller and more modest.

It was not just our society that was destroyed, but our environment as well. Is there any hope of full recovery in this area?

The state of Czecho-Slovakia's environment reflects the state of society. It works as a mirror. It will cost us enormous amounts of money just to stop the continuing devastation of the environment. But even a mountain of money won't help us until something changes in people, and we change our attitudes towards solving this problem.

I come back to the "Slovak Greens" and the "gentle revolution." What do you think was the basic difference between the revolution in the Czech lands and the revolution in Slovakia?

In the Czech lands, the revolution was led by people who had spent long years in parallel, dissident structures. They were people who were practically professional politicians by the time November 17 came. In Slovakia, and particularly in Bratislava, most of the people involved in the revolution were unofficial environmentalists. The dissident movement first blossomed and underground publications first started to appear in the Czech lands. But there was also a parallel culture in Slovakia. As you remember, the first vocal opposition to the government and general social decay was led by the unofficial environmentalists in their publication "Bratislava Aloud."*

Old and new debts between states and peoples have a habit of reappearing whenever they can—even when it's to both sides' advantage to cooperate. What's your opinion of the separatist tendencies of various Slovaks?

Unambiguously negative. It's absurd to think that a small, angry nation like Slovakia has any prospects whatsoever, when Slovaks hate Hungarians, Hungarians hate Slovaks, and everyone hates the

* For a description of "Bratislava Aloud," see "From 1968 to 1989: A Chronological Commentary," 1987.

Gypsies; when Catholics hate Jews, and Jews hate them back; when thirteen various political parties are fighting each other, and so on . . . This is really no platform for entering Europe. On the other hand, you have to admit that we've always had these problems, only we never knew about them. They were drowned in stagnant water. Social life is reemerging, with all its negative aspects as well. I'd very much like to be able to label these separatists "fringe extremists."

What does a forecaster have to say about how our relations are developing with the East (i.e., the Soviet Union) and the West (the U.S. and other countries nearer to us)?

I'd say that for the moment we're fascinated by the prospects for improving our relations with the West, for attracting good investment and establishing contact with Western firms. We tend to forget that there are other countries that have traveled the same road we did, and that now suffer from similar problems. If we don't cooperate with them in solving these problems, we may find ourselves in a troubled region where we have to risk competing with our neighbors. I can't imagine that developments in Czecho-Slovakia, Hungary, Poland and Bulgaria could continue satisfactorily if the Soviet Union doesn't solve its problems. Personally, I'd like to see more visits by correspondents and media representatives from East European countries. More official delegations and working visits to the East. We need to form some sort of democratic alliance between the members of this community.

Could you give us a forecast of your own future? What sort of work are you most looking forward to?

I'm currently trying to establish a "Center for the Research of Social Problems." I hope to collect a group of people who work well together, and who could provide society with information on what ails it, and who could then devise alternative solutions. I'd also like to have a chance, finally, to travel. I've been doing research for a very long time, and I've never once been able to visit the West. I'd love to spend a couple of months at some first-class research institute. I'd also like to perfect my languages.

Do you have any wishes for the future?

The deeper I get into politics, the less I like it. I do think it has its place in life, but I'm trying to come up with ways to make that place better organized. My own wish is that Slovakia in particular, and Czecho-Slovakia in general, enter the twenty-first century with a political landscape made up of social movements; and that these social movements not turn into conglomerations of people with their own membership cards, insignias, oaths of allegiance, rituals and anthems. Instead, I hope that these movements will continue to represent groups of people who are concerned about some problem, and who join together to try to solve it. I hope that these groups will get involved in politics because they see a problem and consider its solution important.

24 April 1990
Interview conducted by Margareta Horáková for *Mladé rozlety*.

The Future of Public Against Violence

DURING A RECENT television interview, I mused that "we don't know where we're headed, but that doesn't bother us." I was thinking of how tomorrow is shaped by what we do today, how the next day depends on tomorrow, and so on. We're living in chaotic times, and it is difficult to predict what tomorrow's concerns will be. But as a sociological forecaster and Public Against Violence activist, I can't help but ask myself two questions. Which of the problems that our victory has produced could sow the seeds of its failure? How can we keep this from happening?

I believe that every social movement (that is not smothered at birth) sooner or later has to deal with one fundamental problem. Let's call it self-renewal. This seems to be the problem that Public Against Violence is currently facing. I see a solution coming in two phases. Before the free elections in June 1990, our job will be to encourage an increasingly weary band of supporters to "hold on." After the elections will be the time to find a new shape for our movement.

I feel that the greatest achievement of Czechoslovakia's civic movements has been to free people of their fear of Communist totalitarianism. The whole structure of social life was improved in one fell blow.

But the speed and manner in which this vacuum was filled has set these movements another task: to free people of fear of the movements themselves. If they are successful, the free elections can only end in victory, and the public will be the winner.

The question is: how to achieve this. The Communists offered us one (unsuccessful) approach. Their model was based on militant ideology, repression and monolithic power. To begin with, the Communist party was also a movement: a movement that won, institutionalized itself, and then made its ideology official, a sort of state religion.

The renewal of today's popular movements hinges on one crucial thing. People have to understand that until the elections, Civic Forum and Public Against Violence have a single aim: to use their coalition forces to improve the social system that we've inherited. When the old, decrepit structures collapse; when truly capable people take over the reins of government; when political freedom, social justice and economic efficiency are established; when the normal means of a society's controlling power begin to work—when all these things happen, Civic Forum and Public Against Violence will have to start the process of revitalizing themselves. There will be three aspects to these changes:

1. These movements will become more like political clubs. This will mean finding a modern form of political organization, without hierarchies, rituals or symbols of allegiance. The members of groups like this will be united by common interest and a shared notion of how this interest should be presented and advanced in society. The basic form of activity for groups like this will be dialogue.

2. The second aspect of this metamorphosis will include the establishment of independent institutes. These will for the most part be devoted to research, the media and publishing. Their independence will not just be defined by their having evolved from either Public Against Violence or Civic Forum, but will depend on their economic self-sufficiency as well.

3. The third and final stage could involve the emergence of a number of particularist movements to defend certain interests: those

of consumers, environmentalists, scientists, cultural figures, teachers and so on. In a "normal" society these groups can fulfill a whole series of functions, from self-help organizations to checking abuses of power. These groups would be interconnected by the network of independent institutes, and would be coordinated by the political "clubs." In the case of some social crisis, movements like this can mobilize their activists and supporters in a relatively short time to defend their political freedom and social achievements.

This approach would give Civic Forum and Public Against Violence an opportunity of regenerating themselves. It ensures their civic, and therefore political responsibility. And it guarantees that we won't exchange one totalitarian system for another.

16 January 1990
Verejnost'

Miroslav Kusy

BORN IN 1931, Kusy is a Slovak. From 1957-68 he was a professor at Bratislava's Comenius University, where he taught introductory philosophy, Marxist epistemology and political science. During this time he published several works, including *Marxist Philosophy, The Marxist Theory of Knowledge* and *The Philosophy of Politics*. He became increasingly active in the mid-1960s as a reform Communist, and supported Dubcek's policies during the Prague Spring. He became head of the Slovak Communist Party ideology department in August 1968 but lost his position after sharp disagreements with Gustáv Husák, the post-invasion "normalizer." He was expelled from the Party in 1970 and lost his university post soon thereafter. He then worked as an archivist until signing Charter 77, whereupon he had to make a living as a construction worker's mate.

Kusy published widely in the underground press, assisted foreign radio stations with reporting, and served as a Charter 77 spokesman. In 1980 he co-authored with Milan Simecka *Big Brother and Big Sister: On the Loss of Reality in the Ideology of Real Socialism.* Kusy was also a signatory of the Movement for Civil Liberties (HOS) (1988). He was the target of repeated police persecution, was twice imprisoned, and was released from his last incarceration by the revolution of 17 November 1989. He was then active in Public Against Violence, and served as temporary chairman of the State Bureau for Press and Information in the new "government of national understanding." He was co-opted into the Federal Assembly, and appointed rector of Comenius University on 18 January 1990.

Nationalism, Totalitarianism and Democracy

An Interview with Miroslav Kusy

PEOPLE ARE TALKING *about a "radical break" with our totalitarian past. What do you think of this? People often mention Czechoslovakia's democratic traditions—but aren't they simply legends? . . . How many working people actually remember the pre-World War II era? How many of them have ever experienced anything other than totalitarianism? Don't you think that the state of our national culture, and what our citizens have grown accustomed to, will stunt the growth of truly democratic politics, at least until our economy is strong enough to satisfy everyone's needs? Aren't you afraid that Czechoslovakia's petit bourgeois may turn their "gentle revolution" into what the Russian bourgeoisie made of revolutionary communism after 1917—revolutionary idiocy, as Sokol'nikov once called it?*

I've been carrying your questions around with me for about a month, and keep giving myself the excuse that there's not enough time to come up with adequate answers . . . Today I decided—what a shame it's April 1st—that I'll finally put it all together and write something down. But now I'm terrified: your questions have become fatally important, urgent, personal. I'd never felt them quite like this before. Vanity keeps me from acknowledging that I was slow to understand. But the times don't. Over the past month the political situation and atmosphere in Czecho-Slovakia has fundamentally changed, and this has given your questions new meaning. So I congratulate you for anticipating so well.

Our thinking has been more deeply affected by totalitarianism than I would ever have thought possible. We celebrate how quickly, elegantly and painlessly we rid ourselves of communism. But now we've got the angry and vociferous builders of a new totalitarianism coming at us with clenched fists. Today it's mostly the nationalists. They've declared a holy "hyphen"* war. "Anyone who's Slovak/Czech should think the way we do, act the way we do, and should always be with us." "Anyone who's not with us is against us" is the central slogan of any totalitarian system.

"What sort of nationalists are we?!" these rabble-rousers defend themselves. "We're simply watching over our national identity, struggling for its interests, advancing its holy cause." But nationalism begins when so-called national interests exclude everything else. Slovakia for the Slovaks! First and foremost a Slovak! It's typical that supporters of slogans like this don't ask people what they want, but impose their own list of national priorities, their own rhetoric about the "only way to save the situation." This all leads directly to totalitarianism. It rejects dialogue ("This point is not up for discussion!"), compromise ("The only acceptable name for our republic is Czecho-Slovakia, with a hyphen!"), and tolerance, which allows for the existence of a reasonable opinion that is not one's own. "Anyone who doesn't think like me is a complete idiot/traitor/enemy." A delegate from a former satellite mini-party shouted at me in parliament, "Anyone who doesn't vote with us is a traitor!" I asked him who he was speaking for. "The people!" came the proud reply.

We seem to be taking democracy, freedom of speech and other basic tenets as purely personal privileges: each man for himself, his clan, his fellow believers. But democracy can only begin when we recognize other people's rights to these freedoms as well. We

---

* For a discussion of nationalist issues, including the "hyphen controversy," see "After the Velvet Revolution" ("The Nationality Question") and Carnogursky's "Physics, Psychology and the Gentle Revolution."

shouldn't just say, "I have the right to vote as I wish!" We need to think, "You have the same right, and I can't deny you that, so I must listen to you carefully and without prejudice." At a Czech-Slovak solidarity meeting, Ivan Hoffman* said that there were two groups of people who should be joining his movement: Slovaks who could support union with the Czech lands, and Czechs who could imagine Slovak secession. Just as in dancing school, so in the school of democracy the first lesson in decent behavior should be to respect one's partner. Schooling in democracy ought to start with an "exchange of views," so that we can experience someone else's situation and think about what it tells us. But I doubt that we're mature enough for this school. We never seem to get any further than working on the framework for change: 1948, 1968, 1990. The bitter arguments of nationalist delusions always get in the way. After everything we've been through, you'd think that people would appreciate reciprocal freedom and democracy. But we never get beyond this stage.

Over the years I learned to defy Communist totalitarianism, but I also learned to function within it. I'm more frightened now by a nationalist totalitarianism that produces "patriotic Slovaks," the sort of people who protest abortion by displaying dead fetuses outside the Slovak National Council building. What they want to turn the "gentle revolution" into is far worse than Sokol'nikov's "revolutionary idiocy," since at least the latter appealed to the future. These new totalitarians look to the past, to the (blessed) legacy of their ancestors, to their inheritance. No, we can't break with the past. Even if everything depends on it, even if we really try. We're in the realm of nationalist totalitarian mythology. And that's the worst totalitarianism of all.

Czecho-Slovak politics seems to be declaring and even promoting the category of morality. Everyone knows that politics can be deeply, unbearably immoral. You've had particularly rich and personal experience of this your-

* Hoffman is a Slovak poet, political activist and independent journalist.

self. Is it possible for politics to be moral? What does it mean to combine politics with morality?

There's a conflict between two different understandings of politics. There's politics as a profession that has its own immanent "political" criteria that define successful achievement of desired ends. This is similar to the way a dentist or tailor can measure their success. Then there's politics as administration of public affairs.

The first type of politics involves the mechanics of power. These mechanics are beyond good and evil, that is, they are neither moral nor immoral, just as these categories don't pertain when we're talking about a dentist's work. The second case has as its single goal the winning of power, but in the name of public service. Power that doesn't carry out this duty, and comes to see itself as its own goal, is barbarous and immoral—as is a dentist who doesn't carry out his duty of tending to people's health. Professional politicians who master the mechanics of power, but reject their duty to people, fall prey to ends in themselves: the achievement of power in and of itself. They give these ends in themselves an ideological framework, which then becomes a taboo. For example: Race, Nation, Socialism. This politics no longer serves the public, but myths. It becomes racial politics, nationalist politics, socialist politics. At this point not only the mechanics of power, but even its goals move beyond good and evil, since Race, Nation, Socialism are presented as ultimate values, or axioms. Politics in the service of Nation or Socialism cannot be moral or immoral—even when it involves murder, dekulakization,* nationalization or impoverishment. It claims to do all this in the name of the Nation's, or Socialism's, ultimate interests, and that it's fulfilling its mystic purpose.

As we emerge from racism, socialism and political ideology, we're returning to an understanding of politics that is based on public service, something along the lines of community service. This is not

* *Kulak* is the Russian word for a rich peasant. Communist collectivization of agriculture was intended to eliminate these rich peasants as a class.

the emasculation of politics, but rather society acting in completely natural self-defense. Political ideology has had terrible consequences, including all sorts of disasters and pogroms. Professional politicians must be placed under public control, just as bakers or cobblers are; otherwise they may deceive or disappoint us. We've endless illustrations of how this can happen. It's not enough for them to argue that they're acting "in the interests of Socialism," or "in the name of the Nation." We want this activity to be in the interests of individual people, the concrete public, the community, society. At this point their political behavior can be measured in terms of good and bad, that is, in moral terms.

This is what we wanted to do as Charter 77 dissidents. It was precisely our attempt to evaluate politics from a moral standpoint that constituted what Havel called "the power of the powerless." And then there was the demand for "moral politics" that gave defenseless students, actors and intellectuals the power that won our "gentle revolution." Morality superceded professional criteria of power mechanics, and subverted ideological definitions of that power's goals. This is apparently a paradoxical meta-politics, or "anti-political politics," as Havel described it in his 1984 essay "Politics and Conscience." This is politics as applied morality, as concern for one's fellow man in human terms. As Havel wrote, "This approach is probably extremely impractical and difficult to apply in everyday life. But I can't see a better alternative." It's a miracle that he got away with it. But the question remains of how long he can hold on. Politics as the practice of morality demands not only a changed understanding of professional politics, but—more importantly—a new understanding of society and its relation to public affairs.

Is our society, whose thinking is still totalitarian, mature enough to understand this morality? Or to reverse the question, how long will it take for a society that has lived so long under totalitarianism to understand what democracy really means? . . . Our system is oscillating, and the more positive (or democratizing) energy one puts in, the more (and longer) it deviates from the desired point of rest. This is what I was talking about before. I wasn't just thinking of nationalism, which at least for the moment doesn't worry me as much. But what if we extrapolate—or interpolate—the sequence you mentioned: Race, Nation, Socialism . . . Isn't there a hint of similar myth-making in the whirlwind of democratic ideology . . . ?

This is at the very least a misunderstanding, if not a confusion of different levels. Race, Nation and Socialism are, in the given context, mystical goals to which totalitarian ideology subordinated all our thinking and actions. It declared, "You live for your Race, your Nation, your Socialism!" (delete what doesn't apply). The community, society and the state exist only to accomplish this Idea. Democracy has nothing to do with this, it's something completely different. Democracy is not, and cannot be, a goal. It always was and is a means. It's a form of condominium that allows different communities, races, nationalities, ideologies and systems to coexist. It's a way for people with completely incompatible stances, opinions and interests to live together in a single community, a single territory, a single state, and it allows people from different communities, territories and states to do the same. This coexistance assumes a natural plurality of attitudes, opinions and interests, as well as their owner's tolerance towards others. This plurality is surrounded by opinions, attitudes and interests that are anti-pluralist: these totalitarian voices advance particular interests, opinions or attitudes to the exclusion of all others. The limit of this tolerance lies in intolerant opinions, attitudes and interests.

Democracy as a form of coexistence is thus a search for compromise between your and my interests. Is it lack of principle? Absolutely not. It involves achieving consensus on society's priorities, and establishing a hierarchy for them. There are some things we have to decide on if we're going to be able to live together. It would be best to agree on them as best we can, so that we can then live peacefully and to mutual benefit. There are other things we shouldn't agree on, so that our lives, way of life, beliefs or convictions aren't placed under threat. Democracy understood this way is thus

„Podívejte, svoji historickou úlohu jste splnil, tak zmizte.“

"Look, you've fulfilled your historic task, so get out!"

incompatible with totalitarianism. To speak of "totalitarian democracy" is just as ridiculous as saying "hideous beauty."

The "ideology of democracy" that you mention is the complete opposite of "totalitarian ideology"; not only in its content, but in the way it's expressed. It doesn't aim to create a single, communal consciousness (nationalist, say, or socialist), but tries instead to find a way for different attitudes to coexist. Certainly democracy can be abused. No demagogue will ever admit that he's attacking democracy when he speaks in the name of democracy. But what sort of democracy is this? You'll notice that the adjectives these demagogues use limit the concept of democracy. They speak in the name of "people's democracy," "socialist democracy," "national democracy." Any sort of limitations on democracy are suspicious, for democracy is by its very nature universal.

The famous manifesto of the Movement for Civil Liberties (HOS)* declared: "Democracy for all." Do we need a genie to help us achieve this, or can it be accomplished through hard work? I feel that every civilized society—that is, every society that's a part of today's global society—is by nature democratic. It may be confused, and consist of people with different backgrounds, lifestyles, needs and interests. But over the generations these people have learned to live together, and even to depend on one another, for this way both sides benefit.

This is elementary, natural, pluralist democracy. Even here in our eternally confused Slovakia, we could never have survived without it. What's forty years of trying to make a universally applicable "socialist man," when you contrast it with the hundreds of years that our people has lived in the natural, pluralist democracy of its communities, towns and societies? In our country, totalitarian thinking is a feature of ideologues and ideological provocateurs, whether socialist, religious or nationalist. But in and of itself it's not a property of our heterogeneous nation and people. If I say that totalitarian ways of thinking have survived, I'm thinking mostly of these ide-

---

* See "From 1968 to 1989: A Chronological Commentary," 1988.

ologues, power-hungry leaders and Party representatives who want to convert the people to their "one true faith." They still have a long way to go before they start to think like democrats. But if we take our society and communities as a whole, I'm nowhere near as skeptical. Elementary, pluralist democracy is part of hundreds of years of experience. The delusions of totalitarianism could suppress this experience for a while, but it could never completely destroy it. This is something we can start building on immediately—only without any totalitarian ideologies.

During the period of post-1968 "consolidation," you were purged from the Communist party and fired from your job as a professional philosopher. For a while after this you lived a more or less normal life: you found work, or something that at least resembled work, that made use of your educational background. Then you signed Charter 77, and went into open political opposition. From what I've read, your life radically changed. Did this change represent something more to you than a simple readjustment in the style, comfort and professional side of your life? Something like Camus' shooting the Arab, an existential Grenzsituation? *Did you find something beyond its political significance, something important for you as an individual?*

You've fallen for the Communist misinterpretation of Charter 77 as a typical political opposition. That's how they saw us, and that's what they tried to force us into being right from the very beginning. The Communists knew how to deal with political opposition. They had their tried and true methods: individual and group terror, persecution, political trials. Class enemies, traitorous elements, agents in the pay of imperialism. But Charter 77 could never be fitted into this framework. It was a qualitatively new phenomenon. It wasn't, and didn't establish, either a legal or illegal opposition. We were crazy, impractical madmen and adventurers who voluntarily gave our names and addresses to State Security. We called on the totalitarian regime to uphold its own laws, and stubbornly kept offering to start a dialogue on solving our society's problems. David and Goliath.

Charter 77's strength was that instead of being an organized opposition, it was a free association of individuals. Instead of a political program it had a moral one. Political slogans were replaced with a moral appeal: Patocka's "Live in truth!"* It was a moral movement, not a political one. Charter 77 didn't fight the totalitarian regime as its opposition, but as its bad conscience. The implication of this moral stance was the philosophy of *als ob*, as if. We'll act *as if* we took our leaders' proclamations seriously, and *as if* we believed that they took them seriously as well (their ratification of the Helsinki agreements, for example). In an article I wrote in 1978 called "Charter 77 and 'Real Socialism'," ** I wrote that "the Charter movement is an absurd reaction to the absurd conditions of 'real socialism'. The absurdity of this reaction is characterized by a certain amount of pure Czech Svejk-ism.† The Good Soldier began taking the monarchy absolutely seriously at a time when it was completely out of fashion to do so. This inevitably led to his being seen as suspicious by both the authorities and the opposition."

The people in power understood the threat that this moral appeal raised. To allow it to survive would have meant the destruction of "real socialism," the political overthrow of the regime. In this context they were right to see morality as politics, that is, as the political consequences of a moral stance.

You ask what Charter 77 meant for me personally. To begin with I saw it as an excellent tactic, a way of using morality in the sphere of politics. In another article, "Charter 77 and Socialist Legality,"

---

* Jan Patocka (1907-77) was one of Czechoslovakia's greatest philosophers, and was a founding member of Charter 77. He died under police interrogation just three months after Charter 77's founding.

** "Real socialism" was the term used by the Communist regime to describe an idealized version of "socialist reality."

† Kusy is referring to Jaroslav Hasek's *The Good Soldier Svejk* (1920-23), a famous Czech novel about the misadventures of a "little man" fighting Austro-Hungarian bureacracy and officialdom with absurdity, wit, subterfuge and passive resistance.

I wrote: "The Charter has discovered an excellent strategem, one it doesn't have to hide or conceal, and it needn't fear that when it is discovered, it will lose its effectiveness." Frantisek Pavlícek once went around a dissident meeting collecting our answers to the question, "What does Charter 77 mean to you?" I tried to answer sincerely. As I remember it now, I wrote: "To begin with I thought that it was a temporary political tactic. Now I know that it has changed my whole life. Charter 77 is not politics, but an attitude towards politics." I still believe this, and that's why I decided not to become a professional politician.

How did all this affect your world-view? How did it change the way you see the world, politics, revolutions, good and evil, even art (something you've also written on)? You obviously see things differently now than you did in 1969. What has become of your Marxist convictions? How do you feel about Marxism and the way it's been applied in the past?

This is the question people have been constantly asking me for the past four months. "How can a Marxist hold these opinions?" I was recently asked. "How can you be a Marxist if that's what you think?" For the twenty years following '68, the Communists kept accusing me: "Kusy's betrayed Marxism." I read some posters at the university yesterday, and now I discover that "the Marxist Kusy has betrayed the nation." When you ask what happened to my world-view, I feel as though I ought to have a world-view hidden someplace secret. Or that I ought to analyze all my political activity and writing. For the only world-view I have is what's expressed in this activity. I don't know, don't recognize and don't need any Marxist talmud to check if my positions and views are sufficiently orthodox.

But when people describe me as a Marxist, I don't refute it: in terms of how my thinking *developed*, that's as much a part of my background as, for instance, the fact that I'm a Slovak. This means that my starting point was Marxism, it "nursed" me, and this I won't deny, just as I wouldn't deny my own father. But as far as my thinking today goes, I'd call myself an independent Marxist. I've always tried to remain independent of political and power structures, and to steer clear of Marxism's official interpreters as well. Long before '68, the censor and ideology department of the Slovak Communist Party's Central Committee considered me an "unreliable, contradictory Marxist." I've also tried to stay independent of the "Marxist classics": I've never thought it worthy to use quotations as crutches. In my last officially published monograph, "Marxist Philosophy" (1967), you won't find a single quotation. I made a point of relying only on my own thoughts. This means that I won't support or defend that sort of teaching and its spokesmen. What I wrote may have been wise, or it may have been foolish; but it was I, Kusy, who wrote it, and not some Marxist who happened to be called Kusy.

As it happens, a few days ago I was going through my dissident writings of the past twenty years. I was amazed at how much they concentrated on harangues against official Marxism. "Marxism and the Ecological Crisis" was about its inability to notice, understand or explain humanity's global problems. "An Un-Slovak Phenomenon" described its pseudo-resolution of our nationality question. "What Happened to the Idea of Social Equality?" examined its utopian approach to this issue. And so on. A book containing all this is coming out soon, so you can check it all for yourself. I'm not saying all this to cast doubt on my Marxist roots, but only to put them in the right perspective.

What has become of my Marxist convictions? They long ago ceased to be the center of my thinking ("What is the correct Marxist opinion on . . .?"). I use Marxist ideas as helpful tools, epistemological and ontological approaches that are universal in terms of logic and methodology ("How can these tools contribute to a truthful understanding of . . .?"). I don't overestimate the value of Marxism understood this way. Others did when they said: "With Marxism we can do anything!" And people are overestimating it today when they fume: "Marxism is responsible for all evil." My complaints about Marxism are humbler, and so my desire to establish Marxism's responsibility will be more careful. Various religions—Christianity or Islam, for example—have shed just as much blood as Marxism. It would obviously be ridiculous to say that Islam was responsible for all the evil in Iran. It's people who are responsible for all good and evil. It doesn't depend on whether they're Marxist or Muslim, for that doesn't change their responsibility for their actions.

While we're on the subject of "worldviews" . . . We're turning to the West with hope and a certain uncritical admiration. This is motivated mostly by economic considerations, and by expectations of a better life. But it may also be happening to the detriment of an important process: our own growing up, which involves defining and utilizing what creative cultural vitality we still have . . .What do you think about what people are calling our "return to Europe"?

I support our return to Europe—but not as a substitute for fully understanding ourselves and discovering our own identity. I support it because if we don't "return to Europe," not even this much will be possible. We've seen what was possible in cultural and political isolation: what little there was has long since been exhausted. These were cooped-up and agonized sorts of possibilities, anyway. The question today is how to join the big, wide world, that noble community of nations. Some people think that all we need to do is make a circus entrance, followed by a good floor-show number. Hyphen-drum rolls, and the Slovak with a capital S steps out into the European arena. "From now on I'm equal with all of you." You can make that sort of entrance in a circus, but not in the community of Europe. Has anyone else in the former Soviet-bloc had a circus act like ours? Perhaps it will help people remember us: "Ah yes, they're the ones who wanted to secede." Perhaps they'll even be so unscrupulous as to add, "God forbid that the Slovaks ever take offense again."

I'm personally offended by this sort of entrance into Europe. And though it is a "return to Europe" for the Czechs, it's the Slovaks' first time around. This is nothing to be ashamed of. If people still talk about us Slovaks as "Czechs," it's not because our republic's name doesn't have a hyphen. Czechs have made their reputation in the world and we haven't. We'll just have to make one for ourselves, that's all. The same way that other nations and nationalities have had to, even though the name of their state didn't contain a hyphen, or even the name of their nationality. Look at the Flemish and Waloons in Belgium, for example, or the Welsh in Great Britain. Where would they put their hyphens?

Of course our entrance or return to Europe is simply the symbolic expression of our desire for full participation in European affairs. It's not that we're simply raving about Europe. We're all beginning to feel that we actually belong in Europe. Let's hope that Slovaks can truthfully say, "We're Europeans." Let's hope that they won't have to stop being Slovak Slovaks, and become Austrian or Canadian Slovaks (which was effectively what happened to our exiles). Let's hope that they won't see Europe as just part of their Slovak turf, which would lead to their feeling too big for their current share of the continent. Then European-ness can perhaps become a higher and more integral value than the need to be an "authentic" Slovak.

4 May 1990
Interview conducted by Peter Gomolcák of *Literárny tyzdenník.*

Milan Simecka

BORN A CZECH in 1930, Simecka did his university studies in Brno (Moravia) and then moved to Bratislava. He has lived there ever since, and is thus as Slovak as a Czech can become. He taught music at the university level and wrote articles and essays on culture, politics and the history of philosophy. In the 1960s he finished his studies *Social Utopias and Utopians* and *The Crisis in Utopianism*. In 1968 he published extensively and provocatively in both Czech and Slovak journals. After twenty years' membership in the Communist party, he was expelled in 1970. From then on he worked in various manual jobs, publishing articles and commentaries in the underground press despite constant police harassment. Although not a Charter 77 signatory, he was active in the human rights movement. In 1980 he coauthored with Miroslav Kusy *Big Brother and Big Sister: On the Loss of Reality in the Ideology of Real Socialism,* a book of dialogic essays on the authors' intellectual past and the experience of their generation. He was arrested in 1981, but after a years' investigation was released without trial. His major works are *The Restoration of Order* (1978), *Our Comrade Winston Smith* (1984) and *Circular Defense* (1985), which describe the post-1968 "normalization" process and the reaction of the population to it. *The End of Immobility* (1988) is a collection of diary entries on the changes in Czechoslovakia that were to lead to the November revolution. He is an independent publicist who participated in the "velvet revolution" through Public Against Violence.

Milan Simecka was named chairman of the president's council of consultants in July 1990. He served until his death on 24 September 1990 [ed.].

Between Danton and Robespierre

ROBESPIERRE WAS A little late coming to the revolution's aid, but he wasn't the one to blame. When the revolution started, he was still in the Bastille; it was the revolution that set him free. Danton, in the meantime, was calling on people to stage demonstrations on the Bastille square. There he spoke to the crowd, and won popularity and a mandate for talks on the city's future with the weakened monarchist regime. When Robespierre was finally released from the Bastille, he embraced Danton, for both men were equally devoted to the revolutionary cause.

We don't know when Robespierre first started to suspect that Danton was being too conciliatory towards the monarchists. His doubts

---

This piece was written at the time of a crisis in Brno which is described in "After the Velvet Revolution" (under "The Political Landscape: Civic Forum"). The issue in Brno was one that the country still faces: whether to retain "cooperative" Communist officials who are professionally qualified for their job, or whether to purge them from all positions of responsibility. The policy so far has been the "velvet" approach of accommodation and reconciliation. This policy has been mostly adhered to, although there have also been calls for sterner treatment of the Communist party (see "After the Velvet Revolution": "The Communist Party").

were probably provoked by the mayor of Paris, who was a moderate monarchist.* This mayor apparently put himself at the service of the revolution and was offered offices in the city hall. Danton declared that the mayor was a work-horse and that he could thus be of use to the revolution.

But Robespierre could never believe that anyone who had once been a monarchist could possibly support the revolution. If a monarchist seemed to be helping, then it was only because he was pursuing his own interests. Robespierre felt that monarchism was a poison, and that once it entered a person's bloodstream his mind was corrupted for ever. They were all the king's flunkies, he said. Yes, they had pinned tricolor cockades on their breasts, but in their heart of hearts they were waiting for the return of the Bourbons, when they could once again sit in the banquet halls of Versailles.

Danton had also been locked up in the Bastille, in fact even longer than Robespierre. But at some point in his youth he had lost faith in things ever being lily-white. This was why Robespierre could not trust him. Danton was experienced in practical politics, which was something that Robespierre despised. Danton had no time for revolutionary purity, morality and incorruptibility. It was Robespierre who mused about "committees for the common good." Ultimately —as we all know—he did set them up, along with courts headed by panic-stricken judges. In the end it was all the same whether it was the pragmatists or the revolutionary zealots who were the first to be sent to the guillotine.

You might think I'm joking, but I'm not. Research on revolutions shows that there are certain similarities in the way people think during great social upheavals. Even when the causes of the upheavals are quite different, certain stereotypes tend to appear. In every revolution, an argument breaks out between more or less moral radicals and pragmatists. The pragmatists agonize over the question, "What next?," which is something that never bothered a radical.

---

* Simecka is alluding to the mayor of Brno, who was one of the Communist officials whom local radicals wanted purged from government.

A question like this shoots off in all directions, but in the end we can see it getting to the heart of the matter. And at the heart of the matter, the question remains: what about the people? What about the inconvenient majority, which is euphoric for a few weeks, but then turns slowly back to everyday affairs? This majority may decide to take part in history writ large, but after a while it returns to history writ small. Life goes on. There's nothing immoral about this: it's simply a social phenomenon with roots deep in centuries-old human behavior. It's essentially a good thing, since it opposes revolutionary romanticism and the temptations of permanent revolution, which have always turned out to be disastrous.

A revolution that decides to build democratic institutions on the arid ground left by totalitarianism has to take history's "little people" into consideration. We're all in the same boat, we went through everything together, including that cruelest disappointment.* We've nothing to hide from one another. It was us, after all, the silent majority, who allowed the regime to drag out history to the bitter end. How many people were there who stood up in a meeting and said, "Stop bothering us with your endless lies and nonsense!" Didn't we go to the May Day celebrations? Didn't we support our "normalization" leadership by giving them ninety-nine percent of the vote? There was always some everyday explanation for this behavior—God forbid that anyone should suspect that we were really Communist believers!

So who today can be the judge of how morally legitimate these reasons were? There was one time in the past twenty years that I too voted for National Front candidates.** This was when, in absolute frustration, I began to wonder if I wasn't ignoring a father's duty by letting my independent activities block my childrens' opportunities for education. I made my sons get dressed up, and we all went off to the elections. There they excitedly photographed

* 1968.

** The National Front was an umbrella political organization controlled by the Communist party.

us and probably reported that I had eaten my words, that I had seen the light and repented. Only that didn't help things either. This is the way most of us still were when we joined our young people in the revolution. Hundreds of thousands of us joined together and celebrated by jingling our keys. Then even more of us went over to Austria to see what was in the shops.

This is why I object to radicals offering people an easy way to cleanse themselves. You're all innocent, and it's only the owners of Party cards who are guilty. There's no great morality in pointing an accusatory finger and thus wiping the slate clean of any shared guilt. Scrutiny of one's own sins, as every believer knows, is the best way to achieve self-improvement. It's dangerous to make such a simple distinction between the majority and some morally irreproachable avant-garde, or between the trustworthiness of the government and that of the people. "Trustworthiness" is a post-war term. Everyone knows an easy way to get a stamped verification that proves one's impeccably "trustworthy" credentials. It's one of our national skills. We've been through all this before.

I support the people who are most concerned with the question of what comes next. I can't accept that the contemporary situation is a struggle between clean and unclean. We've opted for national reconciliation: there's no room for witch-hunts now. It's not a long way from a kick to more drastic measures for preserving revolutionary purity. If we're resolved to abide by the democratic expression of majority opinion, we need to start making allowance for the unradical views of the people who weren't at the demonstrations, because they were working the wrong shift or had to milk the cows. There's always the risk that revolutionaries will lose their contact with the people, and that they'll start to toy with the idea of doing without it altogether. This has happened many times in history. Only today, thank God, is different. We're faced with something else: a sad future of dirty coalition haggling by politicians whose sole virtue is that they've been freely elected. Alternative ways for democracy to function have yet to be discovered.

Robespierre was terrified of the Bourbons' returning. So he began by eliminating all the monarchists, followed by anyone suspected of sympathizing with them, and finally did away with everyone who didn't share his paranoid obsessions. In doing so he paved the way for Thermidor and the Empire, and thus the glorious return to power of the monarchists. Like all radical revolutionaries, Robespierre had no time for arranging United Nations supervision of elections, or for asking his constituents what they thought about the battle between clean and unclean. There are lots of people in Czecho-Slovakia who aren't interested in this battle, and who may not even have a very clear idea about our revolution. But still they are important, because they are the ones who go on baking the bread. Revolutionaries don't usually have the time to worry about jobs like that.

26 April 1990

"I don't have anything against advisors—particularly if they're not Soviet..."

Good Democrats All

IN THE PIECES I wrote over the past fifteen years, I gradually had to eliminate words like "socialism," "communism" and "capitalism." Ideological abuse had colored their meaning to such a degree that I decided to get by without them. Now three months have passed since the beginning of the revolution, and I feel like dropping the words "democracy" and "democratic" as well—or at least stop pretending that we're all good democrats, even the people who aren't. Everything is democratic these days, even things that aren't. Look at how members of parliament were coopted,* for instance: a revolutionary and very necessary step, to be sure, but not one you could describe as democratic.

All our parties—both old and new—are democratic. Even the Communist party is fervently democratic. But what the papers, radio and television are currently giving people is the *illusion* of democracy, and I'm afraid that this will soon have people's heads spinning. Politics is currently about 10 percent more democratic than it was. Even in cooperatives, where democratic methods ought to be as clear

---

* See "From 1968 to 1989: A Chronological Commentary," 28 December 1989.

as crystal, people are simply shouting at one another, as I sometimes read in the newspapers.

People invented democracy so that they wouldn't have to kill each other over their conflicting interests and demands—although such things are not unknown today. The bloody tracks of expedient murder are still easy to follow in our modern history. The rejection of this legacy, particularly by the younger generation, was the great success of our revolution. This is an unquestionably good thing. Less fortunate has been the way democracy has turned into a magic spell, with everyone's distinguishing marks disappearing under a layer of democratic paint. It seems that all our parties are entering the elections with democratic slogans and names. It could happen that voters, overwhelmed by democraticity, will not know how to make their choice. With everyone being such outstanding democrats, what difference does it make whom you choose? This is the explanation for the very strong tendency to vote for individuals, and not for parties.

Democracy is simply a tool. When it's combined with a certain level of political culture, it is an excellent safeguard against the problems of a Lebanon or Azerbaidzhan. Otherwise it is form without content. We all support democracy. What we need to do now is discuss what it actually means. Political parties will have to explain their goals and describe fully the future they envisage. The greatest danger that a democracy can face is vague formulation of political goals. Even in the West it's common for political parties to avoid taking concrete positions. The broader your roof, after all, the more voters you can fit inside.

This is the danger we are facing. This is why political parties need to specify their programs. They must, for example, take a position on the future shape of the Czecho-Slovak state. The way our law on self-determination currently reads, independence for Slovakia is a legitimate goal. But parties should not conceal that goal in such a way that people can't see what they're doing. It would even be legitimate for a campaign to support a return to the old regime; but here again the goods should be clearly marked. And it's the people who were expelled from the Communist party—not the people who expelled them—who should be the ones to advance an idea like this. After all, it was the expellers who were recently receiving their 99.8 percent of the vote. People shouldn't write that they don't like Havel's sweater when what they really mean is that they don't like Havel.

The political center needs to be defined more precisely, in both positive and negative terms. It should announce through its leaders, for instance, that it decries the chauvinist and racist graffiti that is appearing on the walls of Bratislava. Political decency should be supported so insistently that that uncultured voters are frightened away. All our parties seem to agree that we should have a market economy; but they should at least differentiate themselves by saying where they intend to place the responsibility for its social effects. There are many other issues like this that I could mention.

As a student I made a little extra money by working as a librarian. I never had much to do, so I spent most of my time reading magazines of the post-war period. After a while I started believing that everyone was a socialist in those days: almost everyone wanted friendship with the Soviet Union, and virtually everyone (particularly the poets) loved Stalin. I thought socialism had to be a great thing if it was supported by so many grown-ups and intelligent people. This was how I became a devotee of socialism without knowing any more about it than what was written in a few magazines.

With all of us adults suddenly being democrats, I'm afraid that the younger generation may now be in a similar situation. They should ask their elders to explain what they intend to put in democracy's pot, and to give some description of what they think the results will be. We should be able to come up with at least three or four basic ideas on how we want to organize ourselves in the future. "Democracy" is a slippery word; it would be easy to lose our grip on it, as we once did with the idea of "socialism." I say this only out of caution, for from the perspective of global developments I'm optimistic about our prospects. I believe, as Deputy Prime Minister Markus puts it, that we'll knock democracy into shape as well.

May 1990

Jan Urban

BORN IN 1951, Urban is Czech and a self-proclaimed "professional optimist." He is the son of a Communist idealist who fought in the anti-Nazi resistance and subsequently rose to a senior post in the Central Committee of the Czechoslovak Communist Party. Urban's father lost his position for criticizing the regime's inability to reform in the early 1960s, and died of a heart attack after three interrogations by state police in 1988.

Urban has a degree in history and philosophy from Prague's Charles University. After graduating he worked in a theater and taught history and civics at the high school level. He lost his teaching position in 1977 after refusing to sign a condemnation of Charter 77. He subsequently worked in a racehorse stable, as a bookbinder, as a chauffeur and as a construction worker. In 1985 he qualified as a skilled bricklayer. A signatory of Charter 77, he was also Prague correspondent of the Soviet samizdat magazine *Expres Khronika.* He is a member of the Polish-Czechoslovak Solidarity Group, and was a cofounder of the Eastern European Information Agency. During the November 1989 revolution, he was Civic Forum's chief-of-staff, and from February till June 1990 served as its leading representative.

The Politics and Power of Humiliation

I

IN THE COURSE of one week, in November 1989, winter blossomed into spring in Czechoslovakia. A nonviolent mass movement, led by Civil Forum, triumphed. We are in transition from the negation of the old to the building of the new. It is time to seek out the roots of this change.

Czechoslovakia was founded in 1918 on supranational idealist principles. Three peoples—Czechs, Slovaks and Germans—together with various ethnic minorities, united in a perhaps historically naïve belief in the strength of modern political democracy. In reaction to its intimate knowledge of the great size, but also of the darker reaches of the German spirit, formed during a thousand years of living side by side with Germans, the new state oriented itself on an alliance with Great Britain and France, and found its place in modern world culture. The concept of collective security, today generally accepted, was very actively promoted at that time.

Czechoslovakia quickly became a democratic state with respectable economic and cultural achievements. But it would soon become clear that certainties built on idealist principles and enthusiasm easily become false myths without substance. The economic crisis of 1929,

Hitler's chauvinism after 1933 and the trauma of the 1938 Munich Diktat successively and brutally made that point. To this very day, in Czechoslovakia, the Munich settlement is felt to represent a failure by the western democracies and a betrayal by allies. It had exactly the horrible consequences that Winston Churchill predicted. The ease with which humiliated and broken Czechoslovakia submitted to Nazi occupation resulted from, among other things, the loss of faith in democracy that flowed from Munich.

The betrayed Czechs had believed in the strength of parliamentary democracies and in the honesty of their allies. This belief turned into the worst humiliation. For a long time there was no hope for anything more positive. People survived with a "submit, hide or run for your life" psychology. One day before the occupation of Bohemia (14 March 1939), Slovaks formed their own Slovak state. This was felt keenly in Bohemia to be another result of Munich. Humiliation and despair were also the names of occupying powers. Just a few months previously, a strong state had lost most of its territory, its allies, its independence and its hope. This was simply a terrible ten months. It was only when the world war began that a glimmer of hope returned, at least to some.

The year 1945 came, with mass purges, the violent expulsion of 3 million Germans, and a system of selective democracy that allowed only several specific political parties. In 1948, under the passive gaze of citizens who no longer believed themselves capable of defending democracy, the Communist party assumed power.

This episode of betrayal and humiliation forms the essential backdrop to the subsequent history of Czechoslovakia; for humiliation is powerful in politics in two directions. Usually it serves the interests of the oppressor. People live intense, introspective lives, their energies all turned in upon their own miseries and relationships. That is what Milan Kundera has evoked so effectively in his novels, especially in his early books such as *The Joke,* but perhaps best known outside Czechoslovakia through his most recent novel, *The Unbearable Lightness of Being.* Yet occasionally, as happened in November 1989, the energy turns outwards. It pounds upon the oppressor and he simply crumbles.

As President Havel has written, humor as well as honesty had vital roles in the Revolution. So the story of this essay is the power of the absurd to shatter the passivity of humiliation and to liberate the energies trapped within.

But first I must explain how we reached that moment. We had to eat of lot of dirt before we vomited.

II

WHY DID THE Communists succeed so easily in 1948? There were three main reasons. One was the peculiarity of the position of the Communist Party of Czechoslovakia in society. The CPCz had been a legal component of the parliamentary spectrum since 1921. In all other central European states before the war, the Communist parties functioned underground, illegally. Betrayal by the Western Allies, embodied in the disappointment of Munich, was followed by the liberation of most of Czechoslovakian territory by the Red army. This trend towards the Communists was accelerated by the plainly mistaken decision of President Benes to return to Prague with the London government-in-exile via Moscow. All this gave the CPCz great popularity. In the parliamentary elections, on a wave of nationalist populism, they attained more than 40 percent of the vote. They became the most powerful political party in the country. In the struggle for power, they neither had to use force, like Communists in Poland, nor the weight of the Soviet occupation, like the Communists in East Germany. The CPCz had part of the intelligentsia on its side. Industrial workers, profiting from the boom in heavy industry, supported it. Peasants were satisfied with the Communists' land reform and with the redistribution of the property of the expelled Sudeten Germans. The Communists occupied the decisive positions in the army and security services. In February 1948, the Communists seized power without a single shot being fired. With hindsight it is possible to evaluate that event as the failure of an immature, conceited but disheartened democracy faced with threats and force.

Only later we found out that there were two further, important reasons for the ease of the Communist takeover. One was the long term Soviet (or more properly NKVD) plan to occupy the whole of Eastern Europe in an attempt to build a buffer to a possible Third World War. This meant that in 1944, and especially in the spring of 1945, the Soviets sent paratroop groups to Bohemia with only one mission—not to fight, but to organize an information network for the future. After the war, the Communists took on more and more important posts in the security forces and in the army so that at the moment of political crisis in Czechoslovakia they could effectively control the means of power.

The second reason was the growing political pressure exerted by Stalin's Soviet Union. This became visible in July 1947 during a government visit by the Czechoslovak government to Moscow. Stalin simply rebuffed the Czechoslovak desire to receive the Marshall Plan aid. At that moment, even Benes knew that the battle was lost and that Czechoslovakia could not go its own way. Furthermore, historians tell us that the Truman administration was actually working on the assumption that Moscow controlled Czechoslovakia even *before* the spring crisis of 1948 made this control a reality. We can never know what might have been the course of events if the West had vigorously backed Benes and Jan Masaryk with food and other help during the terrible winter of 1947. Only today, after fifty years of the dominance of ideologically driven and repressive regimes, first Nazi then Communist, we stand, perhaps the wiser, on the threshold of the new era. The economist Milos Zeman has offered an apt description of our situation. "We are like emaciated and beaten animals, released from the zoo and looking untrustingly at open country."

Czechoslovakia's experience of communism was bitter for several reasons. A highly industrialized country like Czechoslovakia, with a relatively developed economic infrastructure, was much more sensitive to the extreme unsuitability of the centralized Communist planning system than were the other East European countries managed by Communist governments after the war. There was also a lot more to squander. By comparison with its neighbors, the economy was not damaged by war. There was the property of 3 million expelled

Germans, the nationalization of industry and services, the virtual 100 percent collectivization of agriculture, strictly enforced laws on mandatory labor, and the purges. In short, Czechoslovakia started from a higher material base than its neighbors , and so it was possible for decay to proceed for years without people really noticing, because they did not have to suffer an immediate and commensurate decrease in their standard of living.

The years of Stalin's fury left behind hundreds of executions, tens of thousands imprisoned, millions of damaged and terrified people. The beautiful dream of equality became a nightmare. The social structure was violently turned upside down with the elimination of the private sector in all areas of human activity, and the destruction or entire subjugation of the church to state control. All citizens, without exception, became state employees, because the state owned everything. From the beginning of the sixties, however, it became clear that there was a fault in the system. The economy ceased to function. The intelligentsia, encouraged by the events of the 1956 uprising in Hungary, carefully began to formulate a non-ideological culture. The Writers' Congress and the subsequent student protest at the end of 1967 became the prelude to a revolution in the leadership of CPCz, which prefigured the events known as the Prague Spring. But we are running ahead of our story. First we must ask how people organized their lives to survive under this old regime.

Of course, most people collaborated with the regime, perhaps merely by being passive, but that passivity was very important. In addition there were unknown, but probably large numbers who collaborated actively. The British journalist Neal Ascherson, writing on Eastern Europe, has pointed out that if you lift any flat stone, there are many slimy creatures living beneath it, and so it has proven to be in many countries under occupation. The national shame of the French was redeemed by de Gaulle's successful creation of the myth of resistance, a myth which could only be faced squarely — and the true scale of collaboration in France revealed—forty years after the end of the war in the famous television program *Le Chagrin et la Pitié.* Similarly, more poignantly and painfully, the Italian writer Primo Levi, who survived Auschwitz, explained in terms of sadness and without condemnation how there had been a "grey area" in which victims in the concentration camps were tarnished and compromised, and actually helped to run the death camps. What we in eastern Europe should do about guilt and its management is something to which I shall return. Here I would merely observe that forty years seems to have been a decent time to wait before shining bright lights under recently upturned stones.

For those who did not collaborate in Czechoslovakia, there was only one other choice. This was to live two lives—or a split life. This became a part of everybody's psychology. Children from the age of twelve, thirteen, fourteen, before they were allowed to go to high school, had to understand absolutely perfectly that some things could be said at home, but that something completely different had to be said at school, and the two could not be confused. We call this "the one chance psychology," because you could not afford to make a single mistake, for that would be your last. Living like this became a part of a way of life, part of the nation's understanding of the world.

In this system, you were humiliated by the regime. You were humiliated by its representatives down to the very lowest ranks, by every policeman in the street, by every clerk, by everybody who taught in the schools. Everybody who had even the smallest position of power was part of this system of mass humiliation. People learned to live with it. The regime understood that this perpetual humiliation, punctuated from time to time with demands for proof of loyalty, was the best method for keeping people silent. Everybody listened to the Voice of America, to the BBC and to Radio Free Europe and knew what was going on. But everybody also knew the price to be paid for not playing according to the rules and so kept silent.

How then did we maintain any semblance of public pride? Historically, the arts and the artists in Bohemia and Slovakia have played an important role from the nineteenth century onwards. There was a rebirth of nationalism in the central European states which were then under German or Austro-Hungarian influence. The Czechs, and to some extent the Slovaks as well, restored their pride in their national attitude towards everything through the arts. With this as their heritage, the arts in Czechoslovakia have always run somewhat ahead of politics. As a result, both logically and historically, artists have been taken by the rest of the population to be something a bit special: the nation's pride.

One of the most humiliating features in these last forty and, especially, the last twenty years, is that hundreds of the most gifted artists —writers, actors, singers—were either forced to leave the country, or were degraded even more than ordinary people by playing the role of good Party member and loyal citizen. Millions who trusted them before, who remembered them from 1968, saw these beautiful people produce absolute rubbish.

What I have just described contributed in a way to the Prague Spring of 1968. In 1967, there was a Writers' Union Congress at which the participants all boiled over. Kundera gave a moving speech about the role of culture and ideas as a ping-pong ball bouncing between West and East. The Communists abolished the Writers' Union and a few months later the students went out in protest. It was enough. In 1968, the artists who catalyzed the changes suffered the most in the purges. If you take the Writers' Union list in 1970 and compare it with that of 1968, you will find several hundred names on each list; but you will find maybe only ten that are common to both. The same thing happened in the other arts, but it was most extreme in literature. Louis Aragon talked of Czechoslovakia in those years as a "Biafra of the soul." And so it was.

In 1968, the Party controlled all aspects of life more or less completely; yet it was from within the Party that the first visible signs of reform emerged. With the abolition of censorship, society began to find out about the many political prisoners. Some prisoners had been released gradually during the previous few years. But the last ones were not released until 1968. The dissemination of this knowledge stimulated people, especially writers and students, to question widely, and for the first time, whether the Party was an absolute and infallible force. This feeling was strengthened by the burgeoning public debate about economic reform, which plainly demonstrated the incompetence of the Party *apparat* to deliver what it had promised. So, in a way, this Czechoslovak experience prefigured Gorbachev's *glasnost* by twenty years.

The Party *apparat* reacted quite logically. It could not cope with public discussion and so conspired against its own people and country by asking for Soviet military intervention to crush the flowering of the Prague Spring.

I remember a great deal of optimism before the intervention. Dubcek and the reformist Communist leadership were solidly and creatively part of this reform; and perhaps naïvely, perhaps just because we were used to the fact of state power, we tended to believe that if the "commanding heights" of the system were going our way, we already had the most difficult part of the journey behind us. We used to joke that, "now the water is only up to our knees!"

Everybody of any public stature in Czechoslovakia, the cream of our intelligentsia as well as a broad swath of general public opinion, backed the reform movement. Our mistake was simple and fatal. We failed to realize that for Brezhnev's Soviet Union it was all impossible. It was unacceptably threatening for our springtime to mature into full summer. The Czechoslovaks stood as a constant and potent rebuke to their system, and the worst of it was that the Party structure itself was in the vanguard of reform.

August 21—the arrival of the Russian tanks—came as a complete shock. After the Bratislava meeting there had been a general impression that Dubcek had held, maybe even stabilized the situation, that we could still carry on along our own road. I returned to Prague on the last BEA flight from England on the night of 20 August. I was a student at that time. When I woke up on the 21st, there were tanks in front of my house. Friends telephoned to tell me what had happened elsewhere. I didn't believe it, but it was true. In fury, people tried to block the entrance to Prague Radio with a makeshift barricade of buses and trucks. The tanks rolled over them and drove at the crowd. There were dead and wounded.

We were ready to do anything, but were told to do nothing. Dubcek and the reformist leadership were kidnapped and taken to Moscow in handcuffs, where they were humiliated and imprisoned. President Svoboda announced that he was going to go to Moscow for "talks." What talks? We believed that it was a victory. We thought that he might convince the Soviets that the occupation had been a mistake. When they all came back, still in their positions, we still hoped that we would be able to continue somehow.

In the coming months, the leadership proved to be weaker than we might have feared. It was unwilling to use the popular support it had. It lied to the people. It was supine before the attacks of the most hated collaborators and conservatives in the Communist party. By the end of the year, we finally understood that hope of retaining intact any shred of the Prague Spring reforms was dead.

The self-immolation of Jan Palach on 15 January 1969 near the statue of St. Wenceslas on Wenceslas Square traumatized the nation. Nothing like this had happened before. Palach was immediately compared to Jan Hus, the great Protestant martyr who was burnt at the stake at 1415. But the Party remained unmoved. This was the end of any lingering illusions. We learned from this that the Party cannot be reformed.

III

TODAY ONE OFTEN hears the question: what is the difference between the Prague Spring of 1968 and the Prague Autumn of 1989? I think that while twenty years ago it was predominantly a matter of a crisis of legitimacy within the governing Communist elite in one country of the Communist bloc, in 1989 it concerned a phenomenon of a greater degree. It was the Czechoslovak variant of the crisis of legitimacy of the whole Communist system.

In 1968, the leading role of the Party was only rarely questioned by reformers. The Party intelligentsia alone led the reform process. It did so with vigor and with genuine commitment. In the brief eight months before the August occupation, society, paralyzed by twenty years of Stalinism, was unable to generate an alternative program and movement; there was no power base from which this could have been done. The collapse of the Party elite, around which the nation emotionally united in the days of August, its inability to resist politically and to utilize the virtually unanimous support of the citizens—these were the causes of the abrupt end to the Prague Spring. The terrified leadership of the Communist Party of Czechoslovakia could not institutionalize reform even partially. By April 1969, showing no attempt at resistance, it had ceded its position to the so-called "normalization" led by Gustav Husák. In the purges that followed, about half a million Party members were purged and about 800,000 lost their jobs. From that moment on, the CPCz established itself in opposition to the nationalist and humane forces within society, and so aligned itself with the position taken by the other East European Communist parties. This Party could no longer reform. Henceforth, it could only control the people through corruption and fear. The word "reform" became a curse. The prospect of any solution of basic economic and social problems from that source evaporated.

Humiliation was the spring that drove the last twenty years of Husák's orrery. At some point in their life everyone had to make an agonizing choice: to prove their loyalty to the regime by humiliating themselves or to lose everything. Everybody knew what "everything" meant, for "everything" was defined with delicate cruelty by the Husák regime. It meant to lose not only your own career, but to blight the future of your children, because they would not be allowed to attend university.

After I was thrown out of my teaching job at the Gymnasium, I had this experience myself. At that time, my wife and I were living in southern Bohemia. I looked around the town for another job, which of course had to be a manual job since I was forbidden to teach. I did so for a month. Then a Party official told me that I would only be allowed to work *outside* the town. They intended to drive me out of town, quite literally. So I spent two years as a stable hand in a racehorse stable ten miles from town, riding back and forth on a motorcycle, seven days a week. When my first daughter was born, I wanted to be closer to my family and was allowed to become a forklift truck driver, sweeper and general laborer in a factory in town.

After two more years of this sort of life, I once again began to have problems with state security. I was interrogated and offered the possibility of emigrating. We decided to move to Prague in an attempt to hide in the crowds. It was not easy, and some of our friends, given the chance, did emigrate during that time.

Those of us who were not able to play the game according to the regime's rules learned not to judge others, because we found out how easy it is to break down and how easy it is to blow up. I always maintain that in my own case, when it came to the critical moment when the other side asked me to prove my loyalty, they simply went too fast and I exploded without thinking of the consequences.

This happened in late January 1977. I was teaching history and civic studies. All state employees (including teachers) were suddenly asked to sign "voluntarily" a petition condemning Charter 77. At the time no one actually knew the text of the Charter: it hadn't been published (nor was it, until the end of 1989). The whole thing was simply a crude, mass test of loyalty: don't think; don't ask; just sign. The Party knows best. The newspapers carried libelous articles, defaming Charter 77 signatories, some of whom I knew personally. I just couldn't believe those thing about them. They were called "people who poisoned wells" and "plague disseminators." I couldn't sign their "voluntary" petition. In the evening the director of the school tried to persuade me that it was not only for my own good but for the good of the school that I should sign. I refused. I defended myself by saying that it was immoral to protest against an unknown text. I was afraid to say that I knew some of the Charter people. Ten days after my refusal, in the middle of one of my lectures, I was summoned to the director's office where I was handed a piece of paper which informed me that I was to leave the school premises forthwith and not to return. Shortly after that, state security interrogated me for the first time in my life on my contacts with anti-state activists. Several other interrogations followed in quick succession.

In retrospect, I think that if they had been calmer, or more intelli–

gent, tried to be a little more friendly...who knows? I could have been one of them. Maybe, maybe not. They helped me by being so stupid. They made it so easy. The way they acted forced me to explode and the explosion blew me across to the other side of the barricade. One loses one's work and then finds that it becomes, strangely, very easy. The world becomes black and white. One begins to play one's role on the other side of the barricade.

In the past few years, we have become used to calling our country "Absurdistan." The tradition of Franz Kafka and Jaroslav Hasek loomed ever larger as the ideological blindness of the Jakes regime propelled Czechoslovakia into crisis. In the years following 1968, the problems intensified and the knot tightened. In the course of twenty years, out of a population of 15 million almost half a million Czechoslovaks emigrated. According to the then existing laws, they thereby committed a crime and were forbidden to return. The Husák regime offered its citizens a strange contract: you remain silent and we shall worry about a stable standard of living. Don't ask how and don't probe into the future. For very many the split lives and the humiliation went on, especially after Gorbachev came to power. You could see it especially at the beginning of the 1980s. These were for us the most dark and desperate years.

People went to the cinema or to the theater and they reacted there in a way which was a symptom of occupation. This is reminiscent of how the older generation describe the years of Nazi occupation. In the darkness of a cinema or theater hall, people reacted freely because they were hidden, masked by the darkness. They laughed and reacted to absolutely innocent phrases. Everything was ambiguous and everything was taken in an anti-regime way. When the lights went on, you could see those grey, closed faces, humiliated people who had been happy for a while. It went on and on with no prospect of an end.

Meanwhile, the Communist regime was finding it increasingly difficult to keep its side of the Faustian bargain with the people. With the example of Poland right before its eyes, the Czechoslovak leadership refused to take loans from abroad. Over twenty years it nevertheless created a painful internal debt. It invested insufficiently, so it became impossible to maintain the structure and equipment of industry. The transportation system was old, services undeveloped and the natural environment was devastated. We thus began to live on a more expensive kind of credit, consuming the time and the wealth which should belong to our children.

The old regime neglected investment in our children as well as in our factories and railways. Czechoslovakia, which always prided itself on the education of its citizens, today has one of the lowest per capita expenditures on education in Europe. In terms of the proportion of the population with a post-secondary school education, we have been surpassed by Nepal. We who, with reason, were proud of the quality of our health services, have to admit that the mortality rate is growing and that on average we have a shorter life-span than the vast majority of Europeans.

But at the beginning of the 1970s, a focal point of resistance began to coalesce at the center of the arena in which the battle would be fought. After several political show trials, the opposition concentrated itself in the cultural area, which appeared to the regime to be the most dangerous. Given what I have written already, it should now come as no surprise to learn that this was so. It is in the arts that our deepest politics are played out in Czechoslovakia; and it was out of a battle in the arts that the movement which mobilized a further generation of Czechs, including myself, came into being.

Under the increasing pressure of the state security forces, theater was being performed in private flats, banned rock and roll groups performed in barns in the countryside, and in the cities, *samizdat* (the secret reproduction and illicit distribution of banned texts) was growing. In 1975, Czechoslovakia signed the Helsinki Final Act. This gave the opposition a legal argument for speaking out in public. When the clash came, the pretext was the imprisonment of the musicians of the underground pop group "The Plastic People of the Universe." A broad coalition of people professing the most varied political opinions and beliefs, from former functionaries of the CPCz to Catholics, spoke out in defense of these musicians' right to free artistic expression.

In this way, in January 1977, Charter 77 came into being. It was a historic moment. People, humiliated to the point of desperation about their own powerlessness, were no longer able to remain silent and hide. They had no other option but to offer themselves to the regime as victims of human conscience against violence.

The inspiration for the birth of Charter 77 was obviously also the Polish KOR (the Committee for the Defence of Workers). The regime unleashed a vicious campaign of intimidation and slander against the signatories of Charter 77: imprisonment, beatings, and hundreds sacked from their jobs (including myself). At the majority of workplaces in Czechoslovakia, people were obliged to sign protests against the "anti-socialist pamphlet" whose contents no one knew, and these signed lists were taken to the Party secretariats. Political apartheid again had an opportunity for testing the loyalty of its subjects and for making an example of the disobedient. It was the bull-headed crudeness of this tactic which pitched me over the wall into dissidence, the loss of my teaching job, and everything which has now led to my present task and responsibilities.

However, thanks to the international solidarity which grew as a result of the Helsinki Declaration on Human Rights, the political trials became uncomfortable for the regime. There could never again be so many of them as to frighten the opposition into passivity. In fact, the trials became the absurd barometer of the simultaneous softening and toughening of the political situation in Czechoslovakia at the end of the 1970s and all through the '80s.

Gorbachev and *perestroika* changed the situation in a fundamental way. They accelerated the erosion of the system in all East European countries. The Czechoslovak leadership, however, which took its legitimacy from the Brezhnevite occupation, became increasingly isolated and derided, not least for its attempts to talk about *prestavba*—our *perestroika*. It answered in the only way it knew: with increased repression.

In August 1988, on the day of the twentieth anniversary of the

Soviet occupation, in keeping with what had already become a tradition, several dozen of the more active dissidents were temporarily detained or kept under surveillance at their cottages. No one believed that anything could happen in a city overflowing with police. But on that occasion, suddenly, the streets of Prague were streaming with demonstrators. I remember the panic at the police station where they were holding me. The policemen didn't want to believe the news coming from their police radios, which I overheard from the neighboring detention room. All of us, policemen, politicians, dissidents, had simple forgotten that twenty years is enough time for a new generation to grow up.

The opposition left their flats for the streets, and then it was only a matter of time. The demonstrations occurred with clockwork regularity, and the increased violence of the police had as its consequence the acceleration of resistance and international protest. Hitherto corrupt and silenced groups of scholars, scientists and artists and, increasingly, even the members of the CPCz, openly began to turn against the regime.

Meanwhile, for those of us who were declared dissidents, life was becoming more varied. From the end of 1987, we Czech dissidents had concluded that it wasn't enough to make links with groups in the West, welcome as that was. We had to develop a broader context, and even co-operation, with dissidents in other parts of Eastern Europe. After 1988 we maintained occasional contact with the Polish dissidents. But now we understood that we had to think about joint approaches. So we began to meet regularly with the Poles—Adam Michnik, Jacek Kuron and others—in the mountains on our border. We filmed our woodland picnic and sent it to the Western media, who screened it on television, because we wanted to show that we were now starting a new phase of co-operation.

I myself had gone to Moscow in December 1987 for the First International Independent Human Rights Seminar, organized by Press Club Glasnost. I met there with Lev Timofeev, Andrei Sakharov and other prominent Soviet human rights activists. By participating together with the Soviets in such a public manner, we presented an insoluble conundrum for the Husák regime: not to arrest me for such a flagrant defiance was a mistake; but to arrest me for meeting with Andrei Sakharov at a time of Gorbachev's *glasnost* would be an even bigger one!

To increase the effect of our activities, we launched a so-called "Eastern European Information Agency" which immediately became a great success. We were hated and quoted everywhere, even by the official Czechoslovak mass media. From now on, whatever happened in Eastern Europe, we consulted with our friends in the neighboring countries and were able with them to publish joint comments on events. In all these ways we gradually fused our different efforts into a joint struggle.

In January 1989, we had a demonstration in Prague and some people, including Václav Havel, were arrested for attempting to lay flowers at the place where Jan Palach had immolated himself in 1969. Both the immolation and the honoring were symbolic for Czechoslovaks. I think that it was at this moment that it all became too much for the people in the arts. They started to cross the shadow line. They started to enter the new era: not becoming dissidents, not wanting to take risks, but refusing to go on being silent. They started to sign petitions against Havel's trial. There was an explosion of petitions. Thereafter, we dissidents were absolutely confident that in the moment of crisis, when it came, they would be on our side. Close personal links and friendships were formed at that time.

The open co-operation between dissident groups from various East European states was transformed in a dramatic and incongruous way by the other revolutions of 1989. From illicit forest picnics, we moved to open collaboration between Czechoslovak dissidents and representatives of the governments and parliaments of Poland, Hungary and the Soviet Union. Adam Michnik and Zbygniew Bujak came to Prague in July 1989 as representatives of the Polish *Sejm* (parliament). The StB (the secret police) could only stand by and film the meetings! Andrei Sakharov telephoned us from Moscow. The Polish and Hungarian parliaments condemned the participation of their military units in the occupation of 1968 about which even some Soviet news–

papers began to write critically. In the late summer, two waves of East German refugees passed through a shocked Prague.

Twice in one month, the streets of the Malá Strana district near the West German embassy were clogged with East German cars. Rows of Trabants and Wartburgs, many of them with the ignition keys left in them, were simply abandoned. Remember that these cars were prized possessions, and many of the owners would have waited and saved for ten years to get one. Hundreds of people also streamed from the railway station to the embassy. For us locals, it was very moving. They walked with fixed intent, those East German refugees, quite uninterested in the beauties of Prague; and there was nothing we could do for them except to try to show them where best to cross the Czech police lines surrounding the embassy building. They climbed over the walls of the embassy gardens, handing up their children to others above. Many people cried in the streets.

Very soon the embassy was full and hundreds of them had to sleep outside. The Czech gave them hot tea and blankets and allowed them to use their toilets. That was all that we could do for them; but we understood that if they succeeded in escaping to the West, it would be the end of the illusion of impregnability of the system in which they, and we, then lived. Twice in one month, trainloads of East German refugees left Prague for the West. The buses which transported them from the embassy to the railway station were cheered by hundreds of Czechs in the streets, showing them the "V for Victory" sign.

IV

POLAND, HUNGARY AND now East Germany were moving. What about us? On 9 November 1989 the Berlin Wall was breached. By now it was completely clear that Czechoslovakia would be next on the list. I returned to Prague on 14 November after three weeks' absence. It was a completely different city from the one I had left. The atmosphere was electric. We knew that the Husák regime was desperate enough and isolated enough to contemplate the use of force which, we knew, Honecker had wished to do, but had been restrained from doing, in October in Berlin.

There were two small demonstrations on 15 November, one about environmental issues and the other commemorating the second anniversary of the Brasov massacre in Romania. Both ended in minor clashes with plain-clothes police who behaved with considerable individual brutality. But many of us expected the 17th to be a crucial day. This was because on that day an officially permitted student march, commemorating the fiftieth anniversary of the Nazi crushing of the Czech student movement in 1939, would take place. We thought it might be a turning point. For the Husák regime, it would present another and more critically insoluble conundrum: to forbid the march would be to invite direct comparison between themselves and the Nazis. To allow it, it was already clear, would run the risks of thousands protesting against them in the streets. What would they do?

On 17 November special units surrounded a part of the student demonstration in the middle of Prague. After an hour's wait, during which no one was permitted to leave, the marchers were atrociously beaten. There was blood in the streets. During the night of the 17th, rumors about death spread through the city. It will never be proven for certain whether there were deaths on that day. But there are eye-witnesses claiming to have seen up to three corpses lying in the street. Whatever the truth, the rumors hugely inflamed public anger against the regime. On the following day, students of DAMU (the School for the Dramatic Arts) suggested to other university faculties that they should initiate a strike. This strike was unexpectedly joined in the afternoon by an absolute majority of Czech theaters.

On the 18th, an actor friend took me to their meeting in one of the Prague theaters. When I got there I was astonished to find 400 actors, maybe more, from all parts of the country. They had been telephoning throughout the night of the 17th. They had told others that they all had to come to Prague to decide what to do. After two hours' discussion they had decided to go on strike. It was a crucial moment, because not only in Prague, but also in twenty-five cities in Bohemia and Moravia huge posters proclaiming "On Strike" appeared on the theater buildings. Everyone knew why.

In a country like Czechoslovakia where, as I have tried to explain, actors and people in the arts have great moral authority, no government can survive when that authority is exercised against it. So it was that the actors' strike and the students' demonstration formed the nuclei of the uprising. Different university faculties in different cities did the same. Within twenty-four hours, the uprising had several dozen points of support across the entire Republic, and another twenty-four hours later, it had its own political representation when, in one of Prague's theaters, Civic Forum came together.

Thousands of students and hundreds of actors rushed in cars from Prague throughout the country, talking to meetings. I am certain that frightened people in towns outside Prague were changed into an organized and concentrated party, transformed at the moment when a famous actor stood in front of them and said to them, "Listen people, enough is enough. Now we go against the regime!" And they did.

I ran from the theater meeting with two declarations: one from students and one from the actors, each announcing their strikes. I telephoned the texts to Radio Free Europe and Voice of America. There wasn't time to do more because we heard what turned out to be three unmarked State police cars roaring towards the cul-de-sac where we lived. I quietly slipped away over the rooftops. Eight of my friends who remained in my flat were detained as they left. Two Poles were immediately expelled and not even given the chance to collect their belongings.

I crossed the river and went straight to another theater (in fact, the one where Václav Havel began his career as a stage-hand). I explained from the stage in Russian and in English the reasons why the actors were going on strike. I did this because the scheduled performance for that evening was a pantomime for tourists. To our surprise, none of the foreigners protested! Then began a long period of sleeplessness for us all. That night we discussed means of co-operation with the student leaders.

On 19 November, Havel having just returned to Prague, we discussed in his flat the genesis of what later that evening became Civic Forum. In yet another of Prague's theaters (the reader will by now really understand the central role of theater in our culture, and how important it is to have many theaters!) about 400 people spanning the entire spectrum of political opinion formed a united opposition under that name. I myself was not at that founding meeting in the evening, although I had been at the flat in the morning. I was trapped in another theater, which was surrounded by the state police. Again, this time with the help of the actors, I was able to escape. They blocked the entrance to the passageway and I sprinted down it and away to hide. This was the last time that I saw Them face-to-face.

After two days of constantly changing the headquarters of the new-born Civic Forum, we realized the art galleries which we had been using were not suitable. One was too small and we couldn't monitor the entrance of another. So we ended up, again, in a theater. This time, it was called "The Magic Lantern." We chose it because it was right in the center of Prague, near Wenceslas Square. It had many small rooms suitable for offices and a huge stage for meetings and daily press conferences. The name "The Magic Lantern" has become a kind of shorthand for what was done during those crucial days. Somehow it seems very appropriate that from a place with such a name we negotiated with the collapsing Communist regime, which had so prostituted democracy that Prague people commonly described the Parliament as "something between a theater and a museum" (the buildings which flank it). We met with them on neutral soil in *Obecní Dum*—the building where in 1918 the original declaration of independence was signed.

To stay in a place like The Magic Lantern was a desperate but very logical move. We knew perfectly well that a few dozen riot police could have taken us in five minutes: we were not barricaded in. But from the first moment, we wanted to be aggressively non-violent in our stance—to make a power of our lack of weapons. It worked, even during the mass demonstrations when a quarter of a million people were in the streets. Someone invented a slogan:

"He who throws the first stone is a provocateur." There were no stones thrown. It was magic in the streets.

Meanwhile, down in The Magic Lantern, sixty to eighty people were working twenty-four hours a day, dividing into groups and conducted by a steering group around Václav Havel. Some people were preparing for the General Strike. The objective of the strike had been set in the very first student declaration. Others were preparing the opposition program, later called, "What we Want."

There was also what was called the Crisis Group. This was the busiest group and the one with which Havel spent most of his time. It was located in "Number Ten Wardrobe." This wardrobe room was the real heart of the revolution. The Crisis Group had the responsibility of analyzing the intelligence coming into The Magic Lantern and of making tactical decisions.

We also had a Media Monitoring Group and a Liaison Group for the students, artists and actors. We had printing facilities and (which was rather important) a catering department. Coordinating all these different groups was the HPV department (*Holka Pro Vsechno*, literally, the "Girl Friday" department). This is what I ran. We had to do whatever was needed. So one moment we would be negotiating and the next, we would be trying to find clean shirts for people.

We had this in place within two days of entering The Magic Lantern. On 24 November, Alexander Dubcek, who had made his first major public speech since 1969 at Bratislava two days before, appeared in Prague with Václav Havel. Before they went on to the balcony Marta Kubisová, the singer who had been the voice of 1968 and who had been forbidden to sing since then, preceded and sang "The times, they are a changin'."

Just after seven o'clock that evening the Politburo resigned. Havel and Dubcek were in the middle of giving a press conference on the stage of the Magic Lantern when the news came. I was wearing a T-shirt. The slogan on it was "I'm Czechoslovak and proud of it!" I leapt on to the stage with a bottle of champagne and we all celebrated in front of the world's press.

The streets of Prague now took on, for the first time, a carnival atmosphere. People now dared to believe that the regime really would not use violence. The latent fear of the previous week was lifted like a cloud. The two-hour general strike on the 27th was a pure celebration of victory. It was amazingly successful, mobilizing an entire cross-section of society across the country.

On 3 December, President Husák named the new government, appointing fifteen Communists out of twenty. For him, this was the last throw of the dice. Civic Forum immediately announced the threat of a further General Strike unless the government became properly representative. On 9 December, Husák and the Communist party leadership agreed to all our demands. The one-party system ceased to exist. The absurdity of the situation became even clearer next morning when Husák, still president, had to appoint a Cabinet composed of those whom he most despised, including several freshly released political prisoners.

Shortly after that, Husák resigned and the Old Parliament abolished Clause 4 of the constitution (on the "leading role" of the Communist party). Husák and the Party leadership had fallen victim to what we in Eastern Europe call the old János Kadar syndrome. In the West, people tend to think of Kadar as a hardliner who turned liberal: what the Americans call a "dovish hawk," like Nixon. But that is a misplaced analogy.

For us, Kadar was the first to demonstrate the inability of a Communist hardliner to maneuver in a tight situation when confronted by popular sentiment and unable to have resort to armed force. In this predicament, he lapsed into apathy and then just gave up. (Soon after being ejected from power, he died.) The same happened to other hardline leaders in Eastern Europe, most conspicuously to Honecker. It was evident that during his recuperation from surgery, his will to live collapsed.

With Husák gone, who would be president now? These were the days when we had to rethink and change our strategy constantly, sometimes with a few hours grace, sometimes only a few minutes. The entire political structure collapsed in front of our eyes. We didn't want to allow the state to collapse with it, so we had to act. There was no one else to do so. There were even moments when we had to support some Communist party officials against whom we had just fought.

It was this sort of reasoning which eventually caused Havel to overcome his own deep reluctance and to accept that he had to go Hradcany Castle, as the crowds demanded ever more insistently, in chanting and in posters: "*Havel na Hrad!* ("Havel to the Castle!"). It was very risky. He was the symbol of hope for those who had caused the revolution, but, because of twenty years of hostile propaganda against him, he was for many people who had read the old regime's newspapers or watched television the symbol of evil. But within a few days, it was plain that the positive symbol would prevail. On 29 December, in St. Vitus's Cathedral, a Celebration Mass was held following Havel's installation as the president of Czechoslovakia.

V

I WRITE THIS before the June 1990 election in which according to the most recent opinion polls, the Communist party will have great difficulty in surpassing the obligatory 5 percent threshold. In January 1990 only 8.7 percent of the voters would have voted Communist, and the Communist influence is constantly declining. The principal obstacles to the development of Czechoslovak democracy have now become on the one hand, the difficulties in introducing a market economy and, on the other, the necessity of arousing interest in civil politics from below. The difficulty of this second problem must not be underestimated in a country where the habits of participation in politics have been stifled for so long.

I would like, finally, to turn my attention to the legacy of the Spring in Winter Revolution: possibilities and problems in creating afresh a legitimate civil society in Czechoslovakia. But before I do so, as a way of introducing the political and ideological context created by the 1989 revolution, it is useful to look for a last time at the comparison with 1968. That year, Czechoslovaks created spring in spring, and it was followed by winter in summer. In 1989, we created spring in winter and we must ask what our chances are of regaining a normal European cycle of political seasons hereafter.

It is true, in a strange way, '89 was just '68 turned upside down, as one of the poster slogans put it; for the biggest difference between the Prague Spring and the Spring in Winter was on the place of reform in the rhetoric of dissent. In 1989, it just wasn't there.

I might be mistaken because I don't know much about China, but my understanding is that even the Tiananmen movement tried to use and incorporate the vocabulary of the regime within its own. That was the mistake of 1968 in Czechoslovakia. What was clear in 1989 was that this system could not be reformed. Its ideology could not be reformed. No one discussed doing this. It just didn't appear in any of the discussions about abolishing the leading role of the Communist party. It was beyond discussion. So this was our biggest advantage.

Loss of belief in any ideology has brought a renewed respect for facts. We feel that we have to pay attention to the facts and one has to try to be a realist. But that's not to say that ideas don't matter. In the building of our new perception, we have a playwright for a president who likes to use expressions like "velvet revolution" and "new beginning" and "prosperous Czechoslovakia." Sometimes it sounds funny. But the point is that no one is forced to believe it. No one controls you. This offers the possibility of being flexible, of trying different alternatives. Now, after the revolution, when we are not successful, we don't lose everything. You can say, "This was the wrong choice, let's try another way." Therefore we have a completely different situation.

You might on one hand need a strong state to serve as a tool and a referee. On the other, you have to wake people up to take their share of the responsibility. We don't feel that these are incompatible. But maybe it will be one of those wrong choices. We don't know, we have to try. We must find the mistakes in our history and in the history of the system we have lived through, and we must strive to avoid them in the future. We must find the sources of our recent victory, as I have tried to do in this essay so far, and finally we must ask ourselves whether this victory is really definitive. We may have reached the end of Communist domination, but we must ask whether this means the end of the domination of totalitarian thinking in our country.

Civic Forum came into existence as "a self-defence task force." The phrase has a military ring and that was what we sought in so describing it, deliberately. There came a moment when we had to react and we were desperate enough not to count the cost. In a few hours we had created, from the far left and the far right, a coalition with only one goal: to get rid of Husák. No one would have believed a prediction that it would take us only a week. So there we were. We did it ourselves, and having done so, we found out that it was not enough. Now we had to change the whole system! We decided that the best way to achieve this was through free elections. This is the primary reason why the Civic Forum coalition continued to exist after the revolution had passed its first phase.

The second reason is that people in Czechoslovakia were not only fed up with politicians of any ideological stripe, but with politics as well. Politics were disregarded as a normal way of behavior. Only morally depraved people took up a political career under the old regime, and so according to opinion polling in the spring of 1990, three-quarters of the people supporting Civil Forum did not want it to become a political party. At the time of writing, we want to keep it a political movement, what I call a sort of "primary school" for politics and for politicians. We have eight small political parties within Civic Forum entering the June 1990 election on our canvass list. We will help them to survive the elections, to get their people to Parliament and to give them time, in those two years of constituent assembly which we think will come from this election, to grow up, to build nation-wide stature and to go on. Then, from June to November 1990 we shall concentrate on municipal elections. We think Civic Forum will have to change tactics and to concentrate much more on regional politics. What comes after that, who knows? It depends on people and it depends on the political parties that will grow up in the meantime.

To achieve this change we built a nation-wide network of what we called Civic Forum Election Campaign Centers. There are forty electoral regions in Czechoslovakia and the aim has been to create at least forty of these centers before the June 1990 campaign. Their purpose is to foster discussions with trained people, professionals skilled in organizing elections, able to teach these techniques to other people. In these "primary schools" for politics will be offices with photocopiers, fax machines and publicity materials for the use of all the new political parties. In this way they can recultivate their grassroots political lives to permit the growth of local and regional politics and of local and regional politicians. We felt that it was not enough to destroy the old system from above by having a president and a few other of the active dissidents as ministers. Even more important was to destroy the system from below by destroying the fear and feeling that politics was abnormal.

This leads to an obvious question. What sort of society, what brand of politics do we want? I notice that many people in the West are full of advice to us on these subjects. I would make three observations. First, we want to correct those who think that because we have thrown off the chains of Stalinism, we wish therefore to embrace naked, uncontrolled free-market capitalism. I think very few, if any, Europeans, western or eastern, want that.

Personally I prefer to put it the other way around. There is much that we want and need from the West but there is one thing which I do not want: carelessness with people. The best that I took from those sufferings in my country, the best that I took from the Spring in Winter Revolution last November, and the best that I took from meeting people like Andrei Sakharov was that they cared about others. I would like this caring to remain in my country. I would like society to care for its weak, its socially weak, its economically weak, its disabled. I would like there to be tolerance. I wish to be proud of having my gypsy friends. I do not want to be afraid that my neighbors would mind them visiting me.

So this raises the second question. After communism, is socialism viable in a country such as ours? In a country like Czechoslovakia, and especially in Bohemia, which at the beginning of this century possessed 60 percent of the total industry within the Austro-Hungarian Empire—a region which was often compared to the British industrial regions at that time—it is nonsense to think that socialist thought or concerns for social welfare would disappear simply because of forty years of communism. Of course the idea of left-wing thought is compromised. But I am convinced that when it comes to economic difficulties, we shall find that feelings of social equality, the feeling that the State has a caring role to play and that society should take care of the weak, are still very strong.

I don't know what name it will be given, because the problem is that in Czechoslovakia after forty years of communism we are really fed up with any "ism" at all. We like to do things; we like to change things; but we don't like to give names to things. So it might be called a Democratic Party; and viewed from the outside it could be called a Social Democratic Socialist Party. A problem with names is that there is a Socialist Party hanging about which was, or it used to be for forty years, a lackey of the Communist party. It now spends most of its time proving its anti-Communist beliefs! Aside from this Socialist party, there are other groups which are left-wing. But I must observe that we are not confronting our real problems, our economic problems. It is much easier for them, and for all the forty parties that we now have, to speak about democracy, human rights, free-market economy and not to develop specific policies.

My third observation is that insofar as we can see a new sort of politics forming in Czechoslovakia, it is being driven by newly important issues of ecological and global security; and so none of the old rhetoric or language about "left" or "right" may be appropriate to describe it. However, I shall return to this matter.

VI

HAVEL WRITES THAT honesty was a potent weapon in all the 1989 revolutions. It certainly was in our case, and the playwright-president embodied it both in his earlier suffering under the old regime and in his refusal to become caught up in the trappings of office. Civic Forum was able to use his portrait in the election posters with the simple slogan, "Václav Havel Guarantees Free Elections." That promise from that man was powerful.

But honesty is not an unmitigated political blessing. Indeed, bureaucrats and corrupt politicians everywhere can shroud themselves in secrecy just because there are some issues which people prefer not to bring out into the open. Well, for better or worse, in Czechoslovakia, the government created by the Spring in Winter Revolution could not do this even if it wished it! It would deny everything that we stood for. So in consequence we must face the problems that were previously hidden. Of these, the most entrenched is that of the national relations between Czechs and Slovaks.

In 1918 Czechoslovakia consisted of three major nationalities. The Sudetan Germans have since gone and we now have two nationalities—Czechs and Slovaks. But about 10 percent of the population is still made up of smaller national minorities: Hungarians, Poles, Ukrainians, gypsies. For the first time in our history we have a racial problem. It is now quite obvious that we have no experience in dealing with this. It is logical that after forty years of pretending that there is no problem at all, problems suddenly appear and surprise a lot of people.

All kinds of things are possible. The ethnic violence seen in the USSR in Nagorno Karabakh is one extreme. We may expect anything from that extreme to the other and everything in between; for the situation in which we find ourselves is like that of a swimmer who has swum too long under water. You feel as if you can't go on for another second. Your lungs feel about to burst. You kick and thrash your way to the surface and before you start breathing, you cough. You don't swim elegantly, you just cough. This has been our experience since the November revolution. For forty years we were taught that the Czechs and Slovaks were brothers, that all people were equal, that it was just the imperialist tradition that caused nations to hate each other. When there were any minor problems, it was either the fault of provocateurs or of uneducated people who still had the remnants of capitalism deep inside them. This was the reason why the gypsies were forcefully displaced and scattered among the majority populations in an attempt to educate and civilize them, not taking into account that theirs was simply a different culture.

Now the old regime has gone, but the new one is not yet established. We have surfaced; we cough; and all sorts of racial animosity comes up. We are horrified at how easy it is to inflame national feeling. We have no experience of these things.

The only positive result of 1968 was the so-called federation system, which gave many more rights to the Slovak Republic than it had had before. Still, the Slovaks are not satisfied with the federation and ask for much more equality, which is again quite logical and normal. It is combined with different historical and cultural experiences than those of the Czechs. Slovaks are traditionally much more deeply connected with the Catholic church, while the Czechs felt the Catholic church to have been the tool of German ambitions; so they tend to be either atheist or Protestant. Seventeenth-century German baroque churches in Prague are a witness to the attempts by the Jesuits to proselytize and Germanize the Czechs.

There is furthermore a problem with a minority of 700,000 Hungarian people in southern Slovakia who have, strangely enough, had better relations with the Czechs in Bohemia than with the Slovaks, their nearest neighbors. To complete the ethnic picture, there is a problem in Moravia which is geographically and historically part of the Czech lands; the people speak the same language, but with a slightly different accent. Following the revolution, the Moravians suddenly demanded a three-part federation which very much annoyed the Slovaks and made problems for the Czechs too. It was something like Yorkshire asking to have equal standing with Scotland, Wales and England in the United Kingdom. Nevertheless, we are trying to cooperate by moving some state institutions like the Supreme Court to Brno, which is the capital of Moravia.

When economic difficulties come, as they surely will, the first social groups who lose their positions are women, ethnic minorities and unqualified labor which, in Czechoslovakia means principally gypsies. We could have up to 100,000 unemployed gypsies. This is alarming because the State cannot destroy itself by allowing such potential unrest. We have already had early signs of such danger. In the winter of 1989 there was something close to a pogrom in Slovakia. The only thing that we, the new government, could do, was to ask the church to talk to the people and to convince the heads of Slovak television to show the film "Ghandi." We then tried to convince our Slovak friends that we had to hold a conference on these matters, that they had to have open and frank talks about all of these differences. We asked Havel to go there and use his moral authority, not to say to the people, "Come, you are brothers," but to tell them to talk about their differences.

I have written at length, and frankly, about this question. It may be the first time in recent memory that a public figure in Czechoslovakia had done so in this manner. But I do it deliberately because, looking around, we see that to leave these problems unsolved, not to speak of them, would be the biggest mistake. So we try to be absolutely frank and open about our ethnic and regional differences in order to avoid violence, especially tragedies like Nagorno Karabakh in the Soviet Union.

In fact, I am not pessimistic about solving the nationality problems, because Slovaks played an active and early role during Spring in Winter, in contrast to the situation in 1968. The western press sometimes gives the impression that the revolution was all Czech. This was not so. That impression came from the fact that all the western journalists were concentrated in Prague and were too lazy to drive the four hours to Bratislava.

As I have already observed, the fact is that Slovaks, to a certain extent, were quite happy with the results of 1968 because they got their federation. There were virtually no purges in Slovakia because we always say that in Slovakia, "Everybody is everybody else's cousin." This is a joke, but only to a certain extent. There were very few dissidents in Slovakia. But things started to change in 1987. In that year, there was an upsurge in the Catholic church because of Poland.

The Jakes/Husák regime was stupid enough then to beat some of the Catholic demonstrators. And again, the people in the arts moved into the "opposition."

In November 1989, everything began in Prague because of the concentration of dissidents and because of the theater strike. We understood that it was impossible to play this game without the Slovaks, yet we were astonished by the speed with which that happened. It took only one day, and the Slovak theaters were on strike as well; it was three days after the foundation of Civil Forum in Prague that Public Against Violence was organized in Slovakia. The Slovaks achieved tremendous things in a very short time. At some moments they went even faster than Civil Forum precisely because, "everybody is everybody else's cousin"! There was cooperation even during the revolution, since at those most important round table talks, we always had spokesmen from Public Against Violence with us. This cooperation has continued. I think that relations between Czech and Slovak democrats have never been better than they had become by early 1990. I think things look very promising for Czechoslovak cooperation.

Honesty demands that we are open about our ethnic and nationalist problems. It also demands that we face squarely another issue, a common inheritance of all the post-Communist governments of Eastern Europe. What are we to do with the servants of the old regime; and, equally interesting, what will they do with use? That in turn is linked to another common worry. Could Soviet tanks again restore the old regime?

One wondered at the time whether our new government was brilliant or foolish to give the State Security Police two months' notice before abolishing it in February 1990. Giving them two months meant that the really tough hardliners had time to hide, to run from the country or to prepare for conspiracy. No doubt there were some of them who were sufficiently unrealistic to think of the latter. But they had no chance. It would have made sense only if they believed that the pre-Gorbachev Soviet Union could bring back all the old guard of the Communist party, riding on their tanks. This fear was widespread in the first two months after 17 November. As time went on, it seemed more and more unrealistic. So sometimes I think, with a smile, about someone sitting, hiding somewhere in a flat, and dreaming about conspiracy. I don't rule out the possibility that there might be someone like that hiding somewhere; but the longer he stays there, the less chance he will have of a decent job afterwards, for we shall, very soon, face some degree of unemployment. It will not be the best of qualifications to have been a secret policeman.

I wrote of my conviction that the fear of a repetition of August 1968 had evaporated. This is not least because even in the event of the worst outcome within the USSR, we believe that neither the will nor the means exist to reconquer Europe or even just Czechoslovakia. We see that it is in our interests, however, to maximize the chances of the *best* outcome. This is the reason why Havel himself, a person who lost a lot because of the Soviet occupation, said in the U.S. Congress on 21 February 1990, that the best way to help Czechoslovakia was to help democracy in the Soviet Union. This may sound absurd, but it is the central European way. This is the reason why we use our past contacts with the Soviet dissidents to try to get as much information as possible from there, and to send as much information as possible about our experience to them. We want to tell them how easy it is in some parts of the world to get rid of a Communist regime when you wait for the right moment and when you use no violence to provoke violence on the other side.

The other part of our tactic is to strive not for ending, but for normalizing economic relations with the USSR. We think that it is in the powerful interests of the Soviet Union to show the world its good intentions. This may be done by letting eastern European countries do what they want. Gennadi Gerasimov has famously named this the "Sinatra Doctrine" ("I did it my way...!"). I think all of us in eastern Europe are realistic enough to understand that at the very least for economic reasons, it is unwise to lose the USSR's huge market for our goods, which are still of low quality by world standards. Who else would buy them? This is the reason why we have agreed to conduct trade with the Soviet Union in hard currency. Believe me, it is very hard to trade in hard currency when you don't have it! But it is the only way, and by this we put our context economically and politically on a normal basis, a visible, countable basis; and we suddenly become partners.

Such a policy has a military security dimension also. We achieved an immediate agreement that Soviet troops were to withdraw. Later, we understood when the Soviets proved that it was technically impossible to send 1,700 trains with military equipment and personnel to the Soviet Union before the end of December 1990 using the one railway station at our eastern border. There we have to reload everything because the Soviet railway has a different gauge from ours. Our experts calculated matters and it is indeed impossible to reload more than four trains in one day. The Hungarians are also removing Soviet troops from Hungary and are occasionally using this same railway station, which leaves only three trains a day for Czechoslovakia. Then it is a matter of simple arithmetic. So at a time when we are sure that the Soviets want to remove their troops, for reasons that run beyond our bilateral relations, we can be generous and wait a bit longer. Furthermore, since we count our trade in hard currency, the USSR has to pay for the upkeep of their soldiers in hard currency.

So if, for these reasons, we have not feared what the servants of the old regime might dream of doing to use, the question remains of what we have done with them. The quick answer is that we have used them. No one had anticipated the speed with which the old regime collapsed. We had to take power. We didn't want to participate in taking the ministries and taking a share of power before the elections, but the old regime collapsed so fast that we had to. So, as we say, we had to "parachute" our people to the top posts in the ministries. Remember that for forty years those ministries were deliberately filled with Communists. Thus we had Jiri Dienstbier, a dissident, becoming the foreign minister. A few hours after being named by the president, he had to run to his former workplace to stoke his boiler, for they had not yet found a replacement for him. Dienstbier was alone in the Ministry with about 1,200 Communists who were perhaps the worst sort because they were intelligent servants of the old regime.

He called them all together and told them, "We all know the rules. But I want to tell you that from now on, I will count only your results. We all know that the State Security people have had to leave this Ministry. There is no question about that. But for the rest of you, I want proof of your loyalty to the new government shown by hard work. Again, let me say that I will only count results." As a consequence, the inherited civil servants work harder than ever to prove that they are solely state employees, purely professionals. The same thing happened in Portugal after 1974, and in Spain after Franco. If they could do it, why can't we? It was always the young officers who were the most loyal to the regime because they wanted the higher positions of the really compromised dismissed officers; and this is the way it has happened in Czechoslovakia as well.

VII

IN CZECHOSLOVAKIA, AS in much of the rest of eastern Europe, we have inherited an industrial Rust Belt and a natural environment ravaged by forty years of scornful and systematic abuse. Earlier, I raised the question often put to us of what sort of politics we wanted. I postponed until now a fuller comment on the "New Politics" that I think will follow from the Spring in Winter Revolution.

Pollution in our country is appalling. In parts of northern Bohemia, parents are obliged to sign an agreement when removing a newborn child from the hospital. This is an agreement not to allow him or her to drink tap water for one year. Imagine! We accepted and bureaucratized such poisoning. In northern Bohemia (along with Silesia) there is said to be worse pollution than in any other part of eastern Europe. According to opinion polls, the situation is so bad that the majority of the people (62 percent) think that ecological problems are *more* worrying than economic problems, and close to the same number think that ecological problems should be solved *before* economic problems. It gives you an idea of how broadly informed the population is about ecological problems.

We have high infant mortality. This becomes a very direct political problem because we do not have the resources to solve it. We have to get the people to understand that the government is trying to help them, but our situation is extremely alarming. We have to make choices about how we shall improve our industrial sector. The choices will not be easy, nor will they be easily accepted, for people want an improved standard of living and action on the environment—simultaneously.

Václav Havel is amazing. But we have a lot of problems with him, because he sometimes doesn't count the consequences. He moves very fast. Coming to the most polluted area of Bohemia, he was greeted by crowds of people in the streets. It was at a time of very heavy air pollution, and they said, "Listen Mr. President! It is splendid! For the past few months now we've had information on the environmental situation here, which we didn't have before. That's fine, but the information is horrible. We are told that the children should not leave the houses; that people should not open their windows; that workers should not work too hard outside. What should we do, we who are paid for hard physical labor outside?" Without hesitating Havel replied, "If I were in your place, I would go on strike!"

Three days after that Mr. Pithart, prime minister of the Czech Republic, came to the same area. The people said to him "Listen, Mr. Prime Minister, you have thirty days in which to do something about this pollution. If you don't, we will go on strike, or we'll leave this region in droves." They were serious about it, and we understood the situation perfectly well. No, on second thought, we can't even begin to grasp the whole situation. British producers of monitoring systems have complained to us about eastern Europe and Czechoslovakia in particular. They say that their equipment is too finely calibrated for such high levels of pollution! We simply don't have the money to solve this problem right away.

This anecdote gives both the shape and scale of the challenge that the global and environmental security problems pose in political as well as in physical and economical terms. This is where I think we need specific and extensive western aid. This aid should not just be monetary; indeed, we do not need unattached money anything like as much as we require "know-how" and specific technology which will help us both to reduce pollution and clean up the poisoned land, water and air.

However, we are not just supplicants. We in Czechoslovakia are about to be, at least in this one area, pioneers for the whole of Europe. The Spring in Winter Revolution undermined a tired totalitarianism which fell in upon itself like an empty eggshell, once we pushed. So we've inherited the closest thing to a political *tabula rasa*. The Husák regime was peculiarly obnoxious and illegitimate in the eyes of Czechs and Slovaks for reasons I have explained. It humiliated us, and we struck back. Nowhere else in eastern Europe has the old regime collapsed to the same degree leaving behind a country poised with broad support to construct a new society. This is where we are ahead of the whole of Europe.

At the very moment when the new general agenda of global security is moving to the center of international politics, Czechoslovakia is, in a way, and partly by chance, conducting the first great experiment in the politics of the twenty-first century in Europe. We are trying to create a new political discourse and to promote new political structures responsive to the new agenda. Our people have suffered much and this gives them a depth and a political maturity in which Civic Forum has confidence. So a major lesson of the 1989 Revolution has been the need to combine appropriate Western "know-how" and technology with a fierce desire for an ecologically sustainable improvement in material well-being and a proper grounding of our intellectual life.

From this mixture, we may produce a model upon which other Europeans, both western and eastern, may reflect. A Civic Forum slogan in the June 1990 election was "Come with us back to Europe!" Czechoslovaks feel that they are returning home to Europe not as beggars, but with suffering and experience to offer. Quoting the economist Milos Zeman at the beginning of this essay, I wrote that "We are like emaciated and beaten animals, released from the zoo and looking untrustingly at open country." This time, however, we know precisely what we do *not* want. We therefore have a chance.

We changed it! All of us helped changed it! For the first time in the history of Czechoslovakia, we have escaped that complex of being told by others that the Czechs are always *given* their victories, always *granted* their liberation. This time it was completely our own victory. Because of the problems in our economy and ecology that we will be facing in the near future, we may safely predict that we shall pay a price. Punishment is the wrong word, but the price has an element of punishment within it. It is the price for forty years of silence, and it is fair that we pay it. It is very fair that for the first time we all pay the same share. So I do not think that there is a need to investigate everybody's soul and everybody's personal history because this would cause only more stress and more humiliation. Almost everybody became corrupted under the old regime because it was impossible not to be. There were a few hundred of us dissidents in a population of 15 million. We knew the moment would come. The longer it took, the more dramatic the change would be. We know that there are hundreds, perhaps thousands of deeply compromised people. Should we purge them? On what grounds? This is the not the best way for our society to begin its new life.

Real problems lie before us. This represents an end to the simple role dissidents can play. It is an end to secret meetings and spectacular rooftop escapes. Economic difficulties are awaiting us, clashes with dissatisfied workers, the challenge of environmental destruction. There will be nationalist frictions and the passions involved in the unsophisticated beginnings of a parliamentary democracy.

Sir Winston Churchill once told the British that he could promise them nothing but blood, sweat and tears. Czechoslovakia was able to avoid the blood during the Spring in Winter Revolution; but the sweat and tears will obviously be our lot for a long time. We cannot avoid them. We have to pay the price for too long a silence. If Czechs and Slovaks accept this price without complaint and lamentation, it will be possible for the world to admire them. Not sooner.

Vasil Mohorita

BORN IN 1952, Mohorita trained as an automobile mechanic before studying at the Political Institute of the Czechoslovak Communist Party's Central Committee. In 1972 he began work in the Union of Socialist Youth. One of the Communist party's most influential organizations, the Union's (often mandatory) membership included over 90 percent of Czechoslovak children. In 1987 he became chairman of the Union's Central Committee; in 1988 he joined the Communist party's Central Committee secretariat as well. In January 1989 he supported the violent police action taken to disperse a series of large demonstrations.*

As the climate for change spread across Eastern Europe during 1989, Mohorita distanced himself from the intransigent Jakes leadership, and by early November was calling for acceleration of the reform process. When the police attacked demonstrators on 17 November, Mohorita's office was one of the first to demand an investigation into the violence. When the Communist party leadership began a rapid series of changes in November 1989, Mohorita became secretary of the Party's Central Committee. He was nominated first secretary of the Czechoslovak Communist Party—effectively its leader—at the extraordinary Party conference of 20-21 December 1989.

---

* See "From 1968 to 1989: A Chronological Commentary."

An Interview with the First Secretary of the Communist Party

THE COMMUNIST PARTY *controlled Czechoslovakia for almost forty-two years. Do you agree with what your former member (now federal prime minister) Marián Calfa has said, that this was a period of "moral and material collapse"?*

What happened during these years can't be described as positive. Between 1945 and 1948 there had been discussion of a specific Czechoslovak path to socialism. But what happened after February 1948—as a result of Cold War conditions—was a quick, harsh imposition of the Stalinist model. Decisions about Czechoslovakia were made in Moscow, not Prague. There was only one time when our country tried to extricate itself from the Soviet embrace, acting on the initiative of reformist forces in the Communist party. We all know what happened in 1968. But one shouldn't just see things as black or white. There were also a few substantial successes during those forty-two years: a decent standard of living, for example, or guaranteed social security. Nor is it fair to talk only of cultural decay. Look at our success at the World's Fairs: Expo 58 and Montreal in 1967. We've also made our contribution to world culture, particularly in children's literature and television programs. We've had some great successes in sports as well . . .

What about people who were unjustly persecuted under the Communist regime? What responsibility do you think the Party has towards these people and their families?

The Party as such certainly does hold a certain responsibility. Back at the extraordinary Party congress on 20-21 December 1989 we apologized to everyone who was affected. To apologize is of course one thing, but how to rectify the wrongs and injustices of the past is a matter for society as a whole to judge. Our party is going to see to it that nothing like this ever happens again. Although to look at things from another angle, you could say that Communists are the ones who are being "unjustly persecuted" these days . . .

Despite the Party's apparently iron grip on society, the Communist system collapsed in a matter of days in November and December 1989. What was it in your system that gave way, and why?

In the 1960s our society advanced in a whole series of areas, but after the reversal of 1968 there followed a gradual, pervasive, deep repression and stagnation. Unresolved problems started to build up. In economics we sacrificed intensive development to extensive growth; we missed some important stages in the scientific revolution; and our society started living at the expense of the future, particularly in terms of our natural resources and environment. The administrative, bureaucratic management system relied on command and prohibition, and thus limited people's initiative. Anything that rose above the average was seen as suspicious. True democracy, freedom of opinion and expression didn't exist. The narrow circle of people in charge of the Communist party (and thus society) was incapable of doing anything about this situation, and didn't look for political solutions to our problems. Instead, they started to resort to violent means more and more often and crudely. This increased people's already growing dissatisfaction, and could only lead to the explosion in November.

"Revolution" is a loaded word in the lexicon of Soviet-style socialism, with its overtones of "Glorious October" 1917 and the post-war Communist take-overs in central and eastern Europe. Do you consider what happened in Czechoslovakia at the end of 1989 to be a "revolution"?

It depends on what you mean by revolution. The fact is that long before November 1989 many of us knew that we couldn't carry on in the "old style." We wasted the opportunity that presented itself in 1985 with Gorbachev's rise to power. This was our opportunity to start our own restructuring (*perestroika*) and democratization. Certainly there were proclamations that supported this policy, but no concrete steps were ever really taken. The changes that came after November 17 were inevitable, and were basically aimed at changing the existing system. The majority of Communist party members realized this at the time, and still understand it today. But our previous leadership obstinately stuck to its positions, and as a result our Party lost its chance to influence developments. Events slipped out of our control following November 17, and in many ways are still running against us now. But the fact is that society was yearning for change, even if everyone probably had his own separate idea of what that change should be.

As you say, this "revolution" was basically a rejection of the Communist system and the Party that ruled it. Even after this popular condemnation of your Party and its performance, you decided to accept the post of first secretary of the Communist Party Central Committee. Why?

What the revolution rejected was the neo-Stalinist system, not socialist ideas and ideals. It rejected the way these ideas had been applied, along with the people who had headed these policies. I accepted the post of first secretary because I understood how people felt about the situation in our country, whether they were Party members or not. I knew why they were upset. I could see what they wanted changed in the Communist party. There were, and still are, hundreds of thousands of people who want these changes. As a result, I came to believe that our Party is capable of the truly fundamental renewal that will be necessary, and that its existence in our society is crucial. Particularly now, when rightist forces are once again on the move. I want to offer my services to the Party as it faces a complicated situation.

The Communist party has lost over half its members since November, and at least two parties (Democratic Forum and the Independent Left) have split off from it. They obviously doubt that the Communist party is capable of changing—in your words—into a "modern leftist party." How do you react to this?

Yes, we've lost a lot of members. Some left because they didn't agree with the Party's new policies. Others withdrew their membership after November 17 because they were jumping on someone else's bandwagon. We don't miss these types. Many others left because they felt betrayed and deeply disappointed by what they learned about earlier Party practices that were beginning to come to light. And then there were the people who left because they had different ideas about the sort of political party they wanted to belong to. This was the case with most of Democratic Forum's membership. We're not indifferent to the size of our membership, but it's not the main object of our efforts—which is to become a truly modern leftist party. All our political parties are parting with the past, including the ones we used to work with. The current wave of anti-communism is so great that distancing themselves from the Communist party is virtually a precondition for other parties' existence.

How does today's Communist party differ in ideological terms from the Party of the past? What's your attitude towards the basic tenets of Marxism-Leninism—the dictatorship of the proletariat, democratic centralism, class warfare, and so on?

"When I look at my country, I feel a certain debt.
Something in the range of seven billion..."

We've lost our leading role in society—but I want to make it clear that the Communist party that's now in the process of reform doesn't care about this leading role, isn't trying to win it back and won't in the future. Our Party has also abandoned other dogma and principles that are now out of date. These ideas were born in a different historical situation, and today we feel that they've lost their applicability and usefulness. I'm thinking here of the dictatorship of the proletariat, democratic centralism as a principle for both Party and social organization, and the idea of the Party as the vanguard of the working class. It would be just as nonsensical to keep asserting that we represent everyone's interests. Our future policy will be based on the following principles: We reject any sort of monopoly of power, but we will try to win a share of the decision-making on our country's present and future. We want to win this share through the democratic competition of different parties and movements. We want to represent and advance the interests of people who create material and spiritual value with their hands and minds. We want to be a Party of free people who can think freely. A Party that is open to various opinions and platforms. These basic, crucial ideas and goals are the force that must unite us.

After four decades of unsuccessful experimentation with Soviet-style socialist economics, Czechoslovakia is now moving back to a market economy. What's your reaction as leader of the Communist party to privatization of property and the return of capitalism in general?

Our economy needs fundamental reform. The transition to a market economy is inevitable. But we feel that the market system needs to be effectively regulated by the state. The fundamental question then becomes whether this transition is planned and under society's control, so that it doesn't cause serious social tremors, or take place at the expense of socially weaker citizens. As far as ownership is concerned, we respect and support all forms of property. But we do oppose the selling off of our national wealth and the key branches of our economy, banks and insurance system to private concerns, whether domestic or foreign. I feel that private enterprise should be most important in the service, retail and crafts sector.

Do you still feel that you're a Marxist?

Our Party is currently forming its new intellectual framework. We want to be a Marxist party in the widest sense. Marxism has a whole series of schools and approaches, whether we're talking about philosophy, economics, politics or sociology. In the past many of these have been considered deviations or revisionism; as such they were punishable as the worst sort of heresy. We now want to draw on the whole intellectual legacy of socialism's past, though we also realize that we need to begin with the fact that as a modern leftist party we're taking shape at the end of the millennium, in a completely new domestic and international context. There's nothing that's true once and for all or that applies in all times and at all times.

Do you see any country offering an alternative model for the modern Communist party?

We'll study and be inspired by others, but we're drawing on our own specific conditions, our people's mentality, our traditions and opportunities. I should stress that the Communist party's future may be influenced by how the left develops in Europe and throughout the world.

What do you think of the "government of national understanding"?

Given that it was I who suggested this name at one of the first meetings of all the political parties and forces after November 17, and that the Communist party has had a large share in its work, I'd have to say that I approve. In many ways you could say that this government did some hard work at a difficult time. The Communist deputies in parliament have supported most of the basic economic laws that this government has put forward. If we've had any criticism, it's resulted from our leftist convictions. But it's also clear that the consequences of this government's work are now being reflected in the problems our society is facing.

After decades of totalitarian control, Czechoslovak society is suddenly experiencing freedom and the beginnings of a democratic state. How do you think Czechs and Slovaks are reacting to this newly regained freedom?

First of all, we're all still learning how to deal with it. We're learning about political culture. We also need to know how to cope with the negative features that accompany the first phase of increased democracy and freedom. Some people think of democracy as violent anti-communism, and this can sometimes swell into a frenzy. Some people want pluralism without the Communist party.

Figures have recently come out about the billions of crowns your Party received from the state budget every year, which helped fund vast real estate holdings, fleets of cars and other "Party expenses." There have also been large demonstrations, and even a short strike, demanding that the Communist party return this property to the state. What do you intend to do with your Party's various assets?

We don't want anything that doesn't belong to us. We've already given a significant share of this property back to the state. We only want what every Party needs in order to function properly. Yes, our Party took funds from the state budget, but we also collected over a billion crowns every year in membership fees. When you're judging what should happen with our property, you need to take that into account too. As well as the fact that the Party enjoyed a unique status in society, and was thus involved in every aspect of its running. In other words, it was basically inseparable from state structures and performed a whole series of functions together with the state.

We're having nothing but problems with our property, for our predecessors left it in great disorder. We're giving practically all of it—except what we need—back to the state. Let the state decide what should be done with it: what should be given to schools, medical facilities or other political parties and movements.

Your comrade Jiri Machalík, a Central Committee secretary, has been quoted as saying of the June 1990 elections: "You can safely reckon on our getting 30 percent of the vote; we'll have a majority. Then we'll annex the other parties—the Socialist and People's parties and so on . . ." This sounds more like a dose of the old Communist party system than the approach of some reformed and modern leftist party. How do you react to this?*

Comrade Machalík denies ever having said this. If anyone were to say something like this, particularly if they were members of the Party leadership, then I'd feel that I couldn't work with them. Yes, there are still individuals and groups in our Party who don't understand what's happening in society, or don't see what's important to us. They're hoping for a return of the old system. I argue that such a return is impossible—in the interests of both our reforming Party and society. The Communist party doesn't want to annex anyone. We want to earn people's trust through visible, useful work.

The Czechoslovak press is writing a lot about the problems Czechs, Slovaks, Moravians, Poles, Germans, Hungarians, Gypsies and Ruthenians have living together in one country. These problems rarely surfaced in public during the Communist regime, although they certainly must have existed to have reemerged so sharply and so soon. Were they suppressed by your Party's government? What sort of solution are you suggesting today?

Nationalism is the product of modern history, particularly of the

---

* The Socialist and People's parties were satellites of the Communist party before November 1989. They have since tried to establish themselves as independent parties with new leaderships.

last two centuries. The problems of relations between Czechs, Slovaks and the other nationalities and ethnic groups weren't satisfactorily solved during the First Republic (1918-38) either. Its insensitive, unjust concept of "czechoslovakism"* was one of the reasons for its growing instability and consequent collapse in 1938-39, as were the unresolved problems of Czech relations with the German and other minorities. The federation that was formed in 1968 was obviously a big step forward. Unfortunately, like many other well-intentioned measures, the necessary adjustments in ethnic affairs weren't fully implemented.

The Communist party supports a unified, collective state of Czechs, Slovaks and other nationalities and ethnic groups. This state should guarantee the development of national characteristics, and should provide legal assurances of truly equal status. We also know that nationalist problems aren't only a factor of nations or nationalities, but can also be the fault of politicians, politicians who don't think about the future, and only focus on immediate political success.

Where do you think the disintegration of the Soviet empire is headed? What sort of influence might this have on the future of Czechoslovakia—and on the future of your Party?

I'm not a prophet or a fortune-teller. Internal affairs are the concern of individual countries. But come what may, I think the Soviet Union will remain an important factor in European and world politics. Our country should never again be bound by the decisions of another country or superpower. Whether it's Great Britain and France at Munich in 1938, or the Soviet Union throughout the forty years since the war. The same thing holds true for our Party.

Do you think a revolution like the one you saw here in Czechoslovakia might take place in the USSR?

---

* See Introduction: "After the Velvet Revolution" ("The Nationality Question").

The changes that have taken place in most of the countries of Eastern Europe have many causes and features in common. But there's also a lot that makes each each situation different. I wouldn't want to speculate, but I believe that the Soviet leadership will have to keep the domestic situation under control, and will have to accelerate and expand the reform process, or else the situation will start to develop in such a way that the consequences will be difficult to predict. I for one hope that what happens will be the former.

What does communism mean to you today?

It involves the notion of a certain social formation that has arisen under particular historical conditions: something like the vision of a just society for the broadest segments of the proletariat, that is, for people who are truly exploited by capital. But its concrete shape is much more complicated. Our present task, or intention, is to support democratic socialism. In this sort of a socially just society the individual is the center of interest, along with the greatest possible satisfaction of his needs, whether material or spiritual. In practice this means preserving the right to appropriate work and fair compensation for it—which means compensation according to the quantity, quality and social benefit of the work done. There also needs to be a system of social security guaranteed by the state. Equal and democratic access to education, good, accessible medical care, appropriate public services and a healthy environment.

This sort of a society needs to guarantee the equal rights of all; but people also need to be aware of their social responsibility. This shouldn't be a society of conflict, but one of political and social consensus. A democratic and pluralist society. I'm no utopian, and I've always tried to work in the realm of real politics. Which is why I'm still convinced that a society like this can be created.

11 June 1990
Interview conducted by Tim Whipple.

Index

Freedom House

Freedom House is an independent nonprofit organization that monitors human rights and political freedom around the world. Established in 1941, Freedom House believes that effective advocacy of civil rights at home and human rights abroad must be grounded in fundamental democratic values and principles.

In international affairs, Freedom House continues to focus attention on human rights violations by oppressive regimes, both of the left and the right. At home, we stress the need to guarantee all citizens not only equal rights under law, but equal opportunity for social and economic advancement.

Freedom House programs and activities include bimonthly and annual publications, conferences and lecture series, public advocacy, ongoing research of political and civil liberties around the globe, and selected, on-site monitoring to encourage fair elections.

Focus on Issues

General Editor: James Finn

This publication is one in a series of Focus on Issues. The separate publications in this series differ in the method of examination and breadth of the study, but each focuses on a single, significant political issue of our time. The series represents one aspect of the extensive program of Freedom House. The views expressed are those of the authors and not necessarily those of the Board of Freedom House.

About the Editor

Tim D. Whipple, an expert in East European affairs, currently lives in Prague, Czechoslovakia, where he represents U.S. and West European businesses.

Freedom House Books

General Editor: James Finn

Yearbooks

Freedom in the World: Political Rights and Civil Liberties,
annuals from 1978-1991

Studies in Freedom

Escape to Freedom: The Story of the International Rescue Committee,
Aaron Levenstein; 1983

Forty Years: A Third World Soldier at the UN,
Carlos P. Romulo (with Beth Day Romulo); 1986. (*Romulo: A Third World Soldier at the UN,* paperback edition, 1987)

Today's American: How Free?
edited by James Finn & Leonard R. Sussman, 1986

Will of the People: Original Democracies in Non-Western Societies,
Raul S. Manglapus; 1987

Perspectives on Freedom

Three Years at the East-West Divide,
Max M. Kampelman; (Introductions by Ronald Reagan and Jimmy Carter; edited by Leonard R. Sussman); 1983

The Democratic Mask: The Consolidation of the Sandinista Revolution,
Douglas W. Payne; 1985

The Heresy of Words in Cuba: Freedom of Expression & Information,
Carlos Ripoll; 1985

Human Rights & the New Realism: Strategic Thinking in a New Age,
Michael Novak; 1986

To License A Journalist?,
Inter-American Court of Human Rights; 1986.

The Catholic Church in China,
L. Ladany; 1987

Glasnost: How Open? Soviet & Eastern European Dissidents; 1987

Yugoslavia: The Failure of "Democratic" Communism; 1987

The Prague Spring: A Mixed Legacy,
edited by Jiri Pehe, 1988

Romania: A Case of "Dynastic" Communism; 1989

Focus on Issues

Big Story: How the American Press and Television Reported and Interpreted the Crisis of Tet-1968 in Vietnam and Washington,
Peter Braestrup; Two volumes 1977;
One volume paperback abridged 1978, 1983

Afghanistan: The Great Game Revisited,
edited by Rossane Klass; 1988

Nicaragua's Continuing Struggle: In Search of Democracy,
Arturo J. Cruz; 1988

La Prensa: The Republic of Paper,
Jaime Chamorro Cardenal; 1988

The World Council of Churches & Politics, 1975-1986,
J.A. Emerson Vermaat; 1989

South Africa: Diary of Troubled Times,
Nomavenda Mathiane; 1989

The Unknown War: The Miskito Nation, Nicaragua, and the United States,
Bernard Nietschmann; 1989

Power, the Press and the Technology of Freedom The Coming Age of ISDN,
Leonard R. Sussman; 1989

Ethiopia: The Politics of Famine; 1989

The Imperative of Freedom: A Philosophy of Journalistic Autonomy
John. C. Merrill; 1990

Racing With Catastrophe: Rescuing America's Higher Education,
Richard Gambino; 1990

Soviet Propaganda As A Foreign Policy Tool,
Marian Leighton; 1990

Ireland Restored: The New Self-Determination
Vincent J. Delacy Ryan; 1991

After the Velvet Revolution: Václav Havel and the New Leaders of Czechoslovakia Speak Out
Tim D. Whipple, editor; 1991

An Occasional Paper

General Editor: R. Bruce McColm

Glasnost and Social & Economic Rights
Valery Chalidze, Richard Schifter; 1988

Peace and Human Rights in Cambodia: Exploring From Within
Kassie Neou with Al Santoli; 1990